Learn Linux Quickly

A Comprehensive Guide for Getting Up to Speed
on the Linux Command Line
(Ubuntu)

CodeQuickly.org

& Paul H Bartley

Table of Contents

The Linux Command Line

Introduction

Image: Ubuntu Linux Terminal app window

Imagine someone sits down to use a computer, and on the screen is an empty-looking window with nothing but a cursor blinking on and off. This blank, unidentified window looks like it could be some sort of email program or text editor, except the lack of menus or icons would rule that out. Aside from the cursor, there are just a couple of symbols curiously strung together in what looks like some sort of code or prompt. Assuming the user has never seen a window like this before, what would you guess happens next?

A) The user types something in at the prompt and presses `enter`.
B) The user leaves the window in the background and forgets about it.
C) The user feels a bit uneasy about the window and closes it in a hurry.

Anything is possible, but considering this is the command line interface the user has stumbled upon, C would not be a surprising end to this story. And what about you? What would you do in this situation?

If your answer is anything like C, take comfort that this sort of reaction to the command line interface is not uncommon at all. The feeling of dread at the sight of the "terminal" (as it is affectionately called) is well known, and this has been going on as long as there have been terminal screens to stare at (since the 1970s, when they first appeared). These days, however, the all-text interface can induce an even stronger panic now that we are so accustomed to our graphical user interfaces (GUIs). It would take a lot to pry us away from our GUIs, but if you have ever thought to yourself that you couldn't survive without one (a GUI), we'll let you in on a little secret—you don't have to renounce the GUI to be a command line user. Even the most seasoned Unix authorities shudder at doing certain things on the command line and just reach for their mice instead.

The fact is, no matter the level of experience, command line users need to seek help from time to time. Part of every command line user's routine is consulting the help documentation that lies hidden behind the stark command line interface. Is that documentation for beginners? Not really, unfortunately. This is the documentation that *experienced* users need in order to get their command line tasks done. What about beginners then? Fortunately, it doesn't take long for command line beginners to get enough exposure to start making sense of things. You just need someone to turn on the lights and point out where the essentials are. Before long, you will be charting your own course. In the GUI world, we would expect some kind of tutorial "wizard" to show new users around a platform. Linux, on the other hand, still offers little in the way of a built-in walkthrough for people with no prior command line experience. More often than not, command line users are simply expected to "know" certain things, and this leaves many new users feeling bewildered.

So, why is the Linux command line like this? One explanation lies in the culture and tradition of Linux's forebear: Unix. When Unix was under development in the late-1960s and early 1970s, the notion of the "lone" computer user wasn't really a thing yet. At that time, each computer was shared by multiple individuals in the same locale, and this naturally led to computers as hubs of activity where communities formed and users worked together. Hence, a new user would be welcomed as a new member of the community, and training would generally be a person-to-person transfer of knowledge. Surprisingly, this custom of communal knowledge sharing is reflected in the Unix command line's *lack* of special accommodations for new users getting started. The tacit assumption at the time was that a walkthrough of the basics for brand-new users would be provided by the user community and thus was not the job of the operating system itself. Plus, limited memory resources put a cap on nonessential features, and with Unix manual pages available as early as 1971, there would have been little rationale in trying to amplify the built-in help functionality. This tradition of a "quiet", reserved interface that doesn't impose upon the user runs throughout the Unix design philosophy and has carried over to Linux.

As charming as it would be to have a community of expert users eager to help us with our first steps on the Linux command line, now, in general, people tend to seek help from online resources and books. There are many excellent resources available for beginners, and this book aspires to be one of them. The aim of this guide is to provide a helping hand to readers who want to gain a level of competence on the Linux command line. No previous Linux experience is necessary. We start with the very basics and build from there. We will walk you through the organization of the file system and show you how to navigate it using some of the most common commands. We will equip you with the tricks and techniques that long-time Linux users wish they had known when they started out. And we will take you through a path of guided tutorials where you will get hands-on experience using the command line tools Unix is famous for. Unix and Linux are cultures as much as they are system architectures, and along the way we will be exploring some of the historical and cultural dimensions of these systems' functionality. In the end, you will walk away with an excellent foundation in general Linux command line skills, with enough knowledge to confidently handle most intermediate-level command line tasks. And if at some point you should decide to advance even further, you will be in great shape to progress toward higher-level system administrator skills. We wish you the best of luck in your journey, and we hope you enjoy discovering all of the amazing things you can do on the command line!

What is Unix?

Look around you, and chances are that Unix is not far away. If you use an Android or iOS device, there is a descendant of Unix running at the core. The same goes for all macOS, iPadOS, watchOS, tvOS, Chrome OS, Fire OS, Orbis OS (Playstation), and Nintendo Switch devices. And of course, we mustn't forget the myriad Linux distributions installed in millions of desktop machines, laptops, servers, vehicles, and niche embedded devices all over the planet. The list goes on, and it is not an exaggeration to say that Unix is everywhere now. Unix has even found its way into Microsoft Windows in the Windows Subsystem for Linux (WSL)!

But how did we get here? How did Unix take over the world?

To begin to answer this question, let us explore a bit of Unix history.

Unix is an operating system whose origins date back to the work of computer legend Ken Thompson, who in 1969 at AT&T Bell Laboratories started coding up a new stack of instructions that he knew would lead to better performance from computers. When Mr. Thompson began laying down this early code that would later become Unix, he was addressing a need for a lightweight and reliable operating system. And what software program was to run on this new-fledged operating system? A game, of course! Thompson had earlier developed a game he called *Space Travel* (coincidentally one of the first video games ever created) on a large GE-645 mainframe computer at Bell Labs. When Thompson learned that the project he had been assigned on the mainframe was going to be cancelled (his actual assignment, not the game), he knew this meant he would lose mainframe access and also his means of playing *Space Travel*. So, what did he do? He did what anybody would do—he went to work building his own operating system from scratch (in assembly language) on a different computer so that he and his game could be reunited. This replacement computer was a smaller[1], resource-constrained machine that apparently no one wanted—an older DEC PDP-7 with 9k of RAM. This was

---

[1] The DEC PDP-7 occupied a "small" space of about three full-sized refrigerators.

not very much memory even for those days, but Thompson was confident he could do more with less, building from the ground up. Interestingly, this early requirement for the system to work on limited hardware would become one of the main principles of the Unix design philosophy.

Image: DEC PDP-7

A colleague of Thompson's at Bell Labs named Dennis Ritchie (another person of Olympian stature in computing) was a fan of *Space Travel* on the mainframe, and he too wanted to see the game resurrected with a simpler, sturdier architecture underneath. So, the two joined forces, and they began building atop the foundation that Thompson had laid, adding a filesystem, a command line interpreter (or "shell") with commands for file operations, a text editor, separate memory space for system processes and user processes, and more. Soon, it was clear that as enduring as the game was, their attention had shifted to this revolutionary thing they were building underneath it. And after about a month of intensive work, they had an incredibly efficient, stable, general-purpose operating system that was able to run with just 5k of RAM reserved for the system. What they had created was the first functional version of Unix: an operating system that would go on to change the world. It was a major achievement, and many of the core traits that we see in modern Unix-like systems (Linux, macOS, etc.), we would recognize in this "beta" version of Unix from 1969.

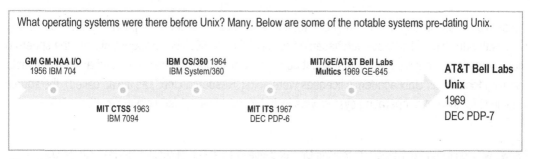

Figure 1 Operating system development timeline (condensed) leading up to Unix

Image: Ken Thompson (seated) and Dennis Ritchie working at a DEC PDP-11 in 1972

From 1970-1973, Thompson, Ritchie, and colleagues at Bell Labs focused all of their efforts on Unix, and the group made a series of advancements that attracted growing interest from the outside. These achievements included the C programming language (courtesy of Dennis Ritchie), a complete re-write of Unix from the ground up in C code (something not thought possible for an operating system), a port of Unix to the DEC PDP-11, comprehensive online documentation (manual pages), a hierarchical filesystem (directory structure with file permissions), multi-user time sharing (multitasking), in/out redirection, pattern searching with regular expressions, and more. Unix began to gain a reputation internally at AT&T as the preferred choice for the company's DEC computers, proving superior to DEC's proprietary operating system that came bundled with the machines. Then, in 1973, the decision was made that Unix was ready to be licensed to academic institutions for research purposes. To introduce their magnum opus to the world, Thompson and Ritchie presented a paper, *The Unix Time-Sharing System*, at a conference at IBM that same year.

Academia started to take notice, and from 1974 onward, Unix saw wide adoption at universities in the U.S., with educational licenses[2] purchasable from AT&T for $150. This brought Unix into the sphere of many computer science departments, and it became both a subject of research and an indispensable teaching tool. When Unix academic licenses were sold ("Research Unix", as it was called), the source code in C for the entire operating system was included, and this helped spawn a culture of Unix

---

[2] AT&T was forbidden from directly marketing Unix because of an anti-trust consent decree with the U.S. Department of Justice in 1956.

enthusiasts making their own modifications and enhancements to the system. Gradually, different flavors of Unix started springing up, each one a unique blend of custom features reflecting a local community of programmers. This spirit of contributing code for the benefit of a shared piece of software set the stage for the free and open-source software (FOSS) movement, which didn't arrive in name until many years later (in the 1990s). Research Unix was arguably the open-source movement's ancestral birthplace—where it first emerged as a phenomenon.

In 1975, Ken Thompson went on sabbatical at the University of California at Berkeley (UCB) as a visiting professor. There he helped the computer science department install the latest version of Unix, gave seminars on the design of the Unix kernel, and took part in the development of several new Unix utilities. Upon Thompson's return to Bell Labs, other people at UCB took up the remaining work on the utilities while also adding some enhancements of their own. One of these people was then-graduate student Bill Joy, who would go on to make many important contributions to Unix, including the seminal Unix text editor known as vi (the predecessor to the vim text editor). Less than two years later, in 1977, the Computer Systems Research Group (CSRG) at UCB released a collection of these utilities for free in a package they named the "Berkeley Software Distribution" (BSD). This bundle of utilities was well-received and became a highly sought-after item in the Unix world (only about 30 bundles were originally sent out). Due to the high demand, the department at UCB continued to release free, updated BSD packages throughout the 1980s.

With BSRG's continued development of extensions and improvements for AT&T Research Unix, by the early 1980s, BSD had become its own entity as a complete operating system[3] bundled together with extensions in one package. The 1970s computers that Unix had been built on were rapidly being outmoded by newer hardware, and several of these BSD extensions became crucial components for deploying Unix in a modern environment. The most important were BSD's support for 32-bit CPUs (then new), virtual memory (hard disks were growing in speed and capacity), and Transmission Control Protocol/Internet Protocol (TCP/IP). The TCP/IP functionality was particularly important with TCP/IP officially becoming the standard internet data transfer protocol in the U.S. in 1983. This standardization set the course for the internet as we know it today, opening the channels that would eventually carry the world wide web. As it happened, BSD was the only viable operating system at the time to offer fully integrated support for TCP/IP. This fortuitous circumstance for BSD instantly placed it in a special category as a game-changing tool, and the Unix userbase in the 1980s expanded from what had mostly been academic circles to a wider radius of users in practically every industry across the board. BSD-based systems with their sophisticated suite of networking utilities became a popular choice for servers. A culture began to form around BSD, marking it as the platform on which the internet was built. Perhaps it is not surprising that Tim Berners-Lee, the person who invented the world wide web, did so on a BSD-variant machine: a NeXTcube.

---

[3] BSD was still based on AT&T Research Unix at this point, but with modifications and added extensions.

Image: The NeXTcube used by Tim Berners-Lee to build and host the first webpage

Amidst the cultural and technological changes sweeping through the 1980s, a number of things went on that dramatically altered the Unix landscape in the coming years. The expansion of the IT industry led several companies to license AT&T Commercial Unix and market their own Unix variants, most notably Sun Microsystems SunOS, HP-UX, IBM AIX, and Microsoft Xenix. Meanwhile, AT&T was in an anti-trust battle with the U.S. Department of Justice, and in 1984 a settlement was reached that resulted in the breakup of the company. This meant that AT&T would be split into several smaller companies, with an agreement allowing AT&T to remain as a (smaller) corporation in control of some of its previous assets, including Unix. AT&T now had the green light to market Unix as a product (something they hadn't been able to do before). With AT&T now competing against the various vendors that had licensed Unix (Sun, HP, IBM, Microsoft, etc.), what came as a result was a fragmentation in the Unix world. Different brands began adding proprietary features to their Unix-based systems, locking customers into platform dependence. This fragmentation of Unix also spread through hardware as companies dug into their proprietary designs, rendering different strands of Unix isolated on separate hardware islands.

But this is never what Unix was about, and this brings us back to our original question: What is Unix? From AT&T's corporate vantage, Unix was a product that they owned, and one that they had the right to profit from after initially being denied the opportunity to do so. But for many Unix users, especially those descended from the academic communities where the roots of Unix had been planted, Unix was a living thing that had been continually evolving for over a decade, with countless contributions from its broader community of users. From this community's perspective, Unix had never been anyone's property, and this virtue, they would argue, is precisely what had allowed Unix to become what it was. To this community, the only way forward would be for Unix to remain what it had been—free. And for that to happen, they would have to rebuild Unix by themselves—from the ground up, taking the essence of its capabilities, its features, its commands, and its behavior, and giving it a new, airy home. This spirit of taking back collective ownership of Unix was famously channeled by Richard Stallman in his 1985 GNU (GNU's Not Unix) Manifesto outlining the goals of the Free Software Foundation (FSF), a non-profit organization which he started. The GNU project and the FSF set an example that inspired many in the Unix community to strike out and find a Unix they could call their own, as in, everyone's.

This exodus would take several years, and despite the lean design that had always permitted Unix to run on bare-minimum hardware, it wouldn't be until the late 1980s that personal computers powerful enough to run Unix would even begin to come within reach for the average computer user. Setbacks and technical hurdles notwithstanding, eventually several varieties of free, Unix-like operating systems started to appear on the horizon—completely untied to any of AT&T's commercial code. It was like the essence of Unix had leapt from one codebase to another and survived. And it wasn't just one, but several new bases where Unix landed.

So, what is Unix? Unix is an operating system, but it is not carried through code alone. It is more a set of standards and guiding principles (technical and otherwise) about how a computer should operate, established through tradition and transmuted across generations of users. Along with the Unix set of ideals and norms comes a culture, and within that culture there are sub-cultures and disagreements between factions. Nonetheless, core aspects remain that all Unix branches share in common, and at the heart of these is something that has been there since the very beginning: the command line.

Figure 2 Unix - Linux lineage (simplified)

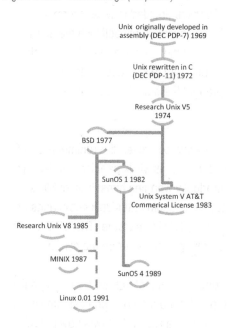

Unix design philosophy redux:

- Build small, simple pieces first.
- Each piece should do one thing only, and it should do that thing very well.
- Make the pieces modular so that the output of one piece can be plugged into the input of another.
- Connect the pieces together to achieve more complex functionality (as needed).
- Strive to keep the system as small and light as possible.
- Suppress system output unless the user demands otherwise.
- Process and store information in raw text to provide a consistent way of handling data from one application to the next.

What is Linux?

Linux holds a special place in the history of computing as the story of a miracle child, born in the most unlikely circumstances. As of 1990, none of the projects to transplant Unix to affordable hardware had produced a viable operating system. There was, however, one fragmentary OS called Minix which came close. Minix offered pieces of a Unix system on floppy disk for the relatively modest price of $69. For students, Minix could be had for the cost of shipping.

Image: Linus Torvalds

In early 1991, a 21-year-old Finnish computer science student named Linus Torvalds received his free student copy of Minix on sixteen floppy disks. Mr. Torvalds had recently purchased an IBM PC clone with an Intel 80386 processor—a Unix-worthy machine with impressive specs. According to legend, Torvalds was put off by the cost of the Sun workstations at his university, where he had just been introduced to Unix in a class several months before. With his 386 PC and Minix, he was determined to see if he could come up with something close to a Sun workstation for a fraction of the price.

Torvalds took a deep dive, learning about the 80386 and testing the low-level interactions between Minix and the CPU. He wanted to be able to remotely log in to the network at his university, but Minix didn't come with a terminal emulator. Without many options, Torvalds decided to write a terminal emulator himself. Never one to shy away from a challenge, Torvalds tasked himself with the extra hurdle of writing a *stand-alone* terminal emulator. This meant his terminal emulator would not make system calls to Minix but would instead run as an independent program talking directly to the PC's hardware, like a mini operating system. It was this step that brought the first shade of Linux into the world.

Satisfied with the results, Torvalds then wrote his own hard disk drive controller, the rudiments of a file system, and then...disaster struck! He accidentally overwrote some of his Minix partition, rendering it useless. Not all was lost, however. By and by, he had been gradually weaning himself off of Minix, building capabilities around his terminal emulator to the point that he could enter Unix commands and a basic shell would interpret the commands into instructions for the CPU to execute. The CPU would then perform its task and spit the output back for the terminal emulator to render on the screen.

Torvalds continued bolting together subsystems, giving the command line interpreter (the shell) a floor to stand on. Eventually, this flooring was strong enough to support more than one process running at a time. What started off as a terminal emulator (functionally similar to a typewriter) was now behaving like Unix wasn't far away. And this wasn't just an act, because underneath the shell, talking to the hardware was a technical marvel that Torvalds had borne into reality. It was something that one day would grow up to run the world: the Linux kernel. Linus Torvalds had single-handedly done what teams of more experienced people had been struggling with for years. He managed to deliver a solid Unix kernel onto modern hardware that was not prohibitively expensive. This achievement was the Holy Grail of the Unix community in their escape from AT&T, and with the inevitable reduction in the price of hardware, it would instill a great hope for the future longevity of the operating system.

Even though the Linux kernel had some kinks to iron out, Torvalds had already given it the firm footing that it needed to run applications such as Bash, and this was too important to keep hidden away. On August 25th, 1991, Torvalds wrote a humble post to the Minix Usenet group announcing that he had developed his own Unix-style OS kernel and that he was getting ready to release it for free. This caught the interest of a small but supportive group of Unix enthusiasts, and in September of 1991, Linux 0.01 was put on an ftp server for all to download with a General-Purpose License (GPL) written by Torvalds himself. Torvalds' intention was and always has been for Linux to be free to use, distribute, and/or modify as users see fit.

At the time when Linux was new, 21-year-old Torvalds might not have thought releasing Linux for free was much of a big deal, but in actuality, it would turn out to be a hugely consequential decision. In 1992, Torvalds replaced his homegrown license with the GNU GPL in Linux .99, integrating the Linux kernel together with a package of GNU utilities. This formed the first beta release of Linux as a general-purpose operating system. It didn't take long for word to spread throughout the Unix community that a new, free Unix-like operating system running on commodity hardware was among its ranks. This sparked a wave of interest, and in the coming months, thousands of people around the world downloaded Linux and began to experiment with it.

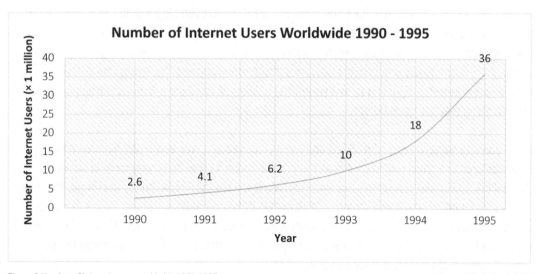

Figure 3 Number of internet users worldwide 1990-1995   *Source: World Bank, ITU*

The timing and circumstance couldn't have been more serendipitous for Linux. The release of Linux .99 directly coincided with the "internet explosion" of 1993-1994 (when internet access began to see enormous growth). Torvalds had always encouraged community feedback and participation in the improvement of Linux, and there had been a small but dedicated team of about 100 developers making contributions to Linux since its initial release. But with the expansion of internet access in 1993-1994 came an inrush of developers—eventually numbering in the thousands—all eager to get involved in Linux kernel development. Torvalds at that point could have thrown up walls around Linux and made it into a more select enterprise, but in fact he met the incoming flood of code with a passion, setting the tone for the Linux developer community as a thriving, self-organizing collective of programmers with diverse expertise. And out of this patchwork of many individual code contributions came a surprisingly efficient system for maintaining and extending Linux.

This surge of activity surrounding the development of Linux became a subject of great curiosity and started getting attention outside the Unix community. Industry leaders were both awed and puzzled by Torvalds' commitment to keeping Linux free. And the way that developers all over the world reciprocated by donating their time and coding expertise was an eye-opening moment that left people stunned. There really was no precedent for it. Some companies saw it as a threat. Some predicted it would never work as a means of producing a viable operating system. But few would dispute that something extraordinary was happening and that a novel movement had begun. When Linux 1.0 was released in 1994, skeptics and nay-sayers would have to relent, because the viability of Linux was clearly on display, and the Linux userbase and developer community were growing.

Linus Torvalds would have secured his place in history as the originator of the Linux kernel even if his involvement had been on a purely programming level. But history would see him for more than just his technical contributions. Torvalds' decision to make Linux free, and his steadfast devotion to this cause would have a world-changing impact and historical significance even bigger than Linux itself. In the transformative period where Linux went from a young programmer's offering to a world-class operating system, Linus Torvalds oversaw the birth of the open source movement, guiding it into a self-sustaining and highly productive model for software development. This would send ripples through every industry, signaling to everyone what a different world the internet era was going to be from anything that had gone before.

In the years to come, through the 1990s and the next decades, Linux saw a steady stream of improvements and continued to evolve as the internet found its way into every facet of society. Several other Unix-like operating systems also materialized in the 1990s, but by and large, the Unix community found its new home in Linux. Of all the Unix-like operating systems, Linux is the most natural heir to the free and open spirit that Unix was founded on. Through Linux, Unix has kept in contact with its community roots, and yet it has grown up, perhaps in a much bigger way than the original creators of Unix could have imagined.

The Unix World

> I think the Linux phenomenon is quite delightful, because it draws so strongly on the basis that Unix provided. Linux seems to be among the healthiest of the direct Unix derivatives, though there are also the various BSD systems as well as the more official offerings from the workstation and mainframe manufacturers. **– Dennis Ritchie, 1999**

When we say that Unix has taken over the world, what we really mean to say is that Unix *like* operating systems have taken over. Linux is one of these Unix-like systems, and it is by far the most widely used of any OS on the planet (Unix-like or not). Linux-powered devices number in the billions—more than all Apple and Microsoft devices combined. Linux is at the core of every Android phone, which explains the high numbers, but that's not all. It is used in a mind-blowing array of things, from cars to calculators to cargo ships. Moreover, 96% of the world's top one million websites are hosted on Linux servers. 90% of the cloud runs on Linux. 100% of all supercomputers in the world run on Linux. And, Linux has been ported to practically *every* modern hardware platform.

Would you agree we live in a Unix-like world? We do, and yet, you would never know it. Unix is often in the background, silently doing its duty without interruption. The Apple macOS, a BSD variant, has a Terminal application where users can access the command line, and this coincidentally makes the Mac the most widely-used desktop Unix-like platform in the world at approximately 15% global market share (at the time of this writing). Linux, on the other hand, is the main OS on around 2% of the world's desktop (and laptop) computers, despite its prevalence in the handheld, embedded, server, cloud, and high-performance computing markets. Unless we happen to use Linux as a desktop OS or interface with Linux in the cloud, we may never see the Linux command line.

This points out an issue that we should address about the semantics of the word "Linux". It is common to hear the term "Linux" to mean—the CLI, GUI, and software utilities packaged together in a distribution (see p. 21). In other words, "Linux" often connotes a complete general-purpose operating system like Windows or macOS. Technically, however, in the most precise use of the term, "Linux" is the <u>kernel</u> of the operating system (see p. 20), and "GNU/Linux" is the official name for the complete operating system with GUI and utilities. **However**, this guide will refrain from using the term "GNU/Linux" and instead use "Linux" to mean <u>the kernel</u>, <u>the command line environment</u>, *-or-* <u>the general-purpose operating system</u>, whichever association fits the context. The main reason for not using "GNU/Linux" is that it is simply not part of the vernacular, whereas "Linux" is widely recognized around the world as the name of the operating system.

What is an OS kernel?

If a computer's hardware is like a road, and a software application is like driving a car on the road, then the OS kernel would be the rubber of the tires supporting the car against the road. It is the layer of instructions that speaks directly to the machine, ushering in requests from programs competing for the computer's resources. The kernel provides a platform where software applications can run without having to know exactly what is happening beneath their feet (or what the next-door neighbor programs are doing). With this layer of abstraction delegating the hardware, it opens the door to the luxuries of general-purpose computing: having a file system, programs (plural) running at the same time, ways to connect to other devices, and so on. To the machine, there are no apps, users, files, or processes; there are just instructions from one step to the next. It is the kernel that dispatches these instructions like a master juggler, spinning together a firm basis for the digital infrastructure we rely on every day.

Figure 4 Linux OS layers (simplified)

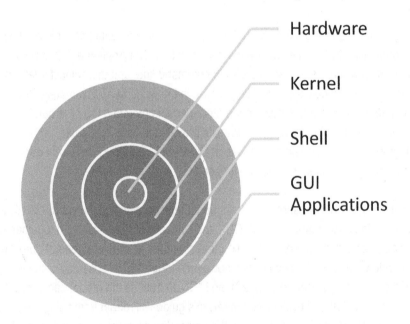

Hardware

Kernel

Shell

GUI
Applications

What are Linux distributions ("distros")?

Taking a cue from the BSD (Berkeley Software <u>Distribution</u>) tradition of bundling Research Unix with a collection of utilities, a "distro" is a packaging of Linux, generally with a package manager, a GUI desktop environment (if applicable), and a utility software bundle. All together these components make for an OS that people can use "out of the box" with minimal fuss. Ubuntu, Mint, and Fedora are all Linux distros.

An analogy can be drawn between Linux distros and the book publishing industry. Distros are to Linux as modern release editions are to classic literature. For example, we can find many printings of Shakespeare's *Hamlet* from different publishers, each with its own look and feel, but all of the editions share the same contents inside (*Hamlet*). Likewise, for different distros, they all contain Linux at their core. Unlike *Hamlet*, however, Linux internals are continually updated.

Why Unix?

One question that arises in the remarkable ascent of Unix is—why Unix and not another operating system? Many other operating systems have sprung up since Unix first appeared, and even before the dawn of Unix in 1969, there were already quite a few operating system designs (now all extinct). Why did Unix survive where others failed?

1. **Stability**
    Since the very beginning, Unix has been legendary for its stability. Unix has a well-defined boundary between the kernel of the operating system and software applications running in "user space". This is achieved through careful management of processes and memory such that one process cannot overwrite the memory belonging to another process. In effect, one application (ideally) cannot crash another application, nor can an application crash the operating system.

2. **Multi-user Design**
    Unix was designed and built from the ground up to be a multi-user "time sharing" system. This was essential when Unix was introduced because computers at the time were all allocated as shared resources. But multi-user capability remained important even after personal computers became the norm. In the early 80s, some in the computing industry underestimated the importance of multi-user design, predicting that we would be living in a one-person/one-computer world. Eventually, when it became clear with the advent of the web that multi-user functionality wasn't going to go away, those who had miscalculated before made an attempt to tack multi-user capability on to their systems as an added feature. Despite their efforts, Unix always had a clear advantage in this area being constructed from the bottom up for multiple users. The system architecture that supports the robust multi-user design in Unix is the same architecture that allows Unix to multi-task gracefully.

3. **Inter-process Communication**

One of the most important features that set Unix apart from other operating systems early on was the way that it allowed communication between processes, making it simple for the user to connect the output of one process directly into the input of another, and so forth. This functionality is referred to as "inter-process communication", and it encompasses things such as Unix sockets, signals, and pipes. Other operating systems have gained ground with similar capabilities, but Unix has always been ahead on this front.

4. **Portability**

When Unix was re-written from the ground up in C in 1972, this positioned it as one of the first operating systems that could be ported to other hardware platforms without requiring a rewrite in assembly language. This gave Unix a tremendous advantage in portability. Likewise, being based in C also made Unix infinitely more maintainable and extensible than systems written in assembly. This symbiosis between C and Unix has served to popularize both the language and the operating system together as a pair.

5. **Networking**

When TCP/IP became the standard in the U.S. for internet communications in 1983, BSD became the platform for server hosting and development. In the future, when the world wide web started becoming popular in the 1990s, Unix systems had an obvious advantage in the maturity of their TCP/IP integration—making them the first choice as web servers. This, on top of their robust multiprocessing backbone, suited Unix systems perfectly for the task of serving websites to multiple visitors at a time. Unix systems have maintained their edge in this area.

6. **Security**

When Unix was new, protecting the system from malicious attack was not the first thing the Unix creators had on their minds; however, very early in its development Unix gained a set of security mechanisms that have proven to be fundamental for keeping operating systems and their users' data safe. The cornerstone of Unix security is in the controlled access that Unix delegates to each user—as determined by the user's status in the system. Every user has a User ID (UID), and this UID follows the user with every action (i.e., every process) the user initiates. As an example, if a user creates a file, then Unix associates the user's UID with the file to establish *that* user as the file's owner. Then, if another user comes along and tries to open the file, Unix checks to see if the file's permissions allow others to access the file, and so forth. No system is perfect, but it is this principle of user ownership that underpins computer security, and Unix[4] got this right where other systems were too restrictive or too lax.

---

[4] Many ideas about user privileges and permissions came to Unix from Multics, Unix's predecessor at Bell Labs.

Why Linux?

Another question we might ask is—why has Linux grown like it has? Why haven't the other Unix-like operating systems such as the BSD variants or Minix[5] received as much interest?

1. **Child of the Internet**
    In August of 1991, there was only one website in the world (the first webpage that Tim Berners-Lee made at CERN). In 1992, there were 10 websites. This is when Linux came into being, and it was at a time of great anticipation for what lay ahead in the digital future. The people who were online at that time were the most computer savvy, and the Unix community would have been well-represented among them. If someone had a 386 PC or PC compatible and the ability to download from an ftp server, Linux was completely free with no barrier to access (Minix had to be mailed on floppy disk and wasn't free). Linux had a terminal emulator included and could be used to telnet into other systems (Torvalds' original goal) whereas Minix at the time had no terminal emulator (not so convenient!). These circumstances, plus the lack of viable alternatives[6], brought Linux to the forefront of the Unix community's attention.

    Then, with the beta release of Linux bundled with GNU utilities in late 1992, Torvalds' mission to keep Linux free gave Linux the boost that sent it into orbit. Meanwhile, BSD was consumed with legal troubles and inner conflict, and this eroded the Unix community's confidence in BSD, causing many to flock towards Linux. As Linux grew up on the internet, it eventually overtook BSD as the web's main host. The permeation of Linux into the server market spread throughout the private and public sector as the world's most powerful interests had an increasingly large stake in the internet. Corporations, universities, financial institutions, and governments became more and more invested in Linux, and over time this cemented the operating system's place around the globe as a crucial piece of civil infrastructure. All the while, what could have easily turned into chaos was masterfully held together by Linus Torvalds himself through his organizational savvy and technical genius. And, he has stayed true to his original mission to keep Linux free.

2. **The source**
    Linux is the culmination of thousands of people's contributions and is the largest open-source software project in the world. The BSD variants are managed under a very different philosophy toward collective software development, preferring an arrangement where a limited number of expert programmers make contributions outside of public view. Linux, on the other hand, is very public, and it embraces the spirit of the free and open-source software

---

[5] MINIX 3 has found its place as the hardware subsystem OS in Intel chipsets post-2015.
[6] The 386BSD OS was made available in March 1992, but a fully functional release wouldn't appear until 1994.

(FOSS) movement that continues to carry it forward to this day. Linux kernel developers generally fall somewhere in a hierarchy of those working on device drivers to those working on kernel extensions to those working on core kernel services (at the lowest levels of the operating system). There are an average eight changes made per minute to the Linux source code repository. This pace of software development is far beyond what Apple, Microsoft, or Google are capable of in their proprietary code bases. Because of the fast pace of development, Linux has seen unparalleled growth and evolution as an operating system. With containerization and virtualization becoming the dominant cloud technologies, Linux has taken the lead in these areas and will likely continue as the world's favorite free and open-source operating system.

Conventions, Concepts, and Terminology

Now that we have covered how Linux made its way into the world, it's time for us to start making our way to the Linux command line.

As we get closer to typing in our first commands, let's take a moment to build up our basic command-line vocabulary so that we can communicate about things in this environment.

The terminal, the shell, and the command line

We need to clarify these Unix-speak idioms we often hear in discussions about the Linux command line interface (CLI):

- The terminal
- The shell
- The command line

What is the "terminal"?

→ In many Linux distros, the application where the command line is accessed is called the "Terminal" app (see p. 34). In general, the "terminal" refers to the window that this app puts up on the screen. The sole purpose of this window is to house the Linux command line interface (CLI). The word "terminal" is an example of language that has outlived its original context (think old-fashioned computer terminals at airports and banks). You will hear mention of the "terminal", the "terminal window", and the "terminal emulator" in discussions about the Linux CLI. All of these refer to the same thing, which is the place where we go to access the command line.

Image: DEC VT-100 terminal

What is the "shell"?

→ The "shell" is the program running inside the terminal window. It receives and interprets our commands as we enter them on the command line. The command line itself is part of the shell program's functionality. When a terminal window is opened, a shell session starts automatically inside the terminal window and remains active until the terminal window is closed. The best way of thinking of the shell is as an environment which provides the user a comprehensive set of tools for interacting with the computer.

Why is it called the "shell"?

→ If you think of the kernel as being at the core of the operating system, then the "shell" would be at an outer layer providing a surface for human access. Depending on the user status, the shell can be made to recede, exposing deeper parts of the system.

What is "Bash"?

→ BASH ("Bourne-Again SHell"), written by Brian Fox and released through the FSF in 1989, is an enhanced version of the original Bourne Shell program $ sh created by Stephen Bourne in the 1970s. Bash is the most widely used shell in Linux. Because of its popularity, "Bash" (as a term) is commonly interchanged with "the shell" in Linux parlance. In this guide, when we refer to the "Linux command line", this can always be assumed to mean the Bash command line.

There are other shells?

→ Yes. In this guide, we will only be working with Bash, but there are other Unix-like shell programs in widespread use. Some of the other shells you will come across are Zsh (Z shell), fish (fish shell), ksh (KornShell), and tcsh (C shell). There are others, and new ones tend to pop up from time to time.

What is the "command line"?

→ The command line is the place where we enter commands in the shell. The cursor marks the position on the command line where we can insert or delete text.

What is the "command line prompt"?

```
me@MyLinuxBox:~$ 
```

→ The "command line prompt", "Bash prompt", or "shell prompt" all mean—the place marker that *prompts* (i.e., comes <u>before</u>) the cursor's starting point on the command line. In Bash, the command line prompt sits on the left side of the terminal window. See the *Command line prompt* section on p. 29 for more information.

Although **the terminal**, **the shell**, and **the command line** are all distinct from each other in meaning, it is common to hear these terms used interchangeably as references to the **Linux command line environment (CLE)**. In this guide, we will be using these (and other) terms interchangeably as they would occur in common practice.

Files, directories, and executables

In Linux, we refer to the part of the operating system that lets us access information on a hard drive (or other storage media) as the **Linux file system**.

In this guide, we will be working with these three elements in the Linux file system:

- Files
- Directories (or "folders")
- Executables (or "programs")

What is a file in Linux?

From a general-use perspective, files in Linux are just like files in other operating systems. A user might have text files, documents, images, audio, video, or other keepsake items on their hard drive, and within a Linux GUI environment (like GNOME[7] in Ubuntu, for example), the user would interact with these files in the same way they would in any desktop GUI environment. That is, double clicking on a file would open the file in an appropriate application.

But if we drill down to the command line level, we find ourselves in an environment where all information is represented in textual form. This has its limitations, but the advantage of handling information in this way is in the lockstep regularity of the plain text medium. Dealing in text lets the characters fill their natural role as standardized capsules of data (think of text characters in Linux as acting like stacked barrels of data). This, in turn, makes the data easier to access and process.

The "Linux file system" is well-chosen as a name. It is appropriate because in Linux (following the Unix tradition), everything in the file system is effectively a text file. But what does that mean? *Everything* is just text? What about images, audio/video, or other binary-encoded data?

One way of looking at this is that in the Linux CLE, with the right administrative privileges, we can use a text editor to open and inspect *any* item anywhere in the file system. It doesn't necessarily mean the files we see will contain human-readable data (image files, for example, will look like gibberish, as will compiled binaries). Still, the information would be viewable in its "raw text" representation if we perused the file system this way. This, in part, is why it is said that "Everything is a file" in Linux.

In other operating systems, we might open a `.txt` file in a text editor, but would we ever use a text editor in a non-Unix-like system to open—a folder? As though the folder were a text file? No, in these other systems, we wouldn't. However, in Linux, if we wanted to, we could use a text editor to open a directory (i.e., a folder—see p. 28) as a file. In fact, directories in Linux *are* files. But even beyond directories, things such as hardware peripherals (like the mouse/trackpad) and other Input/Output channels are represented as <u>files</u> in the Linux file system—with data flowing through them in <u>plain text form</u>. These "special files" in Linux for data I/O aren't files in the "regular" sense like data stored on a hard drive. Instead, they are "virtual files" linked to ephemeral data in transit between different points of connection. Still, these special files show up in the Linux file system right alongside regular files.

Ultimately, the computer deals in data, and in the Linux CLE, the plain text format is the medium through which everything passes. This way, we have a unified interface for storing, sending, receiving, and processing information. The shell gives us a wealth of tools that share this interface, and as we make our way ahead, we will be exploring how to work with files using these tools.

---

[7] GNOME is a popular desktop GUI environment used in many Linux distributions.

What are directories in Linux?

Directories[8] in Linux are what we call "folders" in other operating systems. They can contain files and/or other directories, just as we are familiar with in the GUI world. Unlike other operating systems where the file system is organized based on the names of storage media (e.g., "C: ", "D: " etc.), the Linux file system is entirely contained within one main directory called the **root directory**.

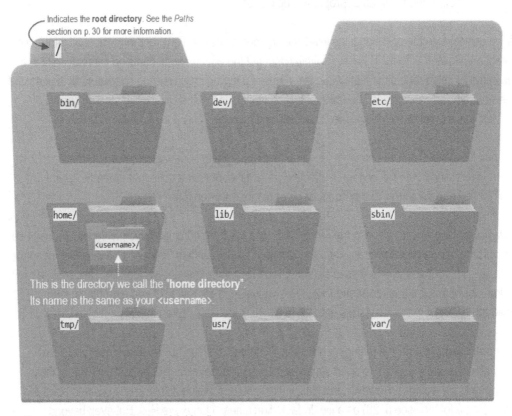

Figure 5 Linux directory structure (abridged)

In this guide, the directory where we will be most active is the /home/<username> directory, otherwise known as the **home directory**.

What are executables in Linux?

An executable is, in general, a file that can be run as a program. Many of the commands[9] that we type into the shell are executables. In the Linux CLE, for executable commands, we "call" the command by name

---

[8] Linux directories are actually files, as mentioned on the previous page. One way of making sense of this is to think of an old phone directory. It is, for all intents and purposes, like a file!

[9] Commands that are "built-in" to the shell are not separate files and are therefore technically not executables.

(i.e., type and press enter), and the shell finds the particular file with that name and arranges for the instructions in the file to be "executed" (i.e., a code interpreter and/or the kernel handle running the program stored inside the file). We "call" the shell's built-in commands as well, although they are not executables[9]. We will discuss in detail what happens in the calling process, and we will compare the different types of commands. We will also be covering the difference between non-executable and executable files.

Command line conventions

As we learn about the syntax of the Bash command line, there are some symbols and formatting conventions that we will see repeatedly. To make things easier to understand, we will need to familiarize ourselves with what these different combinations represent.

Placeholders

In many instances, we will need to indicate where certain types of information go in the command line syntax. For convenience, we will often use placeholders in substitution for specific examples. The following are some of the placeholders that we will be using.

Placeholder	Meaning
<username>	The username that you log in to your Linux machine with
<hostname>	The name that Linux assigned to your machine
<command>	Any shell command in context

The command line prompt

`me@MyLinuxBox:~$`

For this guide, whenever we reference a command as it is entered on the command line, we will use $ to represent the command line prompt. Note that the $ includes a <u>space</u> directly to the right of the dollar sign. This is important, because later we will encounter a different use of the dollar sign where no space appears on the right.

When you open the Linux shell, the command line prompt will display information in this format: <username>@<hostname>:~$. In this guide, we will generalize about the prompt by just showing the trailing end: $.

Note that when you enter your commands to the right of the prompt, you do not need to type $. Bash will automatically place the cursor right next to $.

Paths

A "path" in Linux is like a set of directions that tells us where something is located in the file system. The starting point in a path is always a directory (on the left), and the end point is either a directory or a file (on the right). The end point is the thing we are ultimately interested in, and in the case above, the end point is a directory (`<username>` represents the name of the home directory).

The most important starting point for paths in the Linux file system is the **root directory** (or "root" for short). It is the main directory of the file system, enclosing all sub-directories and files (see p. 28). Root is like the trunk of a tree, and the other directories are its branches.

In any Linux path, if there is a forward slash / with nothing to the left of it, then the forward slash indicates the root directory as the starting point. Below are some examples.

/

This path is quite simple! The starting point and end point are both root.

/etc

Here we have a path to the /etc directory for configuration files. Notice the starting point is root.

/home/<username>

Can you guess where this path leads? It goes from root to the <u>home directory</u> (your special directory for all things you).

When a path starts at root, it is called an **absolute path**. The "absolute" aspect comes from the idea that no location in the file system can descend any farther back than root. If a path does not originate from root, it is called a **relative path**.

Another starting point that is especially important for locating things in the Linux file system is the **home directory** (see p. 28). A path that starts at the home directory is an example of a relative path.

The location of the home directory is /home/<username>. When ~ is on the left side of a path, this indicates that the home directory is the path's <u>starting point</u>. Let's look at some more example paths and see if we can recognize the starting and end points.

```
~
```

Is this a path? Yes. The tilde represents the home directory as the starting point. In this case, it is also the end point!

```
~/Documents
```

Here we have the home directory as the starting point and the Documents directory inside the home directory (i.e., /home/<username>/Documents) as the end point.

```
<username>@<hostname>:~$
```

One more example. Do you see the path here? It is ~ again, this time as part of the command line prompt. The standard Bash command line prompt always displays a path to our current location in the Linux file system. In this case it is the home directory.

The anatomy of a command

The command line gets its name for the way it lets us take control of the machine. And how do we take control of the machine? By issuing it commands!

In English, a command is an "order" we give when we want something to happen. Below are some common patterns used when issuing a command in English.

A)	*"Stop!"*		
	verb		
B)	*"Stop*		*the noise!"*
	verb		**object**
C)	*"Stop*	*all*	*the noise!"*
	verb	**adj.**	**object**

Commands in the shell are similar to English except the machine is our primary audience. Below are the three main components of shell command syntax in the order they typically occur, along with their English grammar counterparts:

`$ <command>`	`[option(s)]`	`<operand(s)>`
verb	*adjective(s)/adverb(s)*	*direct/indirect object(s)*

A `$ <command>` in the shell is just like an imperative *verb* in English: "*Do* this! *Stop* that!"
An `[option]`[10] in the shell is just like an *adjective* or *adverb* in English: "Do *your* task! Stop that *now*!"
An `<operand>` in the shell is just like an *object* in English: "Do *this*! Stop *that*!"

Like natural language, there is flexibility in the way we can form shell commands depending on what we want to express. Some shell commands may have all three components of the syntax, and some may have just the `$ <command>` (i.e., the verb) itself.

Below are some examples of shell commands and their English translations.

Bash:

`$ ls`	`*.xml`
`$ <command>`	`<operand>`

English:

"List	*.xml files!"*
verb	**object**

Bash:

`$ ls`	`-r`	`*.xml`
`$ <command>`	`[option]`	`<operand>`

English:

"List	*.xml files*	*in reverse!"*
verb	**object**	**adverbial**

Let's look at one more example[11].

Bash:
`$ cp -r ~/Pictures ~/Photos`

English:
"Copy the Pictures directory recursively and paste as a directory called Photos!"

In the command above, again we see the three main components of shell command syntax:

`$ cp`	`-r`	`~/Pictures ~/Photos`
`$ <command>`	`[option]`	`<operands>`

---

[10] In Linux-speak, the words "flag" and "switch" are commonly used in place of "option".
[11] Be careful with the `$ cp` command! You could end up accidentally overwriting a file or directory with `$ cp`.

The [option(s)] and <operand(s)> make up the command's **arguments**—collectively called the **argument** of the command. Keep in mind that a command could have any combination of (valid) arguments, or the argument could be implicit if we use the $ <command> by itself.

Three types of commands in the shell environment

There are three different types of callable commands on the Bash command line:

1) **Built-in commands**
    Shell built-in commands, often referred to as "built-ins", are part of the /usr/bin/bash program* itself. This means built-ins are not executable files in the Linux file system (/usr/bin/bash is the executable[12] program file which runs as the shell inside the terminal).

2) **External commands**
    External commands are executable program files generally located in the /usr/bin directory. Ubuntu comes installed with many external commands, and more can be downloaded via Ubuntu's package management utilities.

3) **Scripted commands**
    Scripted commands include executable files programmed in Bash[13] as well as Bash functions loaded and defined at shell startup. It is common to keep the files for custom-scripted commands inside the home directory (~).

*On Ubuntu systems pre version 19.04, the location of the $ bash executable may be /bin/bash rather than /usr/bin/bash.

Getting Started

We are close to being ready to make the jump into the Linux command line environment! There are just a couple of additional things we need to cover in our preparation, and then we will be on our way!

The Linux distro

In this guide, we will be referring to the **Ubuntu 20.04** LTS (Focal Fossa) distribution of Linux. Other versions of Ubuntu should work as well* (see the message above about the location of the $ bash executable in Ubuntu pre-v19.04). If you are using another Linux distribution or another variety of Unix-like operating system, please exercise caution as we cannot guarantee 100% compliance.

---

[12] The /usr/bin/bash executable binary automatically launches every time we open a new terminal window. On some occasions, it may also be necessary to call $ bash as a command on the command line. When we call $ bash, it is like we are launching a shell inside the already open shell.

[13] Aside from Bash, some other common scripting languages used in Linux include Python, Perl, and Ruby.

If you haven't already installed Ubuntu, you can get information about how to do so here: https://help.ubuntu.com/lts/installation-guide/index.html.

For the purposes of this guide, we will assume that you, the reader, are the administrator of your own Linux user account on your own machine with a dedicated Linux boot partition. If you are not the administrator of your own Linux account, then you may need to request admin authorization for certain activities. Please consult with your system administrator and take any necessary precautions.

Opening the terminal window

Assuming everything is installed and that you are logged in and ready to go, let's find the Terminal app and get started! There are several ways of opening the terminal window in Ubuntu.

```
ctrl + alt + t
```
- or -

Click on the GNOME App Launcher, find the Terminal icon in Utilities, and click.

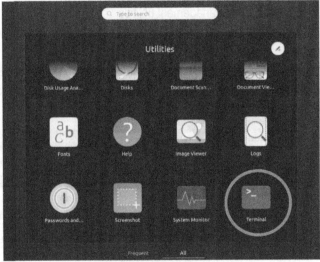

Figure 5 Ubuntu GNOME App Launcher diagram

We recommend adding the Terminal icon to your Ubuntu Favorites dock for easy access.

Some first commands

If you can't wait, here are a couple of commands to try before we go in deep. Just type them in at the shell prompt, press enter, and see what happens!

```
$ date
$ cal
$ echo 'Hello World!'
```

Linux Command Line Survival Kit

There are some things that you should be aware of as you venture for the first time into the command line environment. Bringing these tokens along can save you a lot of frustration.

Linux command line help resources

If at any point you happen to get stuck or are not sure what to do on the command line, there are help resources available at your fingertips. Note that in all but one of the following examples, the $ <command> you want help with is in the <operand> position.

$ man <command>

Here is the key to unlock the vast majority of documentation resources for the Linux command line. Calling $ man <command> will return the command's "$ man pages" (short for "manual pages"). Reading a command's $ man pages[14] will give you virtually everything you ever wanted to know about the command[15]. Plus, $ man pages have info about general Linux operation as well. Sometimes the sheer volume of information in $ man pages can be overwhelming, but with a little practice you will become familiar with the $ man page routine. Try $ man man!

All $ man pages follow this general structure:

> NAME
> SYNOPSIS – Models how to format the command with arguments.
> DESCRIPTION – Details the operation of the command and lists each [option] for modifying the command's behavior.
>
> → Pro tip—when looking through $ man pages, press the Space Bar to page down, and the b key to page up. Press / to search. Press q to quit and return to the command line.

$ <command> --help

Here is a method of obtaining help documents for Bash built-in commands (see p. 33). This style of [option] formatting with two dashes followed by a full word is called a **long option**. Notice with this method you are calling the $ <command> itself, unlike the other examples here. Try this method if you are looking for built-in command (see p. 33) help documents that fit on one page.

---

[14] Historically, "$ man page" (singular) was the standard term, but over time as commands gained more features, the added documentation led to "$ man pages" (plural) becoming common in use.
[15] Most commands do have $ man pages, but if not, you can usually find help using the other methods here.

$ help <command>

The $ help <command> method displays the same help documentation as $ <command> --help for built-in commands (see p. 33). Calling $ help -m <command> tells $ help to check if $ man pages exist for the built-in $ <command> and to display the $ man pages if they are available. Check $ help help for more information and to view other [options].

$ info <command>

If you prefer docs in a hypertextual layout with topics linked to a central table of contents, try running $ info <command>. If a command's info files are available, $ info will present the information in a book-like structure with plenty of cross references to related topics and other information. Press the Space Bar to page forward and the backspace key to page backward.

$ apropos <pattern>

This one will help you even if you don't know the name of the command you want. You can try it with a search keyword (which in shell-speak is a <pattern>), and it will give you a list of suggestions for commands that have related functionality. Try it with something like "backup" and see what you get!

$ whatis <command>

If all you need is a very brief one-line description of what a command does, look no further than the $ whatis utility. In fact, the description that $ whatis <command> returns is taken directly from the one-line abstract found in the beginning of the command's $ man pages. Try $ man whatis and then try $ whatis whatis. While you're at it, you might as well try $ whatis man as well!

Key-command combinations and other useful shell commands

Once you start working in the terminal, you will notice that things aren't quite the same as in the "outside world" (in the GUI environment we are all accustomed to). There are several commands and key combinations you will want to add to your repertoire to make life in the shell a lot easier, especially if you are jumping back and forth between the terminal window and other apps.

1. To Cut, Copy, or Paste inside the terminal window:

    To cut: ctrl + shift + x
    To copy: ctrl + shift + c
    To paste: ctrl + shift + v

2. To page up and down inside the terminal window (on the command line):

> To page up: `shift + pg up`
> To page down: `shift + pg dn`

3. If you don't feel like re-typing something on the command line, these tricks come in handy.

> To run the most recently entered command again: `$ !!`
> To insert the `<operand>` from the argument of the most recent command: `alt + .`
> To flip through previous commands: Up Arrow ↑ & Down Arrow ↓

4. These key commands will help you move the cursor around on the command line more efficiently than with the left ← and right → arrows alone.

> To move to the start of the line (on the left): `ctrl + a`
> To move to the end of the line (on the right): `ctrl + e`

> To move back to the previous word (on the left): `alt + b` -or- `ctrl + ←`
> To move forward to the next word (on the right): `alt + f` -or- `ctrl + →`

5. Sometimes, you just need control. **These commands and key combinations will give you control in the shell when it feels like you've lost it!**

> To interrupt a process in the shell (like pressing "**Cancel**"): `ctrl + c`
> To suspend a process in the shell (like pressing "**Pause**"): `ctrl + z`
> To resume a process directly after `ctrl + z`, enter `$ fg` (for "foreground").
>
> To stop a process from printing to the screen: `ctrl + s`
> To resume printing to the screen directly after `ctrl + s`: `ctrl + q`
>
> To send an "**EOF**" (**End of File**) message when entering text: `ctrl + d`
> To **toggle** between the current cursor position and the start of the line: `ctrl + xx`
> To **clear** the terminal window: `ctrl + l` -or- `$ clear`
>
> To **exit** the shell session and close the terminal window: `ctrl + d` -or- `$ exit`
> To **restart** the computer: `$ reboot`
> To **shut down** the computer: `$ shutdown`

Life on the Command Line

Who am I?

If you haven't already done so, open the Ubuntu Terminal app with the key command `ctrl + alt + t` or click on the Terminal icon in the Ubuntu App Launcher dashboard.

We're here! Our first day on the Linux command line has arrived. We're going to take small steps at first and continue building our concept of how things work in this environment. Take a moment to get situated, and whenever you are ready, try typing something in at the prompt to see how the shell reacts to your input. Go ahead and type anything that comes to mind. For example, you could type, "My name is..." and then press `enter`.

You will see that Bash simply returns a `command not found` error when it receives input that it doesn't know how to interpret. These errors are harmless, and you should never have to worry about causing any problems by mis-typing something or entering an invalid command.

In fact, if you feel at all trepidatious about entering commands for fear of doing something wrong or causing damage to the system, you will be relieved to know that Ubuntu comes set up with limitations on our user privileges such that we will never even get close to causing system-wide damage through anything we do.

As we start learning more Linux commands, we will find certain situations where we have to practice extra caution with actions like `$ touch`, `$ cp` (copy), `$ mv`, (move), and `$ rm` (remove). If we are not careful with these, we could accidentally delete or overwrite our *own* files (and/or directories). With that said, until we get to the point where we actually start using these commands, we can relax knowing that Ubuntu's configuration of Linux will keep our files safe.

How does Linux control which files and directories a user can access?

Linux user status and permissions

The roots of Linux as a multi-user system run deep, and what you can or cannot do in the Linux command line environment (CLE) entirely depends on <u>who you are</u> and <u>what files you own</u>.

$ whoami

So, who are you? Let's find out. Go to the command line and enter the following command:

```
$ whoami
```

You should see your `<username>` directly below in the output. To Linux, this is who you are. Your `<username>` carries a **user status** that defines the limits of what you are permitted to do in the Linux file system.

There are two factors that determine your user status:

Factor #1   What type of user are you (a root user or a regular user)?

→   In Linux, if someone is a **root user** (or "root" for short), there is basically no restriction on what they can do. Just like the root directory contains all files and sub-directories in the Linux file system, a root user has ownership of every single file and directory in the entire system. The root directory might as well be a root user's home directory! A root user can view, open, modify, create, run, and/or delete any file as they see fit—and they can also install programs. This sounds great, except that Linux gives root users the power to <u>irrevocably destroy the system</u>. This is why we have to be very careful with root status.

→   A **regular user** has, as you might have guessed, a more limited set of **permissions** for what they can do in the Linux file system. A regular user is guaranteed to own the files and directories contained in their home directory (the `<username>` 🏠). This ensures that a regular user can view, open, modify, create, run, and/or delete files inside their home directory as they see fit. Beyond that, generally a regular user will have restrictions on what files they can interact with. The exception would be in cases where a regular user belongs to a **user group** with permissions that extend to directories and files outside of the user's home directory.

Factor #2   What user group(s) do you belong to?

→ A root user belongs to the **root** user group by default. Being that root supersedes all other groups, no other group membership has any bearing on the root user's file permissions.

→ A regular user belongs to their own group by default, referred to as the user's **primary group**. A regular user's primary group has the same name as `<username>` (unless the user changes the name). In addition to their primary group, a regular user can belong to other groups if a system administrator authorizes their membership.

$ id

To find out what type of user you are and what groups you belong to, enter this simple command:

```
$ id
```

Assuming you installed Ubuntu on your own machine[16] (or virtual machine), in the output you should see something like this:

```
uid=1000(<username>) gid=1000(<username>) groups=...27(sudo)...
```

You will see other groups listed, but we can disregard them for now. Let's focus on these three pieces of information:

`uid=1000(<username>)` ⟵	Your **User ID** (`uid`) is the number 1000 (user #1000). This is what Linux automatically assigned to you when you installed Ubuntu. The choice of 1000 is customary from the Unix tradition and is largely arbitrary as a "high" valued number. However, if this number were 0, then you would be root. Since it is not 0, this means you are a <u>regular user</u>.
`gid=1000(<username>)` ⟵	Your **Primary Group ID** (`gid`) is also the number 1000 (group #1000). Linux assigned this number to your primary group when you installed Ubuntu. If this number were 0, then you would be a member of the root group. Since it is not 0, this reaffirms that you are a <u>regular user</u>.
`groups=...27(sudo)...` ⟵	This tells us that you are a member of the sudo group (group #27). This is important because it will allow you to use the $ sudo command to temporarily assume root status in order to perform system administrator operations like installing new packages, etc.

---

[16] If you are working on a shared system or you are not the person who installed Ubuntu, you might see very different results when you run the $ id command. Consult with your system administrator if necessary.

Ubuntu disables the root account by default. This is common practice as a security measure to protect the system from attack and other pitfalls. The takeaway from this, as we discovered with the $ id command, is that you are a regular user, *but* you do have the capability to temporarily become root[17] through the $ sudo command[18] (which stands for "superuser do") should you need to for any reason. This is the best compromise between safety (regular user status) and power (ability to act as root). Later in this guide, we will go over how to use the $ sudo command to install programs and perform other elevated-status operations in the Linux CLE. For now, be happy that you're regular!

Summary:

The multi-user foundations of Linux begin at the deepest parts of the operating system. In order to maintain system integrity, Linux reserves full system access for "root" users only (otherwise known as "superusers"). All other users (known as "regular" users) are subject to limitations depending on what files they own and/or what user groups they belong to. As a security measure, Ubuntu disables the root account by default. If an Ubuntu user needs to perform an action requiring root authorization, they can do so with the help of the $ sudo command.

Commands:

```
$ whoami
$ id
```

Concepts:

- Linux command line errors
- Caution with certain commands
- Linux user status and permissions
    - Root users
    - Regular users
    - File ownership
    - Group membership
    - Temporary root status
        - $ sudo

Challenge:

Take a look at the $ man pages for the $ id command ($ man id) and see if you can find two [options] to use with $ id that will produce the same output as the $ whoami command. Try entering the $ id [options] combination on the command line. Did it return your <username>?

---

[17] Depending on context, at times the word "root" refers to the directory, and at other times it refers to the user status (e.g., "that user is root"). In this case, it refers to the user status.

[18] The name "superuser" is another term commonly used for a person with root status.

Where am I?

Now that we have a sense of who we are on the Linux command line, we are going to take a look at where we are in the **Linux file system** and how to move around in this landscape.

We often describe the Linux command line as being integrated within an "environment", as though we actually go somewhere when we use it. This is an instructive way of thinking of the shell because in fact, whenever we use the command line, we are always perched somewhere in the Linux file system. One way to find our current position in the file system is to look at the Bash **command line prompt**.

`<username>@<hostname>:~$`   The ~ here indicates our current position in the file system—the **home directory**. See the *Paths* section on p. 30 for reference.

In the standard Ubuntu Bash command line prompt, the **relative path** (see p. 30) to our current location is displayed between `:` and `$` when we are within the bounds of the home directory.

`$ pwd`

In many situations, we will want a command that reveals where we are in the Linux file system. Bash conveniently provides us with such a command. Try entering this on the command line:

$ pwd

You should see something like this in the output:

`/home/<username>`

The `$ pwd` ("print working directory") command returns the **absolute path** (see p. 30) to the directory where we are currently stationed. Running the `$ pwd` command is like taking a GPS reading of our current position in the file system. Wherever we are, we refer to our position as the **current working directory** (cwd).

Frequently used Linux commands

We're ready to start taking bolder steps on the Linux command line and putting some of its most important tools into service. After working in the shell for some time, you will find there are a handful of commands that you use much more frequently than others. These commands will become so familiar to you that you will type them in without even thinking about it. And even if you go for years without touching the command line interface, these commands will still be with you.

$ ls

As you navigate your way around the Linux file system, you will want to know the contents of the directories you visit. You will develop a reflex for typing in the $ `ls` command to list the contents of the current working directory.

Try it! Type in the following and press enter:

$ ls

The output should be as shown below.

```
                                                    me@MyLinuxBox: ~
me@MyLinuxBox:~$ ls
Desktop  Documents  Downloads  Music  Pictures  Public  snap  Templates  Videos
me@MyLinuxBox:~$ 
```

Congratulations! You have successfully listed (some of) the contents of the home directory. What do we see here? It's a little hard to tell, but we can discern that this is a list of sub-directories[19] inside the home directory. These directories are automatically created for us when we install Ubuntu.

It would be nice if we could see these items in a vertical list format. Thankfully, there is an [option] for that. Try this combination:

$ ls -l

The -l lets us list the contents in long format. Listing this way also reveals other useful information.

```
                                                    me@MyLinuxBox: ~
me@MyLinuxBox:~$ ls
Desktop  Documents  Downloads  Music  Pictures  Public  snap  Templates  Videos
me@MyLinuxBox:~$ ls -l                              ───── owner (<username>)
total 36
drwxr-xr-x 2 me me 4096 Nov 18 19:24 Desktop        primary group name
drwxr-xr-x 2 me me 4096 Nov 18 19:24 Documents      (same as <username>)
drwxr-xr-x 2 me me 4096 Nov 18 19:24 Downloads
drwxr-xr-x 2 me me 4096 Nov 18 19:24 Music
drwxr-xr-x 2 me me 4096 Nov 18 19:35 Pictures
drwxr-xr-x 2 me me 4096 Nov 18 19:24 Public
drwxr-xr-x 3 me me 4096 Nov 18 19:25 snap
drwxr-xr-x 2 me me 4096 Nov 18 19:24 Templates
drwxr-xr-x 2 me me 4096 Nov 18 19:24 Videos
me@MyLinuxBox:~$ 
```

---

[19] One way of identifying directories in Ubuntu Bash is by the neon blue color of the font.

Next, let's go a step further and list all of the contents of the home directory. Try this on the command line:

$ ls -la

```
                                                            me@MyLinuxBox: ~
me@MyLinuxBox:~$ ls
Desktop  Documents  Downloads  Music  Pictures  Public  snap  Templates  Videos
me@MyLinuxBox:~$ ls -l
total 36
drwxr-xr-x 2 me me 4096 Nov 18 19:24 Desktop
drwxr-xr-x 2 me me 4096 Nov 18 19:24 Documents
drwxr-xr-x 2 me me 4096 Nov 18 19:24 Downloads
drwxr-xr-x 2 me me 4096 Nov 18 19:24 Music
drwxr-xr-x 2 me me 4096 Nov 18 19:35 Pictures
drwxr-xr-x 2 me me 4096 Nov 18 19:24 Public
drwxr-xr-x 3 me me 4096 Nov 18 19:25 snap
drwxr-xr-x 2 me me 4096 Nov 18 19:24 Templates
drwxr-xr-x 2 me me 4096 Nov 18 19:24 Videos
me@MyLinuxBox:~$ ls -la
total 80
drwxr-xr-x 16 me   me   4096 Nov 18 19:32 .
drwxr-xr-x  4 root root 4096 Nov 18 19:22 ..
-rw-------  1 me   me     64 Nov 18 19:30 .bash_history
-rw-r--r--  1 me   me    220 Nov 18 19:22 .bash_logout          ──── hidden file
-rw-r--r--  1 me   me   3793 Nov 18 19:31 .bashrc
drwx------ 13 me   me   4096 Nov 18 19:34 .cache
drwxr-xr-x 11 me   me   4096 Nov 18 19:32 .config
drwxr-xr-x  2 me   me   4096 Nov 18 19:24 Desktop
drwxr-xr-x  2 me   me   4096 Nov 18 19:24 Documents
drwxr-xr-x  2 me   me   4096 Nov 18 19:24 Downloads            ──── hidden directory
drwx------  3 me   me   4096 Nov 18 19:24 .gnupg
drwxr-xr-x  3 me   me   4096 Nov 18 19:24 .local
drwxr-xr-x  2 me   me   4096 Nov 18 19:24 Music
drwxr-xr-x  2 me   me   4096 Nov 18 19:36 Pictures
drwx------  3 me   me   4096 Nov 18 19:32 .pki
-rw-r--r--  1 me   me    807 Nov 18 19:22 .profile
drwxr-xr-x  2 me   me   4096 Nov 18 19:24 Public
drwxr-xr-x  3 me   me   4096 Nov 18 19:25 snap
drwxr-xr-x  2 me   me   4096 Nov 18 19:24 Templates
drwxr-xr-x  2 me   me   4096 Nov 18 19:24 Videos
me@MyLinuxBox:~$
```

Wait a minute. The list just became twice as long! What happened? Notice all of the additional items that previously weren't visible have a . as the first character in their names. Items like this are called **dot files** and **dot directories** in Linux. They are hidden from view unless we invoke -a (or -A) as an [option] with the $ ls command. Just think of "dot files" and "dot directories" as code in Linux for hidden files or directories.

Some other [options] that are common with the $ ls command are listed below.

Bash	English
$ ls -S	*List* directory contents arranged by *Size* (largest to smallest).
$ ls -t	*List* directory contents by *time* of modification (most recent first).
$ ls -r	*List* directory contents in *reverse* order.
$ ls -n	*List* directory contents with User IDs and Group IDs displayed *numerically*.

As we saw with `$ ls -la`, it is possible to mix and match `[options]` to display different varieties of information. It generally doesn't matter what order the `[options]` are in as long as they are adjacent to each other as shown. Try these and see what you get!

$$ \text{\$ ls -aS} $$
$$ \text{\$ ls -alt} $$
$$ \text{\$ ls -alnr} $$

One drawback of relying on a pool of `[options]` to output different results is that the `[options]` can be difficult to remember. To alleviate this, Bash comes set up with some useful shortcuts known as **aliases** (which we will explore in detail later) for simplifying the entry of `$ ls` with different `[options]`. These aliases are much quicker to type in than the full commands.

Bash Alias	Full Bash Command	English
$ ll	$ ls -alF	List *all* files in *long* form w/ special *Formatting*.
$ la	$ ls -A	List *All* files except for the **.** and **..** directory shortcuts[20].
$ l	$ ls -CF	List files in *Column* view w/ special *Formatting*.

When we list the contents of a directory, sometimes we want to limit the output to files and sub-directories whose names match specific search criteria. For example, we may only want to list files and directories that start with the letter "D". How would we accomplish this?

One way we can tell `$ ls` which character (or group of characters) to feature in the output is by placing a `<pattern>` of characters in the `<operand>` position (see p. 31) directly followed by *. The * symbol is called a **wildcard operator** when it is used this way. The * wildcard operator will allow <u>any</u> instance of the `<pattern>` to trigger a result in the output of the command.

Let's try it on the command line. First, we will clear the terminal window to start fresh at the top.

$$ \text{\$ clear} $$

Now, enter the following:

$$ \text{\$ ls -la D*} $$

---

[20] When `$ ls -la` returns a list of <u>all</u> files and directories inside the current working directory (cwd), you will see two special entries in the beginning of the list. These entries, **.** and **..**, are symbols representing the <u>current working directory</u> and the <u>parent directory</u>, respectively. We will cover how these symbols function as path shortcuts in the **$ cd** section of this chapter.

```
[⊡]                                                        me@MyLinuxBox: ~
me@MyLinuxBox:~$ ls -la D*
Desktop: ◄────
total 8
drwxr-xr-x  2 me me 4096 Nov 18 19:24 .
drwxr-xr-x 16 me me 4096 Nov 22 09:10 ..

Documents: ◄────
total 8
drwxr-xr-x  2 me me 4096 Nov 18 19:24 .
drwxr-xr-x 16 me me 4096 Nov 22 09:10 ..

Downloads: ◄────
total 8
drwxr-xr-x  2 me me 4096 Nov 18 19:24 .
drwxr-xr-x 16 me me 4096 Nov 22 09:10 ..
me@MyLinuxBox:~$ █
```

Here we see the three directories inside ~ that start with the letter "D". Although each of these directories is empty[21], $ ls seems to think that we want to view their contents. This is because the D* in the <operand> expands to the full names of the three D* directories, and these names become the objects of $ ls (see p. 31). Since we don't want to view the contents of these directories but instead just want to list their names, we'll add the -d [option] to limit the output to the names of these directories.

$ ls -lad D*

```
[⊡]                                                        me@MyLinuxBox: ~
me@MyLinuxBox:~$ ls -lad D*
drwxr-xr-x 2 me me 4096 Nov 18 19:24 Desktop
drwxr-xr-x 2 me me 4096 Nov 18 19:24 Documents
drwxr-xr-x 2 me me 4096 Nov 18 19:24 Downloads
me@MyLinuxBox:~$ █
```

Well done! The $ ls command will follow you everywhere in all your future Linux endeavors, and we will continue to get practice with it throughout this guide. We encourage you to look at the $ man pages for $ ls ($ man ls) and experiment with the many [options] available.

$ cd

So far we have done all of our business right inside the home directory, but there is a whole file system out there that we have yet to explore. It's about time to venture beyond our doorstep and have a look around the neighborhood. And, while we're at it, we can zoom back inside the home directory to get our bearings if we need to.

Although it may not appear so at first, the command line is actually a place of great mobility. With just a single command, we can transport ourselves from the current working directory to anywhere else in

---

[21] They are empty except for the . and .. shortcuts, which we discuss in the $ cd section.

the file system (anywhere we have permission to visit, that is). All we need is the $ cd command (for change directory) and a **path** to tell the command where to take us. Where would you like to go?

Let's start off by jumping to a place whose path is easy to remember—the root directory. Recall that the root directory as a starting point is represented as / on the left side of a path. Since the root directory in this case is also the end point (i.e., our destination), this means the entire path is simply /. Shall we try it?

Enter the following on the command line:

$ cd /

And we're here! Notice the command line prompt no longer displays ~ as the current working directory but rather shows /.

Let's take a current reading of our location with $ pwd and then do an $ ll to list all of the / directory contents.

```
                                                              me@MyLinuxBox: /
me@MyLinuxBox:~$ cd /
me@MyLinuxBox:/$ pwd
/
me@MyLinuxBox:/$ ll
total 2097240
drwxr-xr-x  20 root root       4096 Jul 26 21:43 ./
drwxr-xr-x  20 root root       4096 Jul 26 21:43 ../
lrwxrwxrwx   1 root root          7 Jul 15 17:07 bin -> usr/bin/
drwxr-xr-x   4 root root       4096 Nov 22 09:08 boot/
drwxr-xr-x   2 root root       4096 Jul 15 17:09 cdrom/
drwxr-xr-x  19 root root       4600 Nov 22 04:07 dev/
drwxr-xr-x 133 root root      12288 Nov 22 09:09 etc/
drwxr-xr-x   4 root root       4096 Nov 18 19:22 home/
lrwxrwxrwx   1 root root          7 Jul 15 17:07 lib -> usr/lib/
lrwxrwxrwx   1 root root          9 Jul 15 17:07 lib32 -> usr/lib32/
lrwxrwxrwx   1 root root          9 Jul 15 17:07 lib64 -> usr/lib64/
lrwxrwxrwx   1 root root         10 Jul 15 17:07 libx32 -> usr/libx32/
drwx------   2 root root      16384 Jul 15 17:07 lost+found/
drwxr-xr-x   2 root root       4096 Apr 23  2020 media/
drwxr-xr-x   2 root root       4096 Apr 23  2020 mnt/
drwxr-xr-x   3 root root       4096 Jul 15 17:41 opt/
dr-xr-xr-x 243 root root          0 Nov 22 04:07 proc/
drwx------   4 root root       4096 Nov  6 10:36 root/
drwxr-xr-x  35 root root        980 Nov 22 09:16 run/
lrwxrwxrwx   1 root root          8 Jul 15 17:07 sbin -> usr/sbin/
drwxr-xr-x  13 root root       4096 Nov  8 15:04 snap/
drwxr-xr-x   2 root root       4096 Apr 23  2020 srv/
-rw-------   1 root root 2147483648 Jul 15 17:07 swapfile
dr-xr-xr-x  13 root root          0 Nov 22 04:07 sys/
drwxrwxrwt  21 root root       4096 Nov 22 10:16 tmp/
drwxr-xr-x  14 root root       4096 Apr 23  2020 usr/
drwxr-xr-x  15 root root       4096 Jul 22 18:48 var/
me@MyLinuxBox:/$ 
```

Here we have a wide-angle view of the entire Linux file system. That's quite a lot of directories.

Fortunately, for our purposes we will only need to concern ourselves with a select few of these. You will see a directory named /home. Is this what we call the home directory? Not quite.

The "home directory", as we call it, is actually *inside* /home. The path to the home directory, as you will remember, is /home/<username> (see p. 28). This is where we just came from. Shall we go back for a brief visit?

We could enter $ cd /home/<username> and be there in (almost) no time, but there are even easier ways to teleport ourselves back home. Bash gives us several shortcuts to the home directory that make it a snap to go home if we need to. The first one will be familiar to you. We will simply use ~ as the path for the $ cd command to follow. Try it!

$ cd ~

That was quick. Notice the path in the command line prompt has changed again back to ~. Doing a $ pwd confirms our location as /home/<username>. Let's run an $ ll for good measure.

```
me@MyLinuxBox: ~

me@MyLinuxBox:/$ cd ~
me@MyLinuxBox:~$ pwd
/home/me
me@MyLinuxBox:~$ ll
total 80
drwxr-xr-x 16 me    me    4096 Nov 22 09:10 ./
drwxr-xr-x  4 root root 4096 Nov 18 19:22 ../
-rw-------  1 me    me     142 Nov 18 19:42 .bash_history
-rw-r--r--  1 me    me     220 Nov 18 19:22 .bash_logout
-rw-r--r--  1 me    me    3793 Nov 18 19:31 .bashrc
drwx------ 13 me    me    4096 Nov 18 19:34 .cache/
drwxr-xr-x 12 me    me    4096 Nov 18 19:42 .config/
drwxr-xr-x  2 me    me    4096 Nov 18 19:24 Desktop/
drwxr-xr-x  2 me    me    4096 Nov 18 19:24 Documents/
drwxr-xr-x  2 me    me    4096 Nov 18 19:24 Downloads/
drwx------  3 me    me    4096 Nov 18 19:24 .gnupg/
drwxr-xr-x  3 me    me    4096 Nov 18 19:24 .local/
drwxr-xr-x  2 me    me    4096 Nov 18 19:24 Music/
drwxr-xr-x  2 me    me    4096 Nov 22 10:18 Pictures/
drwx------  3 me    me    4096 Nov 18 19:32 .pki/
-rw-r--r--  1 me    me     807 Nov 18 19:22 .profile
drwxr-xr-x  2 me    me    4096 Nov 18 19:24 Public/
drwxr-xr-x  3 me    me    4096 Nov 18 19:25 snap/
drwxr-xr-x  2 me    me    4096 Nov 18 19:24 Templates/
drwxr-xr-x  2 me    me    4096 Nov 18 19:24 Videos/
me@MyLinuxBox:~$
```

All looks just as we left it. It's nice to know we can always go home at a moment's notice.

Now, let's skip back to root again.

$ cd /

You should see **/** as the path in the command line prompt. Confirm your location with **$** `pwd`.

```
                                                          me@MyLinuxBox: /
me@MyLinuxBox:~$ cd /
me@MyLinuxBox:/$ pwd
/
me@MyLinuxBox:/$ ▊
```

Good. Now we're going to try another method of flying back home. This one is even quicker than the last. Simply enter this on the command line:

$$\text{\$ cd}$$

And we're back! This is an incredibly convenient shortcut and one that is virtually impossible to forget. A **$** `pwd` and **$** `ll` will help us confirm that we have arrived in the home directory.

```
                                                          me@MyLinuxBox: ~
me@MyLinuxBox:/$ cd
me@MyLinuxBox:~$ pwd
/home/me
me@MyLinuxBox:~$ ll
total 80
drwxr-xr-x 16 me    me    4096 Nov 22 09:10 ./   ◄━━━━━
drwxr-xr-x  4 root root 4096 Nov 18 19:22 ../   ◄━━━━━
-rw-------  1 me    me     880 Nov 22 21:54 .bash_history
-rw-r--r--  1 me    me     220 Nov 18 19:22 .bash_logout
-rw-r--r--  1 me    me    3793 Nov 18 19:31 .bashrc
drwx------ 13 me    me    4096 Nov 18 19:34 .cache/
drwxr-xr-x 12 me    me    4096 Nov 18 19:42 .config/
drwxr-xr-x  2 me    me    4096 Nov 18 19:24 Desktop/
drwxr-xr-x  2 me    me    4096 Nov 18 19:24 Documents/
drwxr-xr-x  2 me    me    4096 Nov 18 19:24 Downloads/
drwx------  3 me    me    4096 Nov 18 19:24 .gnupg/
drwxr-xr-x  3 me    me    4096 Nov 18 19:24 .local/
drwxr-xr-x  2 me    me    4096 Nov 18 19:24 Music/
drwxr-xr-x  2 me    me    4096 Nov 23 13:01 Pictures/
drwx------  3 me    me    4096 Nov 18 19:32 .pki/
-rw-r--r--  1 me    me     807 Nov 18 19:22 .profile
drwxr-xr-x  2 me    me    4096 Nov 18 19:24 Public/
drwxr-xr-x  3 me    me    4096 Nov 18 19:25 snap/
drwxr-xr-x  2 me    me    4096 Nov 18 19:24 Templates/
drwxr-xr-x  2 me    me    4096 Nov 18 19:24 Videos/
me@MyLinuxBox:~$ ▊
```

While we're here, take a look at the first two entries in the list: **.** and **..**, both of which appear to be directories. Can we **$** `cd` to those directories? Let's **$** `clear` the terminal window and try the first one.

$$\text{\$ cd .}$$

```
                                                          me@MyLinuxBox: ~
me@MyLinuxBox:~$ cd .
me@MyLinuxBox:~$ ▊
```

If it seems to you like nothing happened, you would be right. Placing . on the left side of a path in Linux always means the <u>current working directory</u> (cwd) as the starting point of the path. So, for $ cd, the . directory shortcut does nothing useful. But for other commands, typing . is easier than banging out the full path to the cwd. And following the . with a forward slash like ./ allows us to define a relative path with an end point inside the cwd. But with the $ cd command, would we ever need to indicate $ cd ./<directory> if $ cd <directory> (inside the cwd) delivers us to the same place? The answer is no, we <u>don't</u> need to indicate a ./ path[22] at all when using the $ cd command.

Something more practical for our use right now is the .. directory shortcut, which represents the **parent directory** (i.e., the enclosing directory). To demonstrate how to use these two dots, let's $ clear the terminal window again, $ pwd to remind ourselves where we are, and then try this:

$ cd ..

Where did we go? Another $ pwd and $ ll will help us get a reading on our position.

```
                                          me@MyLinuxBox: /home
me@MyLinuxBox:~$ pwd
/home/me
me@MyLinuxBox:~$ cd ..
me@MyLinuxBox:/home$ pwd
/home
me@MyLinuxBox:/home$ ll
total 16
drwxr-xr-x  4 root  root  4096 Nov 18 19:22 ./
drwxr-xr-x 20 root  root  4096 Jul 26 21:43 ../
drwxr-xr-x 16 me    me    4096 Nov 22 09:10 me/
me@MyLinuxBox:/home$
```

We took a step back out of ~ and into its enclosing directory, /home (see p. 28 for reference). This is very useful! We can always apply $ cd .. to hop one step back into the parent directory from wherever[23] we are. And a neat trick here is that we can daisy chain these .. directory shortcuts in a path and hop back as much as we like. To see how this works, first let's take a quick trip to the ~/Documents directory with $ cd ~/Documents. Now, try the following:

$ cd ../../..

```
                                          me@MyLinuxBox: /
me@MyLinuxBox:~/Documents$ cd ../../..
me@MyLinuxBox:/$ pwd
/
me@MyLinuxBox:/$
```

---

[22] The ./ relative path to the cwd is sometimes used to launch executable files, which we will explore later.
[23] The only exception to this would be the / directory, which has no parent directory because root, by definition, encloses all other directories in the Linux file system.

We hopped, skipped, and jumped all the way back to root! When we're dealing with layer upon layer of parent directories, this trick comes in very handy.

There's another fantastic shortcut with the $ cd command that all Linux users should know about. Here in the root directory, let's $ clear the terminal window again and give this a whirl (warning: hold on to your hat).

$ cd -

Whoa! Now where are we? We're back in the ~/Documents directory! The $ cd - shortcut always returns us right back wherever we came from, no matter how distant in the file system. This can be a life saver in certain situations, especially if we forget where we were and we need to go back!

At times, typing the names of files and directories can be a little cumbersome on the command line, especially when the names are long or hard to remember how to spell. We can use $ ls to see the contents of a directory, but beyond a certain number of items, it becomes impractical to scroll through the list looking for a file whose spelling we can't remember.

The designers of Unix realized that as hard disk capacity increased, something needed to be done about the issue of large directories becoming so large as to be unmanageable. They came up with an elegant solution that carries on into the Unix-like world of today, and it is the feature known in Linux as **tab completion**.

Since we are currently located in the ~/Documents directory, let's scoot back into the parent directory (the home directory) with the $ cd .. command and do a $ pwd for good luck. Now, enter this as shown on the command line:

Without typing anything else, press the tab key.

```
me@MyLinuxBox:~/Documents$ cd ..
me@MyLinuxBox:~$ pwd
/home/me
me@MyLinuxBox:~$ cd Downloads/
```

Like magic, Bash automatically fills in the last several characters of the `Downloads` directory name, and of course, if we press `enter`, we will be in the `~/Downloads` directory. Tab completion is another one of these practices that will become habitual for you as it makes life so much easier on the command line. You will find some interesting behavior with tab completion if you use it while typing in a path that traverses multiple directories. And there is also something to be discovered when you hold down the `tab` key after typing a partial name that has several potential completions. You can even use tab completion with commands! Try it! When you stumble upon a command that you've never seen before, it's good practice to run `$ man <command>` to get an idea of what the command does. This can be a fun way to learn about the many commands available to us.

Summary:

To get the most out of the Linux command line, we need to know how to locate ourselves and move around in the Linux file system. The file system is effectively the territory where the shell environment is anchored, and the command line itself is like a vehicle that we can use to transport ourselves wherever we need to go in this environment. The commands we use for transportation are the most common shell commands, and there are many useful shortcuts and tricks at our disposal to make it easier to get from one place to another.

Commands:

`$ pwd`	`$ ls`
`$ clear`	`$ cd`

Concepts:

- Linux file system
- Current working directory
- Dot files and directories
- Aliases
- . and .. directory shortcuts
- Parent directory
- * wildcard operator
- Tab completion

Challenge:

Go to the ~ directory and use one of the methods we discussed to list all of its contents so that you can see both visible and hidden items. Now, use the wildcard operator to list only hidden files and directories. Once you accomplish that, as an added challenge, see if you can modify your command to list only hidden directories.

Making contact with files

We have been going back and forth along the path between ~ and /, getting acquainted with commands for navigating the Linux file system. Now we can begin setting up shop in ~ and laying the groundwork for our own files and directories.

If we think of plain text characters as the common currency of data in Linux, then each file in the Linux file system is like a safe deposit box where some amount of the plain-text currency is stored. This would make each directory into something like a vault where safe deposit boxes (i.e., files) and other vaults (i.e., sub-directories) are kept. This collection of vaults within vaults, etc., is entirely contained within the largest vault of all: the root directory.

Being able to gain access to these vaults and view, modify, and/or add to their contents all rests on the **ownership** attached at the file (i.e. safe deposit box) and directory (i.e. vault) level. As we have talked about, what we own in the Linux file system depends on *who we are* and *what group(s) we belong to* (see p. 39). Taking this a step further, what we are allowed or not allowed to do in the Linux file system is determined specifically by the owner and/or group **permissions** attached to each individual file or directory. These permissions establish the "rights" that we have as users to perform certain actions (read, write, etc.) on certain items in the file system.

Here we will be covering the basics of how to view and interpret permissions in the Linux file system. See Appendix A for additional information.

Linux file permissions

When we list the contents of a directory in long form with `$ ll`, the file (and sub-directory) permissions are shown in the left-most column (see p. 53) in a 10-character table layout. These ten characters reveal the filetype[24] as well as the owner, group, and "other" permissions for each item in the list.

For example:

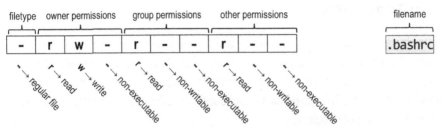

Above is an annotated view of the permissions for the `.bashrc` file in the home directory. The `-` in the filetype slot tells us that `~/.bashrc` is a **regular file**. To be a "regular" file in Linux means the file[25] has no special function[26] and is not a directory. Looking back at the third column in the list on p. 53, we see that `~/.bashrc` belongs to `<username>` (see p. 43), and as we can tell from the **owner permissions** slots (see above), `<username>` can **r**ead from this file and also **w**rite to it. The `-` in the fourth slot indicates that `~/.bashrc` is not an e**x**ecutable program. We also see that the **group permissions** (see p. 40) are **r**ead-only for this file, and the same goes for the file's **other permissions**. These "other" permissions (or "world" permissions) are for anyone who is neither the file owner nor a member of the group connected with the file. Bear in mind that "other" permissions only apply to non-root users as root users always have full **r**ead and **w**rite access to every file and directory in the system.

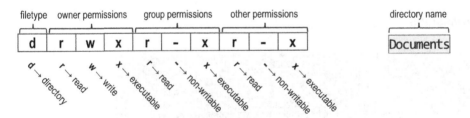

Moving down the list (see p. 53), we spot the permissions for the `Documents` directory. The `d` in the filetype slot indicates that this is indeed a **d**irectory. Looking at the owner permissions slots, `<username>` has the ability to **r**ead from this directory and **w**rite to it as well. And in the e**x**ecutable slot, the `x` lets us know that the `~/Documents` directory is e**x**ecutable.

Wait a minute. What? An **executable directory**? How can that be? A directory isn't a program, is it?

---

[24] For simplicity, we are including filetype here as part of Linux permissions. Technically, however, filetype would be classified as a file attribute rather than a file permission.

[25] The regular-file category includes generic files plus e**x**ecutable program files, which we will investigate later.

[26] Files with a "special function" would include soft **l**inks (which we cover later) and various types of system files.

54

This is one of those secrets about Unix/Linux that you don't learn until you're ready. Yes, access to a directory is affected by its executable permissions settings. No, directories are not programs. You might still have some questions as to what this all means.

There are a variety of explanations, but the best way to make sense of this is to recognize that if a directory is "executable", it means something entirely different from what we normally associate with an "executable" file—as in, a program that we would run or launch. In Unix/Linux, we can think of "executable" for directories as really meaning "accessible"[27].

When the designers of Unix were figuring out what permissions were needed for the file system, they realized that it would be useful to separate the permission to *view* the names of items in a directory (with $ ls) from the permission to *enter* the directory (with $ cd). They determined the best solution would be to repurpose the directory's executable permissions in order to control $ cd access. Hence, a directory that is both readable and executable (i.e., "accessible") from a user's point of view means the user can enter the directory and access the files, whereas a directory that is readable but not executable means the user can only view the names of the items in the directory with $ ls. Surprisingly, it is possible for a directory to be executable (i.e., "accessible") but not readable. In this scenario, the user has to already know the names of items inside the directory to access them. If a directory is neither readable nor executable from a user's standpoint, then the user simply can't see or access what is inside the directory.

The table below shows how permissions for files and directories relate in Linux. See Appendix A for more information.

Permissions	Files	Directories
read	Permits the user to open and view the contents of a file.	Permits the user to run $ ls in order to view a list of the items contained in a directory.
write	If paired with read, permits the user to edit a file. Does not control whether a user can delete or rename a file.	Permits the user to create, rename, and/or delete files inside a directory if the directory's executable permission is also set.
executable	Permits the user to run a program file. Permission to read the file is also required for execution if the file is not a compiled external command (see p. 33).	Permits the user to enter a directory with the $ cd command.

---

[27] Another common explanation of what "executable" means for Linux directories is to say that executable directories are "searchable".

In your time spent with Linux, if you work primarily on systems where you are the only user, then permissions will not play as big a part as they would if you work on multi-user systems. Either way, you will find that there are certain combinations of permissions that are very common, and others that are highly unusual. For example, if a directory is **w**ritable, it will (almost) certainly also be e**x**ecutable (but not vice-versa!). Likewise, if a file is **w**ritable, it will almost always be **r**eadable as well.

Linux file naming conventions

Before we begin making our own files and directories, let's talk about best practices for naming things in the Linux file system. The following are a couple of points to consider when choosing a name in Linux.

- Linux filenames are **case-sensitive**. For example, if you try `$ cd ~/documents` you will get a `bash: cd: /home/<username>/documents: No such file or directory` error. This nitpicky treatment of capital letters can be annoying sometimes, but the upside is that you can use capitalization to distinguish between similarly named items in the same directory.

- It is best not to include spaces in Linux file or directory names. It's not impossible to use spaces, but it's just not recommended as it can wreak havoc with certain commands when a space   occurs in the argument and the shell can't correctly interpret it (see Appendix B).

- As a substitute for spaces in Linux, `underscores_are_common`, although you will also see many examples where `hyphens-are-used`. Alternatively, there is `camelCase`, which uses capital letters to indicate where a space would normally occur.

- If you need to have spaces in a Linux file or directory name, you can put `'the name in quotes'` when the name is in the argument of a command, or you can wield the **escape character** \ to escape[28] spaces in names. For example, `the\ name\ in\ quotes` in the shell's eyes is effectively equivalent to `'the name in quotes'`. Either way, when listing with `$ ls`, names with spaces will show up in single quotes: `'the name in quotes'`.

- Unlike other operating systems, Linux does not need its files to have file extensions in order for the system to recognize filetypes. For example, it's unnecessary to add a `.txt` extension at the end of a filename for Linux to register the file as a text file. With that said, many Linux users do choose to add file extensions because extensions are useful for identifying certain things.

---

[28] When the shell sees the escape character \, depending on context, the shell either ignores the character immediately afterward (such as here where \ "escapes"   spaces from being interpreted by the shell as word delimiters), or the shell regards the character after \ as non-printable and therefore holding some special function (like \u, which represents `<username>` in the variable that controls the Bash command line prompt). Within single quotes, \ has no effect and is treated literally. See Appendix B for more information.

Making files and directories in Linux

We're now going to start putting down some wares of our own in the home directory. The files and directories that we make here are in preparation for our upcoming command line activities. The names for these items are just suggestions, and of course you can substitute any names that you want. It may be less confusing later, however, if you follow the names given here.

$ mkdir

It's time to add another tool to our Bash utility belt. Enter the $ mkdir command, short for "make directory". This command, as the name suggests, lets us make our very own directories. Let's try it!

If you are not already in the home directory, use your favorite method of transporting yourself there. When ready, enter the following on the command line:

$ mkdir Projects

That was easy! Let's do an $ ll to view the home directory's contents.

```
me@MyLinuxBox: ~
me@MyLinuxBox:~$ mkdir Projects
me@MyLinuxBox:~$ ll
total 84
drwxr-xr-x 17 me    me    4096 Dec 13 12:37 ./
drwxr-xr-x  4 root root 4096 Nov 18 19:22 ../
-rw-------  1 me    me    1207 Dec  7 18:31 .bash_history
-rw-r--r--  1 me    me     220 Nov 18 19:22 .bash_logout
-rw-r--r--  1 me    me    3793 Nov 18 19:31 .bashrc
drwx------ 14 me    me    4096 Nov 23 15:03 .cache/
drwxr-xr-x 14 me    me    4096 Dec  5 09:38 .config/
drwxr-xr-x  2 me    me    4096 Nov 18 19:24 Desktop/
drwxr-xr-x  2 me    me    4096 Nov 23 17:56 Documents/
drwxr-xr-x  2 me    me    4096 Nov 18 19:24 Downloads/
drwx------  3 me    me    4096 Nov 18 19:24 .gnupg/
drwxr-xr-x  3 me    me    4096 Nov 18 19:24 .local/
drwxr-xr-x  2 me    me    4096 Nov 18 19:24 Music/
drwxr-xr-x  2 me    me    4096 Dec 13 12:36 Pictures/
drwx------  3 me    me    4096 Nov 18 19:32 .pki/
-rw-r--r--  1 me    me     807 Nov 18 19:22 .profile
drwxrwxr-x  2 me    me    4096 Dec 13 12:37 Projects/
drwxr-xr-x  2 me    me    4096 Nov 18 19:24 Public/
drwxr-xr-x  4 me    me    4096 Nov 23 17:04 snap/
drwxr-xr-x  2 me    me    4096 Nov 18 19:24 Templates/
drwxr-xr-x  2 me    me    4096 Nov 18 19:24 Videos/
me@MyLinuxBox:~$ 
```

And there we have it! You should see a new Projects directory where there was none before.

The $ mkdir command is quite intuitive to use. If called with just the directory's name in the argument (i.e., $ mkdir <directoryname>), then it will place a new directory with the given name inside the current working directory. If we decide instead to specify a path to the new directory and call $ mkdir <pathname>/<directoryname>, then it will place the new directory inside the path's destination directory.

Let's make another directory, but this time with the $ `mkdir <pathname>/<directoryname>` method just to get some practice with this. Enter the following on the command line:

$ `mkdir ~/Projects/MyScripts`

Next, let's use $ `ls` in a similar way. Without going to ~/`Projects` with the $ `cd` command, try this alternative method:

$ `ls -la ~/Projects`

```
                                                    me@MyLinuxBox: ~
me@MyLinuxBox:~$ mkdir ~/Projects/MyScripts
me@MyLinuxBox:~$ ls -la ~/Projects
total 12
drwxrwxr-x  3 me me 4096 Dec 26 16:54 .
drwxr-xr-x 17 me me 4096 Dec 13 12:37 ..
drwxrwxr-x  2 me me 4096 Dec 26 16:54 MyScripts
me@MyLinuxBox:~$
```

You will see something like shown above in your terminal window. Notice the current working directory is still the home directory. Of course, we could have just done a $ `cd` into ~/`Projects` and performed these commands directly inside ~/`Projects`. However, the way we stayed in ~ and performed the commands in ~/`Projects` illustrates that we are not limited to operating on files and directories in our immediate vicinity (in the current working directory). With many commands in Bash, we can specify a path to a **destination directory** in the argument (in this case, ~/`Projects`) and perform tasks in the destination directory as we would in the current working directory—assuming the destination directory is e<u>x</u>ecutable and that we have <u>r</u>ead and <u>w</u>rite permissions. To view the directory's contents with $ `ls`, we only need to be able to <u>r</u>ead.

There is a lot of power hidden behind the $ `mkdir` command's simple operation, and we will be doing more work with it toward the end of this guide. In the meantime, take a look at $ `man mkdir` to get a sense of what the command is capable of.

$ touch

It would be nice if we had a file or two to put into these new directories we just created. At times like these, the command line utility that comes first to mind is $ `touch`[29]. Famous for its simplicity, $ `touch` allows us to create an **empty file** with a name that we provide in the argument of the command (i.e., $ `touch <filename>`).

---

[29] Be careful with $ `touch`! When you use $ `touch` to create a new file, if there is an existing file with the same name in that directory, $ `touch` will overwrite the older file and replace it with the new (blank) file.

As we talked about earlier, files in the Linux file system are just containers of text. If we could make an empty container of text, would this still be a file? Yes it would! With $ touch, we have the ability to simply "touch" wherever we would like a new, empty file to appear in the file system, and the command takes care of the rest for us.

Let's go into the ~/Projects/MyScripts directory with $ cd Projects/MyScripts. When in the directory, enter this on the command line:

$ touch my_first_file

Check with an $ ll to see your shiny new file in the current working directory.

```
                                            me@MyLinuxBox: ~/Projects/MyScripts
me@MyLinuxBox:~$ cd Projects/MyScripts/
me@MyLinuxBox:~/Projects/MyScripts$ touch my_first_file
me@MyLinuxBox:~/Projects/MyScripts$ ll
total 8
drwxrwxr-x 2 me me 4096 Dec 26 16:59 ./
drwxrwxr-x 3 me me 4096 Dec 26 16:54 ../
-rw-rw-r-- 1 me me    0 Dec 26 16:59 my_first_file
me@MyLinuxBox:~/Projects/MyScripts$
```

Good job! We will be using these items as the basis for our upcoming command line experiments.

Getting info about files in Linux

Now that my_first_file has arrived in our shop, let's see what is hiding under the lid. Even though the file is empty, we should still be able to learn about its status as an item in the Linux file system.

There are quite a few ways to get info about files in Linux. One easy way is to use $ ls, which lets us focus on a particular file[30] when we put the <filename> in the <operand> position of the command. For example, $ ls -la <filename> will return the column view as displayed in long format, but with just one file in the list. When we do this for ~/Projects/MyScripts/my_first_file, we see that <username> is the file owner, with read and write permissions. We also know by - in the filetype slot that this is a regular file. No surprises there!

$ stat

When we need additional information about a file or directory in Linux, the $ stat command (short for "status") will return a more explicit version of what $ ls shows us. Let's give the $ stat command a try. In the ~/Projects/MyScripts directory, enter the following on the command line:

$ stat my_first_file

---

[30] Note that if we tried this with a directory, unless we invoke the -d [option], $ ls would simply list the directory's contents ($ ls normally treats a directory in the <operand> as a destination directory).

```
 ⬚                              me@MyLinuxBox: ~/Projects/MyScripts
me@MyLinuxBox:~/Projects/MyScripts$ stat my_first_file
  File: my_first_file
  Size: 0            Blocks: 0          IO Block: 4096   regular empty file
Device: 805h/2053d       Inode: 5768609     Links: 1
Access: (0664/-rw-rw-r--)  Uid: ( 1000/      me)  Gid: ( 1000/      me)
Access: 2020-12-26 16:59:19.152189027 -0500
Modify: 2020-12-26 16:59:19.152189027 -0500
Change: 2020-12-26 16:59:19.152189027 -0500
 Birth: -
me@MyLinuxBox:~/Projects/MyScripts$ ▌
```

We can see that $ stat recognizes my_first_file as a regular empty file and that we have more info about the file's last Access, Modify, and Change times. Later, once we have done some work with my_first_file, we will run $ stat again to see how these details reflect any changes that we make. Of course, feel free to experiment by calling $ stat on any other files or directories you might be curious about as well! This is a great way to make contact with different types of files.

Summary:
In Linux, our user identity and status determine what data we have access to. Permissions based on file and directory ownership govern what we can and cannot do in the Linux file system. When naming files in Linux, avoiding spaces prevents formatting issues in command arguments. If the argument of a command contains the path to a destination directory, depending on permissions, the command operates in that directory as it would in the current working directory when no path is specified. To get info about files and directories in Linux, we can use $ ls, or we can go to the $ stat command for more detailed information.

Commands:
$ ls $ touch
$ cd $ stat
$ mkdir

Concepts:
- Plain text files as containers of data
- Linux filetypes
- File permissions – read, write, executable
- Executable directories
- Linux file naming conventions
- \ escape character
- Single quotes
- Destination directories
- Empty files
- Getting file/directory info

Challenge:
Go to the $ man pages for the $ touch command and find a way to edit the Access and Modify date and time displayed for ~/Projects/MyScripts/my_first_file. You could change the Access and Modify information to reflect the current time (if you like). When you do an $ ll in the ~/Projects/MyScripts directory, you should see the new date and time displayed for the file.

Connecting to streams

With our first file on hand, now we are going to go to the Linux toolbox and look for ways of connecting the file to the world around it. We want to make our file into a staging site where we can hook up commands and funnel text using the Input/Output routing of the Linux shell environment. Our goal is to use these types of connections as building blocks for our own command-line solutions.

Standard Input/Output in Linux

Let's take a moment to talk about how information gets into and out of Linux. When we run a command in the shell, the command first takes delivery of some plain text input, and based on whatever that input is, the command returns its output, also in plain text format[31].

For its main input interface from the outside world, Linux defines the computer keyboard as **stdin** (for "standard in"—as it is also pronounced). The shell itself makes extensive use of stdin in the way the shell constantly "listens" for key-press events (any time we press a key on the keyboard). Because the shell is so good at listening and responding to stdin, many commands don't even bother to take stdin directly as their input.

Instead, commands that operate in this way (such as $ ls) take their input from what the shell sends them only *after* we press enter (when executing a command). Before we press enter, the shell listens to the keyboard and collects the **string** (the line of text) that we type in on the command line. As we type, the shell parses the input string based on wherever we have typed an unescaped space (see p. 56 and Appendix B). Then when we press enter to execute the command, these segments get bundled together and sent to the command as its **argument**, which forms the input of the command. All of the commands we have looked at thus far operate in this way—even when the argument is implied, like with $ ls alone.

There are other commands, however, that do accept direct input from stdin, and they are extremely useful, particularly because they can take their input through an object in Linux called a "pipe" (the | character represents a pipe in Linux). When commands like this in Linux take their input through a pipe, they can effectively take in a stream of text, and Linux lets us chain commands together in this way such that one command can stream its text output directly into the input of the next. Later in this chapter we will be looking closely at how to work with pipes for commands that accept stdin as input.

---

[31] Most of the time in the shell, we are handling human-readable text data, but this is not the only type of information that the plain text medium can carry. Plain text characters can represent binary values in an arbitrary encoding scheme. For example, Base64 encoding ties 6-bit binary values (0 to 63) to the first 64 ASCII characters (A-Z, a-z, 0-9, +, and /). When binary data is represented in Base64 encoding, 4 plain text characters encode 24 bits of data (three bytes).

But before we get there, we have to talk about how commands <u>output</u> information in Linux. Almost all commands in the shell environment are set up to send their output to the terminal window[32]. When a command sends its output to the terminal window, we say that the command sends its output to **stdout** (for "<u>st</u>an<u>d</u>ard <u>out</u>"). All of the commands we've tried thus far send output directly to stdout.

Aside from a command's main output to stdout, there is also another type of output that Linux furnishes for commands, and that is the output called **stderr** (for "<u>st</u>an<u>d</u>ard <u>error</u>"). Stderr is a special output reserved just for error messages. If you are wondering what use this might have, this, like many things in Linux has its roots in the Unix tradition of keeping the shell free of clutter from system messages.

The emphasis in Unix culture on having a "quiet" interface entails that the shell should not burden users with unhelpful alerts or error reporting. In the interest of preserving the quiet, Unix introduced stderr as a separate output stream designated exclusively for carrying error messages.

By forcing the system's error reporting to pass through its own dedicated stream of text, this gives users more control over where to *redirect* the stream in case we want error messages to go somewhere other than stdout. In Linux, it is common practice to divert stderr away from stdout to avoid crowding the shell with unwanted system messages.

All together, these three paths of information into and out of the shell (stdin, stdout, and stderr) are known in Linux as **standard streams**. We will be getting practice working with all of these streams in our upcoming command line tutorials.

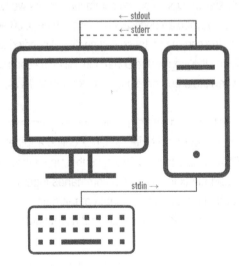

Figure 6 Linux standard streams diagram

In the diagram to the left, we can imagine the display as the terminal window and the computer as encasing the shell. In Linux, stderr is directed to the terminal window along with stdout unless we *redirect* stderr to another destination. In fact, *redirection* (or reconnection) of all of these streams is possible. We will be looking in detail at how to do this, and we will get some practice connecting these streams to (and from) files.

---

[32] While almost all shell commands in Linux send their main output through their stdout interface, this doesn't mean that stdout (i.e., the terminal window) has to be the destination for the output data. In this chapter, we are going to look at how to *redirect* command output to places other than the terminal window.

$ echo

The `$ echo` command performs a simple and important duty: printing text to stdout. We can put text in the command's argument, press `enter`, and the text will appear in the space below the command line. Let's give this a try (we're still in the `~/Projects/MyScripts` directory from last chapter).

$ echo 'something I want to print to stdout'

```
┌─┐                                    me@MyLinuxBox: ~/Projects/MyScripts
me@MyLinuxBox:~/Projects/MyScripts$ echo 'something I want to print to stdout'
something I want to print to stdout
me@MyLinuxBox:~/Projects/MyScripts$ █
```

Good. It will be useful for us to have a way to print things to stdout when we practice redirecting the output to another destination.

$ cat

We need a quick and easy way to view the contents of files, and the `$ cat` command (short for concatenate) will fit the bill perfectly here. As its name suggests, `$ cat` has functionality that goes beyond simply displaying files, and in the next chapter we will be exploring more of what this command can do. For right now, though, we will be using `$ cat` expressly for its ability to print the contents of a file directly to stdout.

To test this, let's `$ cd` back into `~` and do an `$ ll` to view the items in the directory. You should see a file called `.bash_history` in the list. Try the following on the command line.

$ cat .bash_history

```
┌─┐                                              me@MyLinuxBox: ~
cd Projects
clear
ll
cd MyScripts/
clear
ll
clear
stat my_first_file
ll
cd Projects/
ll
cd MyScripts
ll
clear
echo something I want to print to stdout
clear
ll
me@MyLinuxBox:~$ █
```

Look familiar? We're viewing a file that contains a log of all of the commands we have entered on the command line! This is a rather long file, but if you scroll up, you should be able to see everything in its entirety.

$ wc

With the $ wc command, we can get a word count of a file that we put in the command's argument. While we're in the home directory, let's use $ wc to see how many "words" there are in the .bash_history file. We'll use the -w [option], which tells the command we only want a count of the words in the file (and no additional information like a character count or the number of lines).

$ wc -w .bash_history

The exact result you get will likely be different from what is shown here, but the output should look like this with .bash_history next to the number of words.

Redirection in Linux

Now we will begin getting some hands-on experience hooking commands and files together via the shell's standard stream interfaces (stdout, stdin, and stderr). We need some attachments, or adapters if you will, to channel the flow of text in these streams *from* commands *to* files (and vice-versa). Bash handily offers a family of tools for this purpose known as **redirection operators**. These tools are all part of the **inter-process communication** functionality that Unix-like systems are famous for.

The > operator

The > operator is the first redirection operator we will experiment with. When placed after a command, it will redirect the command's stdout output into a new destination file we name on the right side of >. The arrow-like quality of the symbol marks the flow of information from *command > file*.

We could try this on our old friend, my_first_file, but if we did, > would just overwrite it with a new file of the same name, and we don't want that. So instead, in the ~/Projects/MyScripts directory, let's use > to make a new file. When you're all set, we're going to try redirecting some text into a file which we will call my_second_file.

```
$ echo 'hello world' > my_second_file
```

Let's do an `$ ll` to check that everything is in place.

```
                                          me@MyLinuxBox: ~/Projects/MyScripts
me@MyLinuxBox:~/Projects/MyScripts$ echo 'hello world' > my_second_file
me@MyLinuxBox:~/Projects/MyScripts$ ll
total 16
drwxrwxr-x 2 me me 4096 Jan  3 19:31 ./
drwxrwxr-x 3 me me 4096 Dec 26 16:54 ../
-rw-rw-r-- 1 me me    0 Dec 26 06:59 my_first_file
-rw-rw-r-- 1 me me   12 Jan  3 19:31 my_second_file
me@MyLinuxBox:~/Projects/MyScripts$
```

All looks good! And `my_first_file` is waiting patiently, just as we left it. So, now we need a way to view `my_second_file`. The `$ cat` command will do nicely here. Let's try it.

```
$ cat my_second_file
```

```
                                          me@MyLinuxBox: ~/Projects/MyScripts
me@MyLinuxBox:~/Projects/MyScripts$ cat my_second_file
hello world
me@MyLinuxBox:~/Projects/MyScripts$
```

Hello! You succeeded in your first redirection of stdout into a new file. Now let's see if we can stream stdout and *add* to the contents of a file.

The >> operator

If we want to redirect stdout output to an existing file and we don't want to overwrite anything, then we need the >> operator. The >> operator will take what arrives from the stdout output of the command on its left and *append* the data to the file specified on the right. The double arrow-like symbol suggests an accumulation, which is appropriate.

Since we're on a roll with my_second_file, let's keep going and add a bit more to it.

```
$ echo 'this is my second file' >> my_second_file
```

Following up with a `$ cat my_second_file` reveals the new contents.

```
                                          me@MyLinuxBox: ~/Projects/MyScripts
me@MyLinuxBox:~/Projects/MyScripts$ echo 'this is my second file' >> my_second_file
me@MyLinuxBox:~/Projects/MyScripts$ cat my_second_file
hello world
this is my second file
me@MyLinuxBox:~/Projects/MyScripts$
```

Great! Shall we give `my_first_file` its long-awaited text? This will demonstrate how `>>` can be used to populate an empty file.

$ echo 'I am getting good at this' >> my_first_file

A quick `$ cat my_first_file` will show us what is now inside.

```
                                              me@MyLinuxBox: ~/Projects/MyScripts
me@MyLinuxBox:~/Projects/MyScripts$ echo 'I am getting good at this' >> my_first_file
me@MyLinuxBox:~/Projects/MyScripts$ cat my_first_file
I am getting good at this
me@MyLinuxBox:~/Projects/MyScripts$
```

Indeed! But what if we wanted to go *from* a file *to* a command that accepts stdin as input?

The < operator

This one is a little less intuitive than the redirection operators that go from the stdout output of a command into a file. Rather than treating a file as receiving input from a command, `<` makes a file into a source that *outputs* its contents *into* a command that accepts stdin as input. We can think of this as taking the "cable" that feeds stdin from the computer keyboard, disconnecting it from the output of the keyboard, and connecting the cable to the output of a *file* instead!

To see how this works, we need a command that can take input from stdin. As luck would have it, we now have one or two of these in our bag of tricks. Let's go back into the home directory with a `$ cd` and try the `$ wc` command on the `.bash_history` file again, but this time with the `<` operator.

$ wc -w < .bash_history

```
                                              me@MyLinuxBox: ~
me@MyLinuxBox:~$ wc -w < .bash_history
455
me@MyLinuxBox:~$
```

Notice that when we input `.bash_history` directly into `$ wc` via stdin, `$ wc` does not output the name of the file (`.bash_history`) like it does when the file is placed in the argument of `$ wc`. The reason for this, in part, is that when we use `<` to send a file to a command's stdin input, the shell first extracts the text contents of the file and then sends that information (absent of the file itself) to the stdin input of the command. Effectively, this leaves the command oblivious to where the contents came from before they arrived at the command's stdin doorstep. This could be useful in many

66

situations. For example, if we need the output of $ wc to be numerical only and not include the name of the text-bearing file, then we might use the < method ($ wc -w < <filename>).

The 2> operator

With the 2> operator, we have a means of controlling where a command sends its stream of error messages. The 2> operator lets us redirect stderr away from the terminal window—into a destination file we specify on the operator's right side. If you are wondering what the "2" signifies, this is from the Unix convention for labeling standard streams[33] where 0 represents stdin (e.g., the < operator is just a shorthand version of the <0 operator), 1 represents stdout (likewise, the > operator is an abbreviation of the 1> operator), and 2 represents stderr (which shows up in the 2> operator in unabbreviated form).

To get an idea of how to use the 2> operator, we need to elicit an error message from Bash. This shouldn't be hard! Here's an idea:

$ ls /Projects/MyScripts

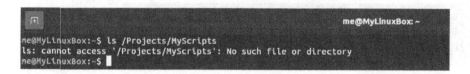

Not surprisingly, this returned an error. Now, let's see what happens if we use the 2> redirection operator to send stderr to a file called /dev/null.

$ ls /Projects/MyScripts 2> /dev/null

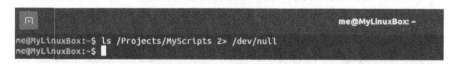

---

[33] When we run an external command in the shell, the Linux kernel treats the command as a <u>process</u>, which is the kernel's way of keeping track of how the command is executed. The kernel equips the process with interfaces for the three standard streams (stdin, stdout, and stderr) so that the process (i.e., the command) can output to stdout, send errors to stderr, and take input from stdin (if needed). Now, believe it or not, the way a process in Linux achieves this Input/Output is simply by writing information to (i.e., outputting to) or reading from (i.e., inputting from) files. Being that "everything is a file" in Linux, this applies even to the I/O devices connected to the computer! For example, the keyboard input itself is represented as a soft link to a file (/dev/stdin), as are the terminal output (/dev/stdout) and the standard error output (/dev/stderr). A process literally writes to or reads from these soft-linked files for I/O. Now, these files are *abstracted* for each process through what are called "file descriptors", which are just numbers representing the different I/O files. From Unix tradition, these file descriptors for standard streams are 0, 1, and 2 (0 for stdin, 1 for stdout, and 2 for stderr).

No more error! Or none that we can see at least. Sending output to `/dev/null` is like throwing the output away into a black hole. Sometimes this is necessary, especially when a command is returning tens, hundreds, or thousands of error messages that are of no use to anyone!

The | operator

The `|` operator, commonly known as a **pipe**, is one of the most powerful tools in the Unix-like universe. A pipe allows us to take the stdout output of one command and directly "pipe" it into the stdin input of another (obviously, the receiving command has to accept stdin as input). The power of the `|` operator lies in its capacity to chain simple commands together, letting us perform more complex operations with relative ease.

While in the home directory, we will first try using the `|` operator with the `$ wc` command (which we introduced earlier in this chapter). When ready, enter this on the command line.

$ man wc | wc -w

Here we are feeding the stdout output of `$ man wc` into the stdin input of `$ wc -w`. Imagine if we removed the `| wc -w` part. Then we would just have `$ man wc`. And, pressing the enter key would send the results to stdout. This is nearly what we are doing, but instead of sending the output of `$ man wc` to the terminal, we are *redirecting* the output of `$ man wc` into the stdin *input* of `$ wc`. This is achieved with the `|` operator, which allows us to *pipe* the output of one command into the stdin input of another. When `$ wc -w` receives the text input, it does a word count, and then sends its output of 237 to stdout. As demonstrated here with the `|` operator, individual commands can be linked up to form a **pipeline**. A pipeline like this can be extended with multiple commands connected one after the other to form an elaborate text-processing chain. As we move ahead, we will be getting practice using `|` to form our own multi-command pipelines.

Linux commands that filter stdin input

It's time for us to get to know two of the most important commands in Linux, both of which accept stdin as input (like `$ wc`, which we just tried above). We call these commands **filters** because they take in a stream of text at stdin and change what they receive—removing and/or transforming portions of the text before sending the result to stdout.

`$ grep`

If the `$ grep` command could ever be renamed, the word "search" would be an excellent candidate because this is essentially what the command does. Originally developed (and named) by Ken Thompson himself, `$ grep` stands for global-search-for-a-regular-expression-and-print (g/re/p).

This iconic command lets us search for a `<pattern>` that we supply in the argument. Okay. But where can we perform this search? One way we can search with `$ grep` is to point the command to a file whose name we put in the `<operand>` position (as in `$ grep <pattern> <filename>`), and `$ grep` will search the file's contents for any instances of `<pattern>`. But in addition to taking input from a file given in the `<operand>`, `$ grep` is also capable of taking input through its stdin interface via a pipe (as in `$ <command> | grep <pattern>`). This way, we pipe the stdout output of the preceding `$ <command>` directly into the stdin input of `$ grep`, and `$ grep` filters down what it receives to the lines of text that contain the `<pattern>` specified in the argument.

Let's get some practice first with the `$ grep <pattern> <filename>` method by doing a search in the `~/.bash_history` file for all of the times we've entered the `$ pwd` command.

<code>$ grep pwd .bash_history</code>

Depending on your own `.bash_history` file, you may or may not get the same results. But whatever is shown, it is due to `$ grep` letting pass only the lines from `.bash_history` that contain the `<pattern>` we have told `$ grep` to look for (pwd in this case). The red text is due to Ubuntu's default formatting for `$ grep` output in the shell.

Just as an experiment, let's pipe these results into `$ wc` and see what number we get in return.

<code>$ grep pwd .bash_history | wc -w</code>

```
me@MyLinuxBox:~$ grep pwd .bash_history | wc -w
8
me@MyLinuxBox:~$
```

It works! Now, it's worth mentioning that $ grep has a -c [option] (for count) that produces the same result as piping into $ wc -w. This goes to show there is rarely just one way to achieve something in Linux. Whatever way you choose is perfectly valid if it does what you need.

Now we'll test the stdin input capabilities of $ grep by piping in a stream of text and letting $ grep search through the text for a <pattern>. We'll use $ man wc again as our source of text, and the <pattern> we will search for this time is the word character. Try this when ready.

$ man wc | grep character

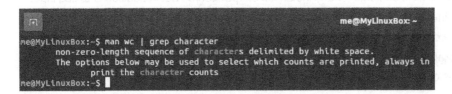

In the output, $ grep lists all of the lines from the $ man page that feature the word character. Putting grep <pattern> after | gives us a powerful device for filtering information, and we recommend you $ man grep to get the big picture of what the command is capable of. In your future Linux learning, you will find many examples where $ grep plays a critical role in the command line toolchain.

$ sed

The $ sed command, short for "stream editor", is another behemoth from the Unix tradition. Like $ grep, $ sed is often found after a | and acts on the stream of text coming into its stdin input. As an "editor", the $ sed command's main function is to filter incoming text by replacing and/or removing characters. The syntax in the argument of $ sed determines the command's filtering behavior.

Let's try adding a $ sed output stage to our previous experiment with $ grep. Pro tip: using the ↑↓ arrows on the command line to flip through the command history will bring back the previous $ grep command (see p. 37).

$ grep pwd .bash_history | sed s/pwd/PWD/

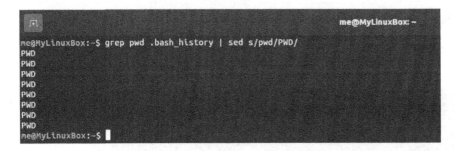

So, what have we done? We have taken the stdout output from $ grep and piped it into $ sed with s/pwd/PWD/ in the latter command's argument. In s/pwd/PWD/, we have some special $ sed syntax in which s indicates that we want to look for the first instance of pwd on each line and substitute the pwd with PWD (in this case, there is only one instance of pwd per line). The $ sed command recognizes / as the delimiter between fields in the syntax. This kind of <pattern> substitution is what $ sed is best known for, and here we have had just a glimpse of what it can do.

As with $ grep, the capabilities of $ sed run deep, and a lot of insight can be gained by perusing the $ man pages and experimenting with the many [options] available.

Summary:
Following the Unix tradition, the three main channels for data to flow into and out of the Linux shell are stdin (the keyboard), stdout (the terminal window), and stderr (a special output just for error messages). We have a set of command line tools for connecting and redirecting these streams of plain text data to files from commands (and vice-versa). With commands that accept stdin as input like $ wc, $ grep, and $ sed, we can use the pipe operator to chain commands together to create our own pipelines for filtering textual information.

Commands:
$ echo
$ cat
$ cd

$ wc
$ grep
$ sed

Concepts:
- Standard streams (stdin, stdout, stderr)
- Input argument string parsing
- /dev/null
- Filter commands
- .bash_history file
- Inter-process communication
- Labels for standard streams (0, 1, 2)
- Redirection operators
  - > operator
  - >> operator
  - < operator
  - 2> operator
  - | operator
- Pipelines

Challenge:
Go back to the error-producing $ ls /Projects/MyScripts command and use some of the tools we have covered thus far to count the number of words in the error message. Does the answer match the number of words you count in the error message by hand? See if you can find at least two different ways to achieve the same result.

Telling text what to do

The deeper we go into the all-text world of the Linux command line environment, the more kinds of files we will be working with. Some of these files are only a couple of lines long, and others will have tens, hundreds, or even thousands of lines of text.

We already know how to use $ `cat` to display the contents of files, but in cases where the length of a file is longer than the height of the terminal window, $ `cat` loses its effectiveness as a file viewer. We need a separate utility to view the contents of longer files. This utility should allow us to advance through text line by line or page by page, and it should also let us easily return to wherever we left off on the command line when we are finished viewing a file.

$ less

The curiously named $ `less` might not sell itself as the obvious choice for viewing longer files, but this is in fact what it is—the go-to command for viewing longer files. Billed as an improvement over an older file viewer command called $ `more`, $ `less` is more than... You can see where this is going.

Using $ `less` will feel oddly familiar. In fact, if you have looked at any $ `man` pages at all, then you have already had exposure to $ `less`. When we enter $ `man` `<command>`, $ `man` calls $ `less` in the background to take care of displaying the $ `man` pages for the `<command>` (see p. 35).

But we can call $ `less` directly with a `<filename>` in the argument and view the file's contents (provided we have permission to view the file). Let's try this in the home directory on the `.bashrc` file (short for "Bash run commands", which we will be investigating soon).

$ less .bashrc

```
                                              me@MyLinuxBox: ~
# ~/.bashrc: executed by bash(1) for non-login shells.
# see /usr/share/doc/bash/examples/startup-files (in the package bash-doc)
# for examples

# If not running interactively, don't do anything
case $- in
    *i*) ;;
      *) return;;
esac

# don't put duplicate lines or lines starting with space in the history.
# See bash(1) for more options
HISTCONTROL=ignoreboth
```

What are we looking at? The `~/.bashrc` file is just a configuration file that tells Bash what to do when we open a new shell session. If none of what you see here makes sense, don't worry about it. It will.

While we're in $ less viewing this file, try scrolling *down* and *up* with the arrow keys ↓↑. Also, you can press the space bar or the f key to page forward, and the b key to page backward.

If you type :, an interactive prompt will appear at the bottom of the terminal window just for special commands that work within $ less. You can type h for help, and there is also a q command to quit $ less. When you are ready to leave $ less and return to the Bash command line, simply press q, and you will be taken back to the familiar <username>@<hostname>:~$ shell prompt as before.

What we have introduced here will probably cover most of your $ less needs for the time being, but there are other things in $ less that you might find useful, like its ability to do a forward search (/<pattern>) and backward search (?<pattern>) through a file's contents. It's also worth noting that $ less accepts stdin and that it is common to pipe into $ less (as in, $ <command> | less) to view the preceding command's output in the $ less page layout. Consult $ man less for more about the command's [options] and other features.

Interactive input in the Linux shell

We have talked about how the shell "listens" to what we type in on the keyboard, and we have also seen how commands that accept stdin as input can take input coming through a pipe. But we still haven't gotten to the bottom of what it really means for a command to "accept stdin as input".

As we approach this topic, let's think about how commands that *don't* accept stdin as input behave on the command line. Take, for example, $ ls, which does not accept stdin as input. The defined behavior when we type $ ls and press enter is for the command to list the contents of the current working directory. But what exactly is the input for $ ls when we run the command? It's not stdin. Why? The input to $ ls is not stdin because once we press enter, $ ls does not listen to the keyboard. Instead, when we press enter, $ ls takes the current working directory as input (which the system provides the command as though the cwd is typed into the argument) and goes about its business listing the directory's contents, oblivious[34] to anything else that we might type in after that.

But for many commands[35] that do accept stdin as input, something else happens when we call them on the command line in their most basic form (as in, $ <command>). A command like this will *start* to listen to the keyboard when we press enter. What we type on the keyboard after pressing enter will

---

[34] Actually, if we send a control signal, for example with ctrl + c, it could affect the $ ls process after it starts.
[35] These commands exhibit this behavior generally when nothing is included in the <operand> position. If an <operand> is given, then the behavior will depend on the specific command's treatment of stdin input. For example, entering $ cat alone puts the command into a mode where it takes input directly from stdin, whereas $ cat <filename> sets <filename> as the command's input.

be funneled into the command's input, and as we continue to type, every time we press enter, the cursor will move to a new line on the left side of the terminal window—like in a text editor. This will go on until we send an **end of file** (EOF) control state change with ctrl + d. Once our EOF message is received, the command will *stop* receiving what we type in and the shell will resume monitoring the stdin input as normal. When a command operates in this way (i.e., takes stdin as input), it effectively allows us to enter a file one line at a time into the command (as the "end of file" message suggests).

To get a feel for how this goes, let's return to ~/Projects/MyScripts and experiment with the $ cat command's stdin input capabilities. We are going to start by simply typing in $ cat and pressing enter.

$ cat

Now, after pressing enter, you will see the cursor appear on the line directly below the command line prompt. Go ahead and type anything that comes to mind and press enter again. Every time you type something and press the enter key, you should see a duplicate of what you typed directly below.

When you are ready to go back to the regular command line prompt, press enter one last time so that the cursor is below the last line of text (as shown above). Then, press ctrl + d and you will be taken back to the familiar Bash prompt (<username>@<hostname>:~/Projects/MyScripts$).

So, what was going on there? We witnessed how the $ cat command can take stdin input and concatenate what it receives to its output destination (stdout in this case). But imagine if rather than outputting to stdout, we could *redirect* the output to a file. In this way, every time we type on the keyboard and press enter, the output would accumulate, line by line, as the file's contents. Shall we give this a try?

We will use the > operator to redirect stdout from $ cat into a new file we'll call my_third_file.

$ cat > my_third_file

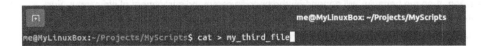

Now, after an initial press of the enter key, we can begin concatenating our redirected stdout to my_third_file. Go ahead and type in three or so lines.

```
                                                        me@MyLinuxBox: ~/Projects/MyScripts
me@MyLinuxBox:~/Projects/MyScripts$ cat > my_third_file
This is my third file.
I'm typing this into the file directly through stdin.
At this point, I'm really starting to get how this works.
```

It's like we almost have a text editor when we use $ cat in this way. Once you've entered a couple of lines of text, press ctrl + d to return to the Bash prompt.

Now let's use $ cat like we did in the previous chapter as a file-viewer to inspect the contents of my_third_file.

$ cat my_third_file

```
                                                        me@MyLinuxBox: ~/Projects/MyScripts
me@MyLinuxBox:~/Projects/MyScripts$ cat my_third_file
This is my third file.
I'm typing this into the file directly through stdin.
At this point, I'm really starting to get how this works.
me@MyLinuxBox:~/Projects/MyScripts$
```

Everything is just as we typed it. Note that my_third_file in the argument supplies the input to $ cat, and in this mode $ cat ignores stdin input.

While we're at it with $ cat as a file viewer, let's check up on my_first_file.

```
                                                        me@MyLinuxBox: ~/Projects/MyScripts
me@MyLinuxBox:~/Projects/MyScripts$ cat my_first_file
I an getting good at this
me@MyLinuxBox:~/Projects/MyScripts$
```

It's time to give this one an update. We'll do this by way of $ cat and the >> operator, which will allow us to append my_first_file with what we type into stdin. Go ahead and add another line this way.

$ cat >> my_first_file

```
                                                        me@MyLinuxBox: ~/Projects/MyScripts
me@MyLinuxBox:~/Projects/MyScripts$ cat >> my_first_file
I'm getting really good at this!
me@MyLinuxBox:~/Projects/MyScripts$
```

With a quick ↑ through the command history back to `$ cat my_first_file`, pressing enter displays `my_first_file` again but this time with its new contents.

```
me@MyLinuxBox: ~/Projects/MyScripts
me@MyLinuxBox:~/Projects/MyScripts$ cat my_first_file
I am getting good at this ◀————————————————missing a period
I'm getting really good at this!
me@MyLinuxBox:~/Projects/MyScripts$ ▮
```

That's more like it! But what if after appending the new line of text to `my_first_file`, we decide that we want to go back and add a period at the end of the first line? The `$ cat` command with the `>>` operator will only allow us to *add* things (i.e., append) to the end of a file, and it looks like we missed our chance to get the period in. Of course, the `>` operator will be of no help in this situation as it only affords a wholesale replacement. If we want to selectively revise something earlier in a file, we are going to have to expand our tool palette.

Linux command line text editors

We now know how to add text to files, but we will also need a way to interactively edit files in the Linux shell so that we can insert or remove text at will—similar to the way we handle text in our favorite mobile or desktop user environments. Lucky for us, Unix has a long history of text editing tools going all the way back to the first iteration of the operating system in 1969, and Linux has carried this tradition forward with an impressive list of text editors built up over the years. Here we will be covering two of the most beloved Linux command line text editors.

`$ nano`

Originally released in 1999, the `$ nano` text editor is relatively new as far as Linux utilities go. Derived from another text editor called `$ pico`, `$ nano` is known for its ease of use, reliability, and practical set of features. Editing text in `$ nano` feels almost like editing text in a GUI-based text editor, and this has earned `$ nano` its reputation as a "beginner-friendly" editor in Linux.

To open a file in `$ nano`, we simply call the command with the `<filename>` in the argument. Let's try this on `my_first_file`.

`$ nano my_first_file`

After pressing enter, you will see the `$ nano` interface occupy the entire terminal window, and toward the top you will see the two lines of text that make up `my_first_file`. Use the arrow keys as you normally would in a GUI-based text editor to move the cursor to the end of the first line. When there, add a period.

So far so good. Now we need to save `my_first_file` with its brand-new period. In `$ nano`, when we want to save something, we enter the key command `ctrl + o` (for Write Out). If you find this strange, you would not be the first one. But it does work.

`ctrl + o`

You will be prompted as shown above. Simply press `enter` and `my_first_file` will be saved. One thing to be aware of is that the `M` displayed in the beginning of these key commands doesn't actually mean `M` but rather, the `alt` key. Historically, the `alt` key was labeled as the "meta" key.

When you press `enter`, you should see `[ Wrote 2 lines ]` just above the key-command guide at the bottom of the terminal window. When you are ready to exit `$ nano` and return to the Bash command line prompt, press `ctrl + x`.

After some time in `$ nano`, you will get used to its unorthodox key commands, but if you do ever forget any of them, it's helpful that `$ nano` always displays key combinations at the bottom of the terminal window. With its emphasis on simplicity and usability, you may find that `$ nano` becomes your favorite text editor in the Linux shell.

$ vim

Descended from the seminal `$ vi` text editor first introduced as part of BSD in 1979, `$ vim` (for vi improved) has a deserved reputation as a powerhouse editor in Linux. In this first look at `$ vim`, we will be going over just the basics so you can get a handle on how to use `$ vim` for everyday editing tasks.

To start with, let's call `$ vim` to check up on `my_second_file` and see if there is anything we can edit or add. Just like with `$ nano`, we can open a file in `$ vim` by calling the command with the `<filename>` in the argument.

```
$ vim my_second_file
```

Alright. You will see that `$ vim`, like `$ nano`, takes up the entire terminal window. You will also notice that `$ vim` has a less inviting, more traditionally spartan Unix feel to its interface. Just imagine it's 1979 and editing text this way is a major improvement over using a typewriter.

Like in `$ nano`, you can use the arrow keys in `$ vim` to move the cursor around. Try adding an exclamation point at the end of the first line.

Right. If you find when trying to type the exclamation point that the cursor is unresponsive, just take a deep breath. It's not broken. This is actually a feature. When we launch `$ vim`, it starts off in what is called **normal mode**[36]. To be able to edit, we need to tell `$ vim` that we wish to switch to **insert mode**. To change to insert mode, simply type a lowercase `i`. Now you should be able to add an exclamation point at the end of the first line.

While we're here, go ahead and add a period at the end of the second line. And why not type in a third line to mark the occasion.

Making progress. Now we need to save our changes to `my_second_file`. When you are ready, press the `esc` key, and this will take us back into normal mode. After pressing the `esc` key, type in a single `:` and you will see a colon prompt appear at the lower left corner of the terminal window. With the `:` prompt at the bottom of the terminal window, we are now in what is confusingly called **command-line mode**[37] (within `$ vim`). Finally, type in `wq` at the `:` prompt (for write and quit), press `enter`, and this will take us back to the Bash command line prompt.

---

[36] In some Linux circles, the default mode when we open `$ vim` (or press the `esc` key) is referred to as "command mode" rather than "normal mode".

[37] Not to be confused with the Bash command line, which is external to `$ vim`.

Whew. It's no secret that $ vim has a tendency to scare people away on the first meeting. If this is you, don't give up on $ vim just yet! It does get easier with practice. Below is a recap of the procedure we follow for basic editing in $ vim.

Opening and editing a file in $ vim

1. Launch $ vim <filename>.
2. Press the esc key (just to make certain you are in normal mode).
3. Press lowercase i to switch to insert mode.
4. Edit the contents of <filename>.

Saving a file and quitting $ vim

1. Press the esc key.
2. Type in a single colon :
3. Type in w at the : prompt and press enter to write the file.
4. Type in another single colon :.
5. Type in q at the : prompt and press enter to quit $ vim.

Here are some important key commands in $ vim:

$ vim key command	Result
→ esc	normal mode (use this to pivot to/from other modes)
→ i	insert mode (accessible from normal mode)
→ :	command-line mode (accessible from normal mode)
→ n	next instance of <pattern> (in a search—see below)

And here is an abridged list of $ vim commands to enter in command-line mode (at the : prompt):

$ vim command-line mode command	Action
▪ :e <filename>	open <filename> for editing
▪ :tabe <filename>	open <filename> for editing in a new tab
▪ :tabn	go to the next tab
▪ :w	write (i.e., save) the current file
▪ :w <filename>	write the current file as <filename>
▪ :q	quit $ vim
▪ :wq	write the current file and quit $ vim
▪ :q!	quit $ vim without saving changes
▪ :/<pattern>	forward search for <pattern> in the current file
▪ :?<pattern>	backward search for <pattern> in the current file
▪ :set number	show line numbers
▪ :set nonumber	hide line numbers

Whole books have been written about advanced use of $ vim and its deep extensibility through plugins as this editor's power is like an operating system in itself. Even if we don't have need for all that $ vim offers, it is still good for us to be familiar with basic $ vim usage because it is the *de facto* text editor in Linux. One thing we can be sure of is that $ vim (or $ vi) will be available in nearly every Linux shell. At some point you may find yourself in a situation where you are logged in to a remote shell on a server, and you need to edit something in a file. It is not uncommon for $ vim (or $ vi) to be the only editor available in this type of restricted, containerized[38] shell environment. To prepare yourself for these situations, it is important to know your way around $ vim.

Aliases in the Linux command line environment

We're going to turn our attention now to Bash aliases as our first application of the command line text editing tools we have been looking at. Of the aliases we have seen so far, do you have any that you prefer for $ ls? We have made frequent use of $ ll (alias for $ ls -alF), but there are others, like $ la (for $ ls -A), and $ l (for $ ls -CF), to name a few. Really, any command can be represented as an alias in Bash. This is especially convenient when we have a long or complex command that we might have difficulty remembering how to type.

$ alias

The $ alias command is the tool we use for reserving our own custom aliases in Bash. To get an idea of how to use this command, let's take a step back into the ~ directory and have another peek inside the .bashrc file. This time we will use $ vim to view the file's contents.

$$ \$ \text{ vim .bashrc} $$

In $ vim, scroll down through the file to find the section shown below (or do a search in $ vim using :/'alias ll'). Notice that normal mode (via the esc key) in $ vim acts as a kind of shield protecting us against making accidental edits in a file like this.

---

[38] Containers are used as a method of securely allocating system resources for running an application in an isolated, controlled environment. When we "spin up" a container running a Linux web server, for example, we are effectively launching a completely contained web server that works in isolation from other web servers running in their own containers on the same host machine. To conserve shared hardware resources, container environments are often stripped down to a minimum set of command line utilities.

See how the three aforementioned aliases ($ ll, $ la, $ l) are defined using the $ alias command in the ~/.bashrc file? When we launch a shell session, Bash looks to the .bashrc file in the home directory and runs commands included in the file. Since Bash only remembers aliases for the duration of a shell session (i.e., when we close the terminal window, Bash forgets all aliases), we need to have Bash run these $ alias commands at the beginning of every shell session for the aliases to persist from one session to the next. Hence, these $ alias commands are included in ~/.bashrc.

If you continue to scroll down in the ~/.bashrc file, you will see another segment where Bash gets instructions to look for a .bash_aliases file in the home directory. If a ~/.bash_aliases file exists, Bash is told to open it and run[39] any commands contained therein.

But do we have a .bash_aliases file in the home directory? We'll have to check on this when we go back to the command line. Once you are done perusing ~/.bashrc in $ vim, let's quit $ vim and return to the Bash command line in the home directory. A quick $ ll confirms that in fact there is no ~/.bash_aliases file (yet). We will come back to this in a short while.

We are about ready to experiment with creating our own alias. Despite already having several aliases for the $ ls command, we can certainly make room for one more. There is a -t [option] for $ ls that instructs the command to list the contents of a directory by time of modification. Viewing files organized this way is often key for understanding what is going on in a directory, so we will take this opportunity to make our own alias for $ ls -alt.

Now we need to choose something to represent $ ls -alt. How about $ lt? This sounds like it could work, but first we need to make sure there isn't an existing alias or command by that name. Let's get a list of all currently active aliases by entering $ alias on the command line.

$ alias

---

[39] In this segment from the ~/.bashrc file, the first . in . ~/.bash_aliases is a synonym for $ source, which is a Bash built-in used to launch commands contained in files. We will cover the $ source command when we take a closer look at the difference between executable and non-executable files.

```
                                              me@MyLinuxBox: ~

me@MyLinuxBox:~$ alias
alias alert='notify-send --urgency=low -i "$([ $? = 0 ] && echo terminal || echo error)"
;&|]\s*alert$//'\''")"'
alias egrep='egrep --color=auto'
alias fgrep='fgrep --color=auto'
alias grep='grep --color=auto'
alias l='ls -CF'
alias la='ls -A'
alias ll='ls -alF'
alias ls='ls --color=auto'
me@MyLinuxBox:~$ █
```

Sure enough, there is no existing alias by the name of $ lt. OK. Next, we will take a chance[40] and enter $ lt on the command line to see if any command goes by this name (we could also try $ man lt, but this is not guaranteed to prove the absence of a command since not all commands have $ man pages). Upon trying $ lt on the command line, you should receive an extended error message that starts with Command 'lt' not found. This is everything we need to know.

We're all set to create our own alias. When ready, enter the following.

$ alias lt='ls -alt'

Let's now test our new alias in the home directory. Enter $ lt and you should see the directory's contents listed by time of modification. Nice work! Now, we are going to $ exit the shell, and then after the terminal window has closed, we will open a new shell session and enter $ lt again on the command line. In doing this you should receive the same Command 'lt' not found error as before. This happens because Bash does not remember aliases from one shell session to the next. We need to remind Bash in the beginning of each shell session what aliases we want it to keep track of.

As we saw before, we can give Bash the reminder it needs by creating a new file, ~/.bash_aliases, and putting our $ alias command in the file. Let's take care of this with $ vim in the home directory.

$ vim .bash_aliases

In $ vim, type in the $ alias command as shown below. Then save ~/.bash_aliases and quit.

```
                                              me@MyLinuxBox: ~

alias lt='ls -alt█
~
```

---

[40] In this case, because we happen to know that $ lt is not an existing command, this is safe to do. In other cases, you may want to use $ compgen -c to list all active commands and check for availability. Because this is going to return a long list, it is a good idea to view the results in $ less with $ compgen -c | less.

To test this alias, close the current shell session and open a new one. Enter $ lt, and you should see ~ organized by time of modification. Great job! You now have your own persistent alias. If for whatever reason you ever need to remove an alias in a shell session, simply type $ unalias <alias> and the alias will no longer work (in that shell session). To permanently remove an alias, delete the alias <alias>='<command> [option(s)]' definition in .bashrc or .bash_aliases (and then open a new shell).

Summary:

The $ cat command is useful for taking a quick look at shorter files, but as we start working with longer and more complex files on the command line, we will need a different set of tools for viewing and editing file contents. For browsing through longer files, the $ less command shows the contents in full-page view and offers some useful navigation features. For editing raw text, the $ nano and $ vim text editors cover practically every conceivable use case—$ nano being the easier of the two to learn, and $ vim being more powerful. One use of these command line text editors is to view, modify, and/or create configuration files in Bash. Making adjustments in configuration files (e.g., with $ alias) gives us a means of making persistent changes to our command line settings.

Commands:

$ less $ vim
$ cat $ ls
$ nano $ alias

Concepts:

- Viewing larger files
- Interactive input in the shell
- Commands that accept stdin as direct input
- End of File control state (ctrl + d)
- Editing text on the command line

- Bash configuration files
  - ~/.bashrc file
  - ~/.bash_aliases file
- Persistent aliases in Bash

Challenge:

Use a | with $ ls and $ wc to form a command that outputs the number of visible and hidden items in the current working directory. For this item count, we want to exclude . and .. from the list, so you will need to find the right [option] for $ ls that will output everything in the directory except for the . and .. shortcuts. Consult the $ man pages for $ ls if necessary (or look on p. 45). For $ wc, check the $ man pages for the [option] that outputs the number of lines received in the input. Once you have assembled a command that correctly outputs the number of items in the current working directory (minus . and ..), make an alias for your command (you can choose how to name this alias) and add the alias to the ~/.bash_aliases file.

About the shell environment

We've been living our life on the command line inside this environment for a while now, blissfully without a care for what is going on around us. This is one of the nice things about the shell environment—to be able to use the command line and not have to concern ourselves with every detail the shell keeps track of—like what directory we last visited or what commands we entered since we opened the terminal window. The shell stores this kind of information for us so that if, for example, we type in a command like `$ cd -`, we can arrive at our destination without having to think about it.

But sometimes we may want to delve deeper into this information that follows us around in the shell. As we have seen in creating our own persistent alias, there is more behind the command line than just a "stock" list of commands that operate in a prescribed way. The real power in the command line lies in the potential to tap into its resources and shape things as we want. This includes creating our own commands, which we will be doing as we progress through this guide. In order to reach that goal, first we need to learn how to take full advantage of the environment that surrounds us.

The command line environment

This thing we call the **shell environment** still has its secrets, and it is time we did a little forensic work to uncover what lies beneath the surface.

We use this term "environment" as an intuitive way of describing the context in which our command line activities take place. Things such as *who we are*, *where we are*, and other determining factors are all part of the shell environment. These pieces of information altogether define the space we inhabit on the command line.

So, how are pieces of information like *who we are* and *where we are* stored in the shell? Each piece of information[41] in the shell environment is assigned to its own **variable**. In terms of computers, a variable is like a storage box of information, and we can access that information by calling the storage box by name.

Let's try a little experiment on the command line to demonstrate how Bash lets us store information in a variable. We will define a variable named a and then retrieve the information it stores by calling the variable's name. Go to the command line and enter the following[42].

$ a=3

---

[41] It is possible for more than one piece of information to be assigned to a single variable in Bash, such as in an array variable like `$ array=(1 2 3 … N)`.

[42] In assigning a value to a variable in Bash, there should be no spaces surrounding the =, as shown.

We are telling Bash that we want to assign the value 3 to a variable we are naming a. The name we choose for any variable in Bash must begin and end with an alphabetic character or _ (underscore).

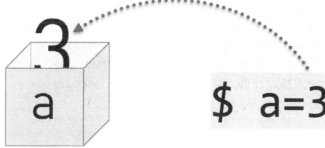

Figure 7 Variable assignment diagram

Now, in the same shell session, if we call the variable a by name, for example in the argument of the $ echo command, Bash will return the value we assigned to a (in this case, 3). One thing to know about calling the name of a variable in Bash is that a $ has to be placed directly before the <variable> (as in, $<variable>[43]) for Bash to return the assigned value (see p. 29).

$ echo $a

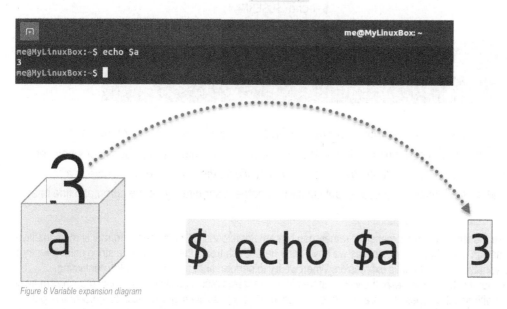

Figure 8 Variable expansion diagram

---

[43] As a general rule, when we have a $<variable> expansion in the <operand> of a command (like shown here), it is best to put the $<variable> in double quotes (e.g., $ echo "$a") to prevent the shell from misinterpreting any spaces or other special characters that *may* be stored in the variable. Here the $<variable> is safe to expand without double quotes, but this will not always be the case. See Appendix B for more information.

When we invoke this `$<variable>` form with the `$` prefix to get the variable's stored value, we are performing what is called **variable expansion**[44] (formally known as "parameter expansion" in Bash). You can think of variable expansion as the act of "opening the box" (i.e., the variable) that contains the stored value. In this guide, when we talk about specific variables, sometimes we will refer to a variable just by its name (e.g., a), and at other times if we mean to refer to the value stored inside the variable, we will use the `$<variable>` form (e.g., $a).

Variables in Bash can contain **integer** values[45] (as we just demonstrated), or we can assign other types of data to variables, such as letters and/or special symbols. In general, a stored piece of information that consists of letters and/or other symbols is called a **string** (e.g., `'abc'`, `'A+'`, `'y'`, `'Hello there!'`, and `'3D'` are all strings). Most of the variables that we will be looking at contain strings, but we will see some that do store integers, like our variable a.

Bash environment variables

Now let's find out exactly what kind of information the shell maintains in our presence. We are going to use variable expansion to unpack some of the **environment variables** that accompany us wherever we go on the command line. Take note that environment variables in Unix/Linux are customarily labeled in <u>all caps</u>. Go ahead and see what comes up when we print $USERNAME.

$ echo $USERNAME

In the output, you should see your `<username>`. This looks like the `$ whoami` command all over again! Printing $USERNAME and running `$ whoami` will return the same result unless, for whatever reason, we choose to *switch to another user account while on the command line.* There is a command, `$ su`, that allows a user to <u>su</u>bstitute for another <u>u</u>ser directly on the command line in a

---

[44] We use the term "variable expansion" rather than "parameter expansion" because the former is more intuitive.
[45] If we assign a number to a variable as we have done here, Bash treats the number as a <u>string</u> unless we try to use the variable in an arithmetic expression. When we try to perform arithmetic on variables containing numbers, for this to work in Bash, the values stored in the variables must consist of <u>digits</u> only (i.e., they must be integers) with no other types of characters (the exception being a possible minus (-) sign to indicate a negative integer). So, for `$ a=1` and `$ b=-2345`, `$ echo ((\$a + \$b))` would be treated as valid for arithmetic in Bash, whereas `$ a=1.0` and `$ b=-2345.0` would <u>not</u> be treated as numeric but rather as strings. This behavior exposes one of the main limitations of Bash, which is that it is only capable of doing math on pure integers—with integer results. To do floating-point math in Bash requires elaborate workarounds or the use of `$ bc` (for <u>b</u>asic <u>c</u>alculator)—an external command with scientific calculator capabilities.

multi-user system (without logging out of GNOME). For example, on your machine, if root were enabled and if you had the root password, you could use $ su to become root on the command line (which you shouldn't do unless you have a good reason to). In this hypothetical scenario, if you ran $ whoami after switching to root, $ whoami would return root, while $ echo $USERNAME would still print the original <username> that you logged in with. Meanwhile, the shell stores info in *another* environment variable, USER, which would mirror $ whoami (i.e., root) in the event that you $ su as root.

So, Bash keeps track of *who we are* in at least two environment variables (one of which sometimes stores *who we were*!). Let's see what Bash has in store in another environment variable.

$ echo $PWD

In the output you will see /home/<username> (assuming you are still in the home directory). This PWD variable seems eerily familiar, doesn't it? It's as though there's no difference between $PWD and what we get from the $ pwd command! In fact, there is virtually no difference[46] between these two. The biggest difference would be in the acronyms themselves: "Present Working Directory" (PWD) vs "print working directory" ($ pwd), which of course is neither here nor there.

In addition to *who we are* and *where we are*, there is a lot of other information that gets stored in the Bash environment. We are now going to see about taking this information in as a whole.

$ env

In its simplest application, calling the $ env command returns a list of all active environment variables in the current shell. Try entering the following and see what comes back in return.

$ env

The output will be a rather long list that probably extends beyond the height of your terminal window. If this is the case, you will have to scroll up to see the beginning of the list.

---

[46] When called with the -P [option] (for Physical), the $ pwd command does not report soft links in the path to the current working directory, whereas $ pwd with no [options] does observe soft links, as does the PWD variable. Later we will be going into detail about how to work with hard and soft links.

A better way of viewing a long list of information like this is to pipe the output of the command (in this case, $ env) into $ less and use the latter command's page-view layout. Let's try this.

$ env | less

Better. But even better yet would be a way to view these environment variables in alphabetical order. Having a way to condense the list would be helpful too.

Other filter commands in Linux

$ sort

The $ sort filter answers a need for a simple command line utility that can organize textual information in alphabetical or numerical order. Like $ wc, $ grep, and $ sed, $ sort takes stdin as input and transforms what it receives according to a set of rules. The rules that $ sort operates under are to reshuffle the lines of text[47] that arrive at its input based on the order of the leading characters. Let's see what this means for our list of environment variables.

$ env | sort | less

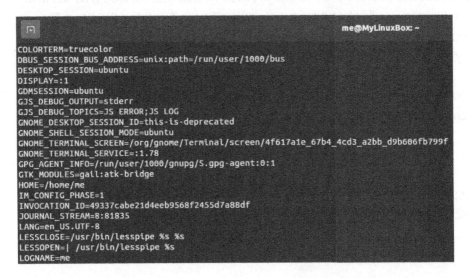

```
                                                          me@MyLinuxBox: ~
COLORTERM=truecolor
DBUS_SESSION_BUS_ADDRESS=unix:path=/run/user/1000/bus
DESKTOP_SESSION=ubuntu
DISPLAY=:1
GDMSESSION=ubuntu
GJS_DEBUG_OUTPUT=stderr
GJS_DEBUG_TOPICS=JS ERROR;JS LOG
GNOME_DESKTOP_SESSION_ID=this-is-deprecated
GNOME_SHELL_SESSION_MODE=ubuntu
GNOME_TERMINAL_SCREEN=/org/gnome/Terminal/screen/4f617a1e_67b4_4cd3_a2bb_d9b606fb799f
GNOME_TERMINAL_SERVICE=:1.78
GPG_AGENT_INFO=/run/user/1000/gnupg/S.gpg-agent:0:1
GTK_MODULES=gail:atk-bridge
HOME=/home/me
IM_CONFIG_PHASE=1
INVOCATION_ID=49337cabe21d4eeb9568f2455d7a88df
JOURNAL_STREAM=8:81835
LANG=en_US.UTF-8
LESSCLOSE=/usr/bin/lesspipe %s %s
LESSOPEN=| /usr/bin/lesspipe %s
LOGNAME=me
```

Sometimes it's so satisfying to see a nicely ordered list where before there was chaos. If you scroll or page through the list, you will come across the environment variables that we've already mentioned, plus some others that you will probably recognize, like HOME, LOGNAME, OLDPWD[48], and SHELL.

---

[47] The $ sort filter takes in a stream of raw text and looks for <newline> characters, which it uses as markers to slice the text up into discrete lines. Then it reorders the lines lexicographically.

[48] This one could qualify as an oxymoron—OLDPWD (for "Old Present Working Directory")! The value stored in the OLDPWD variable reflects the destination directory for the $ cd - command (effectively *where we were*).

Viewing a list like this in $ less is better than reeling out loads of information directly to stdout, but if we just want to get a quick snapshot of a couple of lines of text, we may turn to a different solution.

$ head

Another member of the filter family of commands that you will want to keep nearby is $ head. Just like its cousins $ wc, $ grep, $ sed, and $ sort, $ head takes input through stdin—most commonly after a pipe. Like all others in this family, however, $ head is perfectly capable of being called on the command line with a <filename> in the argument. Either way, with stdin or not, the default behavior for $ head is to display the first ten lines of text that arrive at its input. If we want to see a different number of lines, this is configurable with the -n [option] followed by an integer (as in, $ head -n [#]). Give the following a try on the command line.

$ env | sort | head

Now, see if you can display just the first five lines of text from the list.

$ env | sort | head -n 5

```
me@MyLinuxBox:~$ env | sort | head -n 5
COLORTERM=truecolor
DBUS_SESSION_BUS_ADDRESS=unix:path=/run/user/1000/bus
DESKTOP_SESSION=ubuntu
DISPLAY=:0
GDMSESSION=ubuntu
me@MyLinuxBox:~$
```

Excellent! The $ head command works in classic Unix fashion as a simple, modular tool that does one thing very well. See the $ man pages for other useful [options].

$ tail

The $ `tail` command is like $ head but stationed at the trailing end of a stream of text. Try running the previous two commands with $ `tail` in place of $ head. The environment variables you will see in the output all start with the letter X.

By combining $ `tail` and $ head together in a pipeline, we can filter arbitrary ranges of text. One such trick is to use a +[#][49] with the -n [option] in the $ `tail` command's argument. For example, if we try $ env | sort | tail -n +1, this will treat the entire list as the "tail"; hence, the entire list will be shown. If we try $ env | sort | tail -n +2, the "tail" will be everything in the $ env list *except* for the first line. If we wanted to create a filter to show, for example, just the second line from the $ env list, we could do so with $ env | sort | tail -n +2 | head -n 1. To show only the second *and* third lines, it would be $ env | sort | tail -n +2 | head -n 2 (and so forth). Try it!

Modifying the Bash environment

As you were looking through the environment variables returned by the $ env command, did you happen to notice our variable a anywhere in the list? Take another look if you want. You will see that it is not there.

Why is this? Doesn't it seem like a is part of the "environment" in the way we can call for it and retrieve its value—as if it's just floating around somewhere nearby? It certainly does! For all practical purposes, a is floating around nearby in our current shell (figuratively speaking)!

To understand why a is not on the list returned by $ env, we need to go a little deeper into what constitutes the "environment" on the command line. If you think about our physical surroundings, what we call our "environment" could vary in scope depending on context. We could describe our environment in terms of our immediate surroundings, or we could expand outward and speak about the environment on a larger scale.

Similarly, the shell is not just one monolithic thing but rather a multifaceted domain where variables have different **scope** depending on how they are defined. By defining a in the way that we did, which was to enter $ a=3 in our current shell, we cast a as a **shell variable**. A variable created in this way[50] is called a "shell variable" because its meaning is local (i.e., limited) to the shell where it is originally defined.

---

[49] With no + sign in front of the [#], $ `tail` -n [#] filters out *everything* except for the last [#] lines of text.
[50] By "this way", we mean by using $ <variable>=<value> to define a new variable. Unless an additional command is used to *export* the variable outside of the local scope, the variable a remains a shell variable. In the $ **export** section of this chapter, we will talk about how to define variables whose meaning extends beyond the local scope.

Here is where this gets a little tricky. By "local", we don't simply mean the home directory or even any particular location in the Linux file system. In this frame, we have to think vertically. A "local" shell variable lives inside what can be thought of as a dome (a shell!) covering the entire file system[51]. Within this shell where our variable a has meaning, running certain commands like $ bash will cause the shell to spawn[52] a **child shell**, not unlike a matryoshka (or Russian nesting doll) "spawns" its internal offspring. For example, if we were to $ su as another user on the command line (as we talked about earlier—see p. 86), this would take us into a child shell effectively contained under the original **parent shell**. Now, in this child shell, the variable a would have no meaning because as a shell variable, the scope of a is confined to the original parent shell in which it was defined.

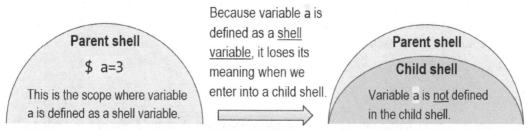

Because variable a is defined as a shell variable, it loses its meaning when we enter into a child shell.

Figure 10 Parent shell and child shell diagram

However, if we had *exported* a as an **environment variable**[53], then a would be **inherited**[54] by any child shells that we spawn from the original parent shell.

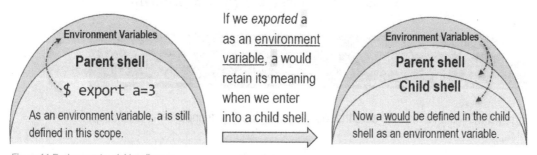

If we *exported* a as an environment variable, a would retain its meaning when we enter into a child shell.

Figure 11 Environment variables diagram

The $ env command lists all currently active environment variables; hence, a (as a shell variable) was not included on the list. In the next section, we will create another variable and see how to *export* it as an environment variable.

---

[51] As in, any part of the file system to which we have access, as determined by user status and file permissions.
[52] Another way this is expressed in Linux is to say that a parent shell "forks" off a copy of itself as a child process.
[53] Keep in mind that by convention, environment variable names should be in ALL_CAPS.
[54] Note that while a child shell inherits environment variables from its parent shell, the reverse is not the case. If we define an environment variable in a child shell, it will be forgotten when we $ exit back into the parent shell.

$ export

If we want to have a variable retain its meaning beyond the local shell, the `$ export` command will help us accomplish this. To `$ export` a variable to the environment, we simply need to put the variable assignment in the `$ export` command's argument (or put the `<variable>` alone in the argument if the variable is already defined). Let's try this on the command line with a new variable we will call **A**.

$ export A=my_first_environment_variable

First we will test this to make sure that our new variable **A** is defined in the local scope.

$ echo $A

This is encouraging. Let's also confirm that our shell still remembers the variable **a** that we defined earlier.

$ echo $a

```
me@MyLinuxBox:~$ echo $a
3
me@MyLinuxBox:~$ ▮
```

Everything looks good. Now we are going to experiment with something that we haven't tried yet on the command line. We are going to use the $ bash command to enter into a child shell. By doing this, it is as if we are running Bash (a child shell) "under" Bash (the parent shell). Although this might seem like an obscure thing to do, this happens automatically with a lot of commands in Linux (such as $ su, for example). For right now, we are doing this to demonstrate how going from our local shell into a child shell plays out with the two variables we created.

$ bash

```
me@MyLinuxBox:~$ bash
me@MyLinuxBox:~$ ▮
```

And we're in. That was easy. But what happened? It appears as though nothing has changed, right? Nevertheless, we are now inside a child shell spawned from the parent shell. We can prove we are in a child shell by checking if our variable a has made the journey with us or not.

$ echo $a

```
me@MyLinuxBox:~$ bash
me@MyLinuxBox:~$ echo $a

me@MyLinuxBox:~$ ▮
```

As expected, our variable a is unknown in this child shell. This is because a was defined as a shell variable in the parent shell. Put another way, in this child shell we are now outside[55] the scope of a.

How about our variable A?

$ echo $A

---

[55] In this child shell, even though our location in the file system hasn't changed (we're still in the ~ directory), it is *as if* we have gone somewhere else now that we are no longer within the scope of a. Being in a child shell like this is analogous to being in the *Twilight Zone* (the 1950s TV show), where we might be in the same place, but certain things are not the same as before.

```
me@MyLinuxBox:~$ bash
me@MyLinuxBox:~$ echo $a

me@MyLinuxBox:~$ echo $A
my_first_environment_variable
me@MyLinuxBox:~$
```

There we go! This confirms that $ export does indeed allow us to create environment variables.

Now you can type $ exit or use ctrl + d to leave the child shell and return to the parent shell. Once back in the parent shell, run $ echo $a one more time to make sure that the parent shell hasn't forgotten about our variable a. You should see 3 again in the output.

Summary:

When we use the Linux command line, there is a set of information that follows us around and forms the backdrop of our command line user experience. Bash stores this information in a number of variables, and depending on how these variables are defined, they will either only exist in our current shell, or they will extend into child shells spawned from our current shell. When a variable's meaning is limited in scope to the current shell, we call this kind of variable a "shell variable", whereas when a variable is passed down from a parent shell to a child shell or process, we call the variable an "environment variable". As a technical term, the "environment" refers to the body of information stored in all currently active environment variables.

Commands:

$ echo	$ tail
$ env	$ export
$ sort	$ bash
$ head	$ exit

Concepts:

- The shell environment
- Variables in Bash
  - Integers
  - Strings
  - Variable expansion
  - Scope
- $ su command
- Environment variables
- Shell variables
- Parent shell
- Child shell
- Filter commands

Challenge:

Form a command pipeline in which you filter the output of $ env to show only the first five environment variables that begin with the letter X. There are several ways you could do this, but one could be to use a +[#] with $ head (and not $ tail). Check the $ man pages if necessary!

Your new prompt

As we form a complete picture of the variables that live on the command line, we're now going to be focusing on some pieces of information stored in **shell variables**. As we talked about in the last chapter, shell variables only have meaning in the shell where they are defined. We will be thinking about why this might be preferable for certain types of information, and along the way we will have some fun dissecting the shell variable string that determines the Bash command line prompt.

$ set

When we want to see a complete list of all active shell *and* environment variables, we call the `$ set` command to give us a 360-degree view of the information. The list it returns is long, so again it's a good idea to pipe into `$ less`. Try the command below.

$ set | less

You'll see that `$ set` does its own alphabetical sort, and you'll recognize some familiar environment variables that we talked about earlier. You will also see some variables that weren't in the `$ env` list, such as `HISTFILE`, `HOSTNAME`, and `PS1`. Because some of the variables returned by `$ set` contain a lot of data, let's modify the output of `$ less` with two [options].

$ set | less -SN

The `-S [option]` chops off the end of all multi-line entries so that each item in the list occupies just one line, and `-N` tells `$ less` to display line numbers. The list will still be quite long, but the number[56] of lines with variable definitions (shell or environment variables) now should be around 87. The lines in the rest of the list contain shell function code returned by `$ set`, which we can disregard for now.

It's great to be able to see all of the currently defined variables, but what if we just wanted to view the shell variables (and not the environment variables)? The `$ set` command alone will not do this for us; however, if we combine the output of the `$ env` *and* `$ set` commands together, then we can filter out the repeated environment variables and isolate just the shell variables.

$ uniq

To remove adjacent duplicated lines from a stream of text and only show lines that are "unique", we bring out the `$ uniq` filter command for its talents in this area.

---

[56] This number can vary depending on what type of Linux install you are working with (local install, VM, etc.).

Here we will form a command where first we combine the output of $ env and $ set into a merged list. Then we will send the list through a pipeline of filters with $ uniq -u in the chain to remove the duplicated environment variable entries, leaving only a list of shell variables (the -u [option] is to filter out non-unique items). Note that with $ sort, the duplicated environment variables are adjacent.

```
$ echo "$(env)" "$(set)" | tail -n +1 | head -n 129 | sort | uniq -u | less -SN
```

Starting from the left, we have the *output* of both the $ env and $ set commands concatenated together in the argument of the $ echo command. Then $ echo prints the lists from both $ env and $ set as one long list to stdout output (which is then piped into the stdin input of $ tail).

The way we capture the output of the $ env and $ set commands is through a shell technique called **command substitution**. By invoking the $(<command>) form, we are telling Bash to *substitute* (i.e., replace) $(<command>) with the *output* of $ <command> (as in, the output we would get if we called $ <command> on the command line). This leaves us with the output of both commands concatenated together in the argument of $ echo.

We put $(env) and $(set) in **double quotes** because we want to prevent Bash from turning the <newline> characters in the output of $(env) and $(set) into spaces. This effectively preserves the list nature of the $ env and $ set outputs (as seen when calling these commands on the command line).

Piping into $ tail -n +1 and then $ head -n 129 filters out everything in the list but the first 129 lines. The $ tail -n +1 trick (see p. 90) is used to take in the whole list from the output of $ echo (over 2000 lines) *before* piping into $ head -n 129. This use of tail -n +1 provides a makeshift buffer in the pipeline and prevents problems that can occur when piping large streams of text.

The line numbers that you see in $ less might not match up exactly with those shown here, but around line #18 you should see the HISTFILE shell variable containing the path to your /home/<username>/.bash_history file (see p. 63 for reference).

```
17 HISTCONTROL=ignoreboth
18 HISTFILE=/home/me/.bash_history
19 HISTFILESIZE=2000
20 HISTSIZE=1000
21 HOSTNAME=MyLinuxBox
```

Shell variables in Linux

To get some perspective on why shell variables are better for holding certain types of information, let's consider how Bash makes use of the HISTFILE variable.

Whenever we have a shell open, Bash allocates a special block of memory (RAM) where it stores a running log[57] of the commands that we enter during that session. If we terminate the session (e.g., if we $ exit), right before we leave the shell, Bash will take the commands that we entered in that session and *append* them to the file specified in the HISTFILE variable (which for regular users is /home/<username>/.bash_history).

You've probably noticed that if you flip through your previous commands with the ↑↓ arrows on the command line, Bash remembers your commands from the current session *in addition to* everything from your previous sessions (up to the limit defined in the HISTSIZE variable). Bash has your past commands readily available because, at the onset of each shell session, Bash goes to $HISTFILE (i.e., /home/<username>/.bash_history) and pre-loads the command history list into the special block of RAM reserved for logging commands. Then as you type things in, Bash continues to add your latest commands to the log (in RAM) until the session is terminated.

Now, let's imagine that you are working on a multi-user system and that something on your machine requires a system administrator's attention. In certain cases, this may require the system administrator to take control of your machine and do an $ su to act as a "substitute user" directly on the command line, thus entering into a child shell. In that event, when the sys admin comes to your machine and does $ su, because the shell variable HISTFILE is limited in scope to your shell only (and not exported to the environment), your $HISTFILE will not transfer to the sys admin's child shell. Instead, when the sys admin does $ su, HISTFILE will be freshly defined as a shell variable inside the sys admin's child shell. In that scope (in the child shell), HISTFILE will contain the path to the sys admin's own unique .bash_history file. Keeping HISTFILE as a shell variable so that it remains local to each shell where it is defined is key for keeping your and the sys admin's command histories isolated from each other.

But just imagine if rather than storing HISTFILE as a shell variable, we *exported* it to the environment with the $ export command. Any child shells spawned thereafter would *inherit*[58] your HISTFILE variable as an environment variable. This is not what we want to happen. Why? Well, for one thing, the sys admin's child shell could load your .bash_history file into the child shell's RAM, thus making your command history appear when the sys admin flips ↑↓ through past commands. Furthermore, the commands that the sys admin enters could end up in your .bash_history file when the sys admin exits the child shell.

---

[57] This is assuming that $ set -o history is enabled, which it should be by default.
[58] The reason that HISTFILE is inherited directly from the parent shell in this case is that HISTFILE, unlike many other shell variables, is not defined with a statement like HISTFILE=<value> in a configuration file that gets loaded during shell startup. Rather, HISTFILE is set to its default value (~/.bash_history) in the execution of the shell binary (/usr/bin/bash) when the shell launches (i.e., the value is essentially hard-coded in the shell binary). If we $ export HISTFILE to the environment, that value of HISTFILE as an environment variable takes precedence over the shell binary's hard-coded HISTFILE value.

There are safeguards in Linux that can prevent these types of things from slipping through, but the most failsafe way to avoid such issues with command histories is to simply store HISTFILE as a shell variable (as it is by default). Obviously, on a single-user system this is of less concern, but in case you do ever work on a multi-user system, it is something to be aware of.

Basic Linux account administration

Speaking of multi-user systems, by entering just a couple of commands, it is possible for us to add user accounts in Linux. Shall we try this? We can make another user account for ourselves and then practice with $ su to get some hands-on experience substituting as another user on the command line. This will help in developing our understanding of the parent shell/child shell relationship, and we will see first-hand how variables behave in these different contexts.

First, in order to perform elevated-status actions like creating a new user account, we have to be able to temporarily assume root-user status on the command line.

$ sudo

It is a major turning point in anyone's Linux journey when they start using the $ sudo command. Short for "superuser do", $ sudo (which is pronounced "Sue-Do") gives regular users like us a chance to know what it feels like to have superpowers—one brief command at a time.

Becoming a "superuser" comes with big responsibility. The $ sudo command temporarily allows us to execute commands reserved exclusively for root users. This is why we should never $ sudo without first thinking carefully about what we are doing. With that said, if we exercise good judgement, we should be okay.

For any command that requires root status to run, we simply put the command in the argument of $ sudo, press enter, type in our account password, and the command will execute. This is all possible because, as we found out in the first chapter, we belong to group27(sudo), which means Ubuntu placed us in the sudo group with permissions to temporarily act as root (see p. 40). You can list your $ sudo permissions by running the command with the -l [option] and entering your account password when prompted.

$ sudo -l

In the output, you should see the following:

```
User <username> may run the following commands on <hostname>:
(ALL : ALL) ALL
```

$ useradd

Making new user accounts in Linux is easy thanks to the $ useradd command. We will be taking advantage of $ useradd to create a second user account for ourselves. Enter the command as shown below with a <newusername> of your choosing. We are including the -m [option] to tell $ useradd to make a /home/<newusername> directory (a home directory for the new account), and -s with /usr/bin/bash as an [option-argument][59] to set up Bash* as the default shell for the new account.

$$ \$\ sudo\ useradd\ -m\ -s\ /usr/bin/bash\ <newusername> $$

When prompted, input the password for your <username> account (the password you used when you logged in).

*On Ubuntu systems pre version 19.04, the location of the $ bash executable may be /bin/bash rather than /usr/bin/bash.

That's all there is to it! Now you have an account for <newusername> on your system.

$ passwd

You can set a new password for your <newusername> account with the $ passwd command as shown below[60]. Because we're changing a password on an account other than our current <username> account, we need to use $ sudo for elevated privileges[60].

$$ \$\ sudo\ passwd\ <newusername> $$

Now we can experiment with using $ su to switch back and forth between accounts.

---

[59] For some commands, certain [options] can be accompanied by their own argument(s) for specifying the command's behavior. When an argument follows an [option] like this, we call this type of argument an [option-argument].

[60] If you perform this command within fifteen minutes of the previous command, $ sudo will not ask you to re-enter your <username> password for access.

$ su

With the $ su command (short for substitute user), we can switch between user accounts directly on the command line. On Linux systems with root enabled, entering $ su alone with no argument allows the user to switch to root if they type in the root password. Because logging into the root account is disabled in Ubuntu, fortunately for us we won't be "substituting" as root with $ su (since it's dangerous).

Instead, we will be using $ su to switch back and forth between our current regular-user account (<username>) and our other regular-user account (<newusername>). Let's give this a try! Enter the command below, followed by your <newusername> password.

$ su <newusername>

Welcome! If you are still in the /home/<username> directory, you should see the prompt change to <newusername>@<hostname>:/home/<username>$. Since you now have a different $HOME directory, you no longer see ~ displayed for the current working directory.

A quick $ whoami confirms your (new) identity.

$ whoami

Just to test some environment variable behavior we mentioned in the last chapter, try the following.

$ echo $USERNAME

As previously discussed, USERNAME retains *who we were* when we $ su (see p. 86).

$ echo $USER

And USER stores *who we are* (see p. 87).

While we're here as <newusername>, let's also check the shell variable HISTFILE.

$ echo $HISTFILE

This is as it should be. The HISTFILE shell variable is initialized by Bash when we open a new shell (including every time we $ su into a child shell).

Let's $ exit out of this child shell and go back into our parent shell where we started as <username>.

Variables in parent shells and child shells

We're now going to test the behavior of the HISTFILE shell variable, which we talked about earlier in this chapter (see p. 96). If we print $HISTFILE in our current shell (where we reside as <username>), we get the result shown below.

$ echo $HISTFILE

This /home/<username>/.bash_history path is the $HISTFILE connected with our <username> account—in the same way that the /home/<newusername>/.bash_history path shown earlier is the $HISTFILE connected with our <newusername> account. Because each account's HISTFILE stores a unique <pathname>/.bash_history file path, everything is in good order.

Now, we're going to try something that is not recommended in "real life". For the sake of demonstration only, we're going to *export* HISTFILE to the environment from our <username> shell (i.e., we're going to make HISTFILE into an environment variable).

Then, we will $ su as <newusername> again into a child shell. In the child shell, we will check the string stored in HISTFILE to see if it has the correct <pathname> associated with <newusername>.

Type in the following command. Since HISTFILE is already defined in the current shell, we can type in $ export HISTFILE to export the variable to the environment without having to assign a value in the $ export command's argument.

$ export HISTFILE

Now HISTFILE is an environment variable. You can confirm this with $ env | grep HISTFILE if you like.

Next, we will do an $ su as <newusername> again and enter into a child shell. Then, once in the child shell, we'll check one more time to view the stored HISTFILE information for <newusername>.

$ su <newusername>

$ echo $HISTFILE

Uh oh. That doesn't look right! We are in this child shell as <newusername>, but the HISTFILE variable contains the wrong file path (it contains the path to the file belonging to <username>). When we tested this before (see p. 101), this wasn't the case. What happened?

Beforehand, `HISTFILE` was stored as a shell variable in the parent shell. When we entered the child shell via `$ su`, `HISTFILE` was reinitialized—again as a shell variable but with a different value. This made each instance of `HISTFILE` discrete to the shell in which it was defined.

This second time, however, `HISTFILE` was *exported* to the environment from the `<username>` parent shell, so in the `<newusername>` child shell it was *inherited* along with other parts of the parent shell's environment. Child shells inherit their parents' environment variable values unless a variable is defined in a configuration at shell startup that overrides the inheritance. As an example, in the case of the `USER` environment variable that we looked at earlier (see p. 101), we confirmed that when we `$ su` into a child shell, the child shell does not inherit the parent's `USER` value. Instead, when we `$ su` into a child shell, `USER` is reconfigured to reflect the user's account inside the child shell. On the other hand, as we also found out, the `USERNAME` environment variable is not reconfigured and thus we do inherit `USERNAME` when we enter into a child shell via `$ su` (`USERNAME` preserves a record of *who we were*—as in, *who we were logged in as* in the parent shell).

If `HISTFILE` is exported to the environment, it works similarly to `USERNAME`—that is, the parent shell's `HISTFILE` becomes the child shell's `HISTFILE`. When this is undesired (as is the case with `HISTFILE`), there are many ways to prevent this kind of thing from happening, but one possible solution (aside from avoiding unnecessary `$ export` of shell variables!) would be to use `$ su -` (with the bare hyphen argument as shown) rather than `$ su` with no bare hyphen. If we had invoked the command as `$ su - <newusername>`, this would cause Bash to forget all environment variable values from the parent shell so they could be reset when we enter into a child shell.

Doing a reset on all environment variables with `$ su -` may be effective in some situations, but it may produce unwelcome side effects in others. It's generally preferable to let the shell variable policy control what is or is not passed on from a parent shell to a child shell. Variables in Bash are ephemeral things, so if we wish to return to the shell's initial variable settings, one tried and true method is to simply `$ exit` (or `ctrl + d`) all the way out of our parent shell and then open a new shell session. This way, our environment and shell variables are sure to be reset to their startup configuration.

Modifying the Bash command line prompt

Our loyal companion the Bash command line prompt is with us every step of the way. We rely on it to indicate our status on the command line, and the more we get out and about in the shell, the more the prompt becomes a critical piece in our command line workspace. One of the most useful shell customizations that we can make is to modify the prompt to display information in just the way that we like. Here we will be looking at the shell variable that controls the Bash command line prompt, and we will see how redefining this variable results in changes to the prompt's display of information.

To start off with, let's make sure that we are back in a "fresh" shell environment as our good old <username> self. If you haven't already done so, $ exit all the way out of any active shells and then start a new shell session afresh with ctrl + alt + t.

Once you have done that, let's return to the $ set command to view the list of all currently active shell and environment variables (see p. 95).

$ set | less -SN

Around line #56, you should see a variable called PS1.

```
 ┌─┐                                                    me@MyLinuxBox: ~
 54 PIPESTATUS=([0]="0")
 55 PPID=3596
 56 PS1='\[\e]0;\u@\h: \w\a\]${debian_chroot:+($debian_chroot)}\[\033[01;32m\]\u@\h\033[00m\]:\[\033
 57 PS2='> '
 58 PS4='+ '
```

Yikes. What is that? Depending on the size of your terminal window, you might not be able to see the entire string contained within this variable. No matter, though.

The PS1 shell variable (for "Prompt String One") holds the information that determines our familiar Bash command line prompt. How do you feel? Maybe like you've had enough for today? Wait! The PS1 variable can look intimidating at first, but once you get an idea of what the symbols represent, it will start to make sense.

As we come to terms with PS1, first let's talk about how this variable is defined. Like most shell variables, for the variable to take effect, a statement such as $ <variable>=<value> needs to be made somewhere in the shell session—either directly on the command line or in some configuration file that Bash loads at the start of the session (in every parent or child shell).

The configuration file where PS1 is defined happens to be a file that we have already looked at. Remember the ~/.bashrc file (see p. 72)? Let's open this file again in $ vim and have another look to see if we can find where PS1 is defined as a shell variable.

$ vim ~/.bashrc

In $ vim, you can scroll down, or you can enter :/<pattern> (see p. 79) to do a forward search through the file's text (in this case, <pattern> would be PS1). Pressing the n key will let you jump from one instance of <pattern> to the next. In doing so, you will find three lines that contain the PS1 variable in ~/.bashrc. Find the line where PS1 is defined as shown (see the next page).

```
                                              me@MyLinuxBox: ~
if [ "$color_prompt" = yes ]; then
 ➤  PS1='${debian_chroot:+($debian_chroot)}\[\033[01;32m\]\u@\h\033[00m\]:\[\033[01;34m\]\w\[\033[00m\]\$ '
else
     PS1='${debian_chroot:+($debian_chroot)}\u@\h:\w\$ '
fi
```

When Bash loads the ~/.bashrc file at the start of a new shell, PS1 is defined in the if statement[61] we see above. For right now, we will concentrate on just the part of PS1 featured inside the frame.

Before we experiment with any changes to PS1, let's look for some clues into how this sequence of characters translates into what gets displayed.

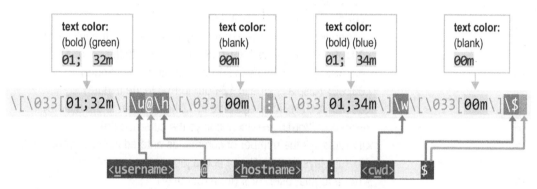

Figure 9 PS1 command line prompt variable diagram

In the figure above, the highlighted codes and characters[62] determine what we see in our prompt. Notice the @, :, and   (the space at the end of the prompt) are **string literals**, meaning that they show up as themselves when the prompt is printed in the terminal window. The \$ looks like it could be a string literal, but this is actually a **special character** that displays as $ when a regular user is on the command line, and # (in place of $) if the user is logged in as root. The \u, \h, and \w are also special characters. When the prompt is rendered on the screen, these characters get expanded to the shell or environment variable information they represent. All of these backslash-escaped (see p. 56 and Appendix B) special characters only have meaning within a shell prompt string (such as PS1). In any other context, they are treated as generic characters with no special significance. If we were to redefine PS1—either directly on the command line by entering $ PS1=<value> or by editing ~/.bashrc and saving the file before starting a new shell session, we could exchange these codes, special characters, and string literals for other ones, thereby modifying our shell prompt.

---

[61] Under if ["$color_prompt" = yes], PS1 is defined based on whether the terminal emulator in use is capable of displaying characters in different colors. Since the Ubuntu Terminal app can display text in different colors, our PS1 variable is set by the first definition (and not the definition under the else part of the statement).
[62] The non-highlighted \[\033[...\] escape sequences surround the text color codes and prevent (i.e., "escape") the color codes from being interpreted as printable characters (see p. 56 and Appendix B).

Saving the ~/.bashrc file with changes to PS1 would make our customizations persist from one shell session to the next. We certainly do want to try this (soon!), but at first let's experiment by making temporary changes to the prompt using the $ PS1=<value> method directly on the command line. This way we will be able to "audition" our changes before committing them to the ~/.bashrc file.

Below is an abridged list of PS1 special characters and the information they display when expanded in the shell prompt.

Special Character (PS1)	Information Displayed (expanded in the shell prompt)
\u	<username>
\h	<hostname>
\w	<current_working_directory>
\W	<basename_of_cwd> (<directoryname> without the full path)
\t	<00:00:00> (displays time in 24-hour format to the second)
\A	<00:00> (displays time in 24-hour format to the minute)
\T	<00:00> (displays time in 12-hour format to the minute)
\@	<00:00_AM/PM> (displays time in 12-hour format to the minute)
\d	<Weekday_Month_Year> (displays the current date)
\#	<#> (displays the number of commands entered in the current shell)
\j	<#> (displays the number of active jobs in the current shell)
\$	$ (for a regular user) or # (for a root user)

And here is a list of codes that work inside the \[\033[<colorcode>\] escape sequences. These color codes can be swapped in place of one another to change the color of text in the prompt.

Color Code	Text Color (displayed in the shell prompt)
00m	Blank/White
30m	Black
31m	Red
32m	Green
33m	Brown
34m	Blue
35m	Purple
36m	Cyan

Also note that the color codes can be prepended by 01; to specify **bold** text. On the next page is an example of how to define the PS1 shell variable with string-literal characters displayed in **bold** green followed by the special character \$ in regular blank/white. As always, a string-literal space   is included at the end.

Example PS1 shell variable definition:

```
PS1='\[\033[01;32m\]MyCustomShellPrompt\[\033[00m\]\$ '
```

Resulting prompt displayed in the terminal window:

```
MyCustomShellPrompt$
```

Because for now we will be defining PS1 directly on the command line, any changes we make will be temporary. To restore the default prompt, we can simply $ exit (or ctrl + d) and open a new shell session.

Ready to try this? We'll start with something simple. Go ahead and enter the following on the command line.

```
$ PS1='MyNewPrompt: '
```

Wow! This is quite different, isn't it? Try entering a couple of commands to see how things feel. If you stay in the current shell, your new prompt will remain active.

It's fun to experiment with special characters in PS1. Try anything[63] you like! Below is one possibility for adding \@ into the works. Notice that everything aside from \@ is a string literal.

```
$ PS1='MyNewPrompt @ \@ '
```

In the next chapter, we will discuss how to set changes to PS1 so that they persist across shell sessions.

---

[63] If while trying to redefine PS1 on the command line you happen to get stuck with a > prompt, this is perfectly normal. In this scenario, the shell displays PS2 (for Prompt String Two), which is the prompt we get when we press enter to continue a command line entry that extends from one line to the next. This can happen by hitting \ and enter when typing in a command, or by pressing enter before typing a closing ' at the end of a PS1 string definition. Sometimes we may do this intentionally, but it often happens by accident. In this situation with the PS1 string and the > prompt, if you type a ' and press enter, you will be taken back to the PS1 command line prompt (with redefined PS1). Otherwise, you can do a ctrl + c to go back to the PS1 prompt unchanged.

Summary:

For multi-user setups in Linux, it is best to store certain pieces of information in shell variables so as not to upset anyone's user configuration when switching between accounts on the command line. If we want to set up a new user account, in Ubuntu we can use `$ sudo` to perform this kind of elevated-status action. With more than one account on the system, one way of switching between user accounts directly on the command line is through the `$ su` command, which takes us from our current shell (the parent shell) into a child shell. When we switch users with `$ su`, this change is reflected in several shell and environment variables—most visibly in the updated command line prompt. If at any point we wish to customize the Bash command line prompt for our current shell, we can modify the `PS1` shell variable using a mix of formatting codes, special characters, and string-literal text.

Commands:

`$ set`	`$ passwd`
`$ uniq`	`$ su`
`$ sudo`	`$ echo`
`$ useradd`	`$ export`

Concepts:

- Shell variables vs environment variables
- Command substitution
- Double quotes
- Linux system administration (basic)
  - Temporary root status
  - Adding user accounts
  - Switching user accounts
- `HISTFILE` shell variable
- Parent shell/child shell relationship
- Bash command line prompt
  - `PS1` shell variable
  - String literals
  - Special characters
  - Text color codes

Challenge:

Make a modification to the standard Bash command line prompt so that each of the six elements (i.e., `<username>`, @, `<hostname>`, :, `<cwd>`, and `$`) is given a different color (notice we are lumping `$` together as one element). Then, add two more elements between `<hostname>` and : so that `<username>@<hostname>@<time>:<cwd>$` displays in the prompt. Choose whichever time format you like. This will bring the total number of elements to eight, which also happens to be the number of text color codes available. Try formatting the prompt so that a different color is given to each of the eight elements.

Making things persist

It's a good thing the shell is so easy to reset by doing an $ exit (or ctrl + d) and re-opening the terminal window. This gives us assurance that if we make some change on the command line in a way we don't like, we can always just restart the shell and our settings will snap back to their prior state.

But when we come to a point where we would like a change to remain as a "permanent" feature of our shell, we find that Bash doesn't make things quite as automatic as it does when it wants to forget something for us. This is also good, because making permanent alterations to our shell is serious business and shouldn't be "too easy". The extra steps we must go through guarantee that if we are going to be making any non-temporary modifications, they are going to be done deliberately.

So, how do we make persistent changes in the shell? Generally, to get Bash to remember anything requires some tinkering with **Bash configuration files**. This involves going into ~/.bashrc or another configuration file, making edits, and then writing our changes to disk (i.e., saving the file). To see our changes take effect[64], we then just restart the shell to get Bash to load the new settings. This is essentially what we did when we defined our custom alias $ lt, except in that case, rather than changing ~/.bashrc, we created a new configuration file: ~/.bash_aliases (see p. 80).

Making direct edits to ~/.bashrc does come with the risk of overwriting (i.e., losing) the Bash default settings, so before we go full bore into modifying ~/.bashrc, first we need to make a backup of the file. Once that is complete, then we can pick up where we left off with re-doing our shell prompt.

Copying, moving, and deleting files in Linux

For some users, the commands for handling basic file management functions like copying or moving files are among the first commands they learn in Linux. This makes sense, considering how important it is to know how to do these things.

In this guide, we take a different approach, preferring to let ourselves get some experience on the command line before easing our way into Linux file management. As simple and fundamental as these commands are, they really do require a great amount of caution on our part. Linux doesn't give us any second chances if we, for example, mistakenly copy or move a file into a directory that happens to contain another file with the same name. If we do this, the other file with the same name will

---

[64] If we want changes to take effect immediately without restarting the shell, Bash gives us an easy solution for this. After editing the ~/.bashrc file, we can call $ source ~/.bashrc, and this will cause Bash to relaunch all commands and variable definitions stored in the file. We will be going over $ source in more detail later.

invariably get deleted. And by deleted, we don't simply mean moved into the "trash" like in the GNOME desktop environment or other GUI-based operating systems. When a file is deleted in the Linux shell, the file is gone, as in, permanently[65] deleted. We will be taking precautions to make sure this kind of thing doesn't happen unintentionally.

$ cp

As our introduction to the $ cp command (short for "<u>c</u>o<u>py</u>"), we will be making a backup of the ~/.bashrc file. We want to preserve ~/.bashrc in its "stock" configuration if at some point in the future we need to restore the shell's default settings.

Go to ~, do an $ ll if you like (just to get a look at what's there), and when ready, enter the following on the command line.

$ cp -n .bashrc .bashrc.bak

Check with $ ll again, and you will see that .bashrc has a new neighbor: .bashrc.bak . Try listing ~ with $ lt (see p. 80), and .bashrc.bak should appear at (or near) the top of the list. The .bak extension is used to indicate a "<u>bak</u>up" of a file and is just to help us keep track of things (.bak doesn't mean anything in particular to Linux).

The syntax for $ cp follows a template that applies in general to Linux file management commands: $ <command> [option(s)] <source> <target>. Conveniently, $ cp packs the familiar GUI *copy* and *paste* operations all in one go from <source> to <target>. Note that in the case above, because <source> and <target> are both in the cwd, it is not necessary to specify a path to either one. For any <source> or <target> not located in the cwd, a path would be needed. If we are operating with $ cp on a file as <source>, and a path to a destination directory is given in the <target> position with no <filename> specified as the end point (see p. 30), then a copy of the <source> file is pasted as the <target> inside the destination directory. On that note, with $ cp and other file management

---

[65] When a file is deleted in Linux, for example by calling $ rm <filename>, the file is unlinked from the kernel's database that keeps track of where the file is located in the storage medium. In theory, the file's data could still be present on the physical storage device even after the file's location is removed from the database, but recovery of the file would be a matter of luck at that point.

commands in Linux, we can also operate on directories[66] as <source> and <target> in addition to files.

On the previous page, when we used the $ cp command, we included the -n [option], which stands for "noclobber". The -n [option] invokes **noclobber** in several Linux commands and generally means "do not overwrite an existing file (or directory) when placing a <target> somewhere." This is a safety measure that will cause $ cp to simply do nothing if it is put in a position where it could "clobber" something. That is, $ cp -n will quietly leave an existing <target> alone.

Another important safety [option] for $ cp and other file management commands is -i (for "interactive"). The -i forces an extra step where the user is given an **interactive prompt** for y or n confirmation before an overwrite occurs—cp: overwrite '<target>'?.

Between the noclobber and interactive [options], we should be able to protect ourselves against accidental deletions with $ cp and other file management commands. The main stumbling block here is that we must remember to take these precautions when performing file management operations[67] in Linux. Our hope is that at least one of these [options] finds a permanent place in our muscle memory by the time we start pointing these commands at important files and directories.

About file management commands in Linux:

There is a debate in the Linux world over how best to approach these file management operations. In some camps, the prevailing attitude is that users should make aliases for these commands so that the safety [options] are the default behavior. For example, this way of thinking would recommend that for $ cp, we should make an alias named $ cp (just the same as the base command) and include the -i [option] (or -n) as part of the alias. This way, they say, we would never have to worry about accidentally deleting something. Others in the Linux community, particularly from the Ubuntu sys admin side, argue that using aliases in this way would make us too reliant on a "non-standard" configuration, and that if we are going to work on the command line in a variety of situations (servers, containers, virtual machines, etc.), it would be better if we stuck with the base commands and disciplined ourselves to remember to type in a safety [option]. This way, they argue, we would be proactively guarding against an unpleasant surprise when issuing commands in a shell environment other than the one we are used to.

---

[66] When using $ cp to copy a non-empty directory (e.g., $ cp <source> <target> where <source> and <target> are directories), Bash will return an error unless we include an [option] such as -r (for recursive) to instruct the command to operate on files *and* sub-directories contained within the directory. The -a [option] (for "archive") is like -r except that it also preserves <source> metadata and permissions.

[67] Note that while the -i [option] works with $ cp, $ mv, and $ rm, the -n [option] only works with $ cp and $ mv.

$ mv

The $ mv command (for "move") is very similar to $ cp except that the <source> gets changed into the <target> (unlike with $ cp where the <source> is left alone[68]). When the $ mv operation does its business on the <source>, coming from a GUI perspective, it's startling to see the <source> suddenly vanish from its original listing in a directory. This "disappearance" challenges our GUI notion of how a file persists "in flight" when dragged from one place to another. Using the command line reveals the level of abstraction that goes into creating the GUI user experience.

To give ourselves some practice moving files around on the command line, let's $ cd into ~/Projects/MyScripts and take a peek at the files inside this directory. Here we will find the three files we created a few chapters ago. Since these files aren't doing anything very important at the moment, we're going to have a little fun moving them around with $ mv.

When ready, type in the command as shown.

$ mv -n my_first_file ~/

Now, let's do an $ ll to check on the files in the cwd (~/Projects/MyScripts).

```
                                              me@MyLinuxBox: ~/Projects/MyScripts
me@MyLinuxBox:~/Projects/MyScripts$ mv -n my_first_file ~/
me@MyLinuxBox:~/Projects/MyScripts$ ll
total 16
drwxrwxr-x 2 me me 4096 Apr 23 07:47 ./
drwxrwxr-x 3 me me 4096 Apr 21 05:14 ../
-rw-rw-r-- 1 me me   70 Jan 31 18:30 my_second_file
-rw-rw-r-- 1 me me  135 Jan 24 08:42 my_third_file
me@MyLinuxBox:~/Projects/MyScripts$
```

You will see that my_first_file is no longer there. We moved it right out of the cwd and (hopefully) into ~. Go and confirm the file's arrival in ~ if you want.

While we're on this moving spree, let's try using the $ mv command again but this time with the * **wildcard operator** in the <operand> (see p. 45 for reference). When we place the * operator directly

---

[68] The exception to this would be if we use $ cp to copy from <source> to <target> within the cwd and the <target> overwrites an existing file. In this scenario, $ cp removes the <source> as though we intended to perform a $ mv operation to change the name of the file from <source> to <target>.

adjacent to a <pattern> (as in, <pattern>*), this expands in the <operand> to every[69] <filename> in the cwd whose first characters[70] match the <pattern>.

This is best illustrated through an example. Try the command as shown below, and then do an $ ll again to take inventory of the cwd.

$ mv -n my* ~/

Before we ran this command, since the two remaining files in the directory had the my <pattern> in the beginning of their names, both of them got swept up and included in the <operand> during execution. In effect, we have used the $ mv command here to operate on two <source> files. This is quite handy! This demonstrates how we can use file management commands to operate on multiple <source> files at once. We can do this either manually by placing each <filename> in the <source> position or by assembling a **glob**[71] of files–like we have done here with * as the globbing operator.

Now, we need to check up on our three itinerant files to make sure they made it to their destination directory (~). Let's go back into ~, and once there, do another $ ll. You will see our three files sitting safely in the ~ directory list.

---

[69] If no <filename> in the cwd matches the <pattern>, then nothing is returned by the * operator.
[70] The * operator treats the first character in the <pattern> as a leading character, which by definition has to stand at the very beginning of a <filename> for a match to occur at all. Note that the * operator ignores the delimiting space before <pattern> as the space is used by the shell to parse the argument of the command and is not part of the <pattern> itself.
[71] As a noun, the term "glob" in Unix/Linux means a <u>set</u> of zero or more item(s) returned from a <pattern>–matching operation. In the $ mv -n my* ~/ command above, the glob is the set of <filenames> returned by the * operator (specifically, my_second_file and my_third_file). As a verb, to "glob" means to "collect" or "assemble", so in this context, we have used the "globbing" operator * to "glob" the <filenames> from the cwd whose spelling matched the my <pattern>. In this case, this happened to be all of the files in the cwd.

It's time for these three wandering files to pack up and head back to the ~/Projects/MyScripts directory. We'll use the * operator as before in the <source> position of the $ mv command.

$ mv -n my* Projects/MyScripts

Go ahead and check on ~/Projects/MyScripts without $ cd-ing into the directory. The alt + . key command comes in handy here if you don't feel like typing in the destination directory (see p. 37)!

$ ll Projects/MyScripts

```
me@MyLinuxBox: ~
me@MyLinuxBox:~$ mv -n my* Projects/MyScripts/
me@MyLinuxBox:~$ ll Projects/MyScripts/
total 20
drwxrwxr-x 2 me me 4096 Apr 23 07:51 ./
drwxrwxr-x 3 me me 4096 Apr 21 05:14 ../
-rw-rw-r-- 1 me me   60 Jan 29 12:43 my_first_file
-rw-rw-r-- 1 me me   70 Jan 31 18:30 my_second_file
-rw-rw-r-- 1 me me  135 Jan 24 08:42 my_third_file
me@MyLinuxBox:~$
```

Good. There is another important function that $ mv handles in the shell aside from flying things across directories, and that is—**renaming items in the Linux file system**. The standard way to rename a file (or directory) in the Linux shell is to call the $ mv command with the original <filename> as <source> and the new <filename> as <target>—all within the cwd.

Let's use $ mv to give our trusty my_first_file a new name. Go into the ~/Projects/MyScripts directory, and once there, try the following command.

$ mv -n my_first_file my_very_first_file

```
me@MyLinuxBox: ~/Projects/MyScripts
me@MyLinuxBox:~/Projects/MyScripts$ mv -n my_first_file my_very_first_file
me@MyLinuxBox:~/Projects/MyScripts$ ll
total 20
drwxrwxr-x 2 me me 4096 Apr 23 07:54 ./
drwxrwxr-x 3 me me 4096 Apr 21 05:14 ../
-rw-rw-r-- 1 me me   70 Jan 31 18:30 my_second_file
-rw-rw-r-- 1 me me  135 Jan 24 08:42 my_third_file
-rw-rw-r-- 1 me me   60 Jan 29 12:43 my_very_first_file
me@MyLinuxBox:~/Projects/MyScripts$
```

An $ ll shows us that all is well with my_very_first_file. As an exercise, you could do a

$ stat my_very_first_file

and compare the results with what we got when we introduced the $ stat command back on p. 59.

$ rm

If there is one command in Linux that we should try to avoid if at all possible, it would be $ rm (for "re̲move"). All of the file management commands we have looked at are potentially destructive, but with $ cp or $ mv, if we, for instance, make a mistake with the * operator, at least it is unlikely for *every* <source> file to catastrophically overwrite a <target> file.

However, with $ rm, if we, for example, use the * operator to glob files in the <operand> and we make some sort of mistake, the command will unfailingly delete *every* file for which there is a <pattern> match. With * alone in the <operand>, this translates into deleting *every* non-hidden file in the cwd (and possibly every non-hidden directory too if we include the -r [option]).

How unfortunate that would be. So if we do use $ rm, we should do so with great care. One good use of $ rm is to "empty" the trash from the GNOME desktop environment. We will demonstrate how to do this on a generic screenshot file that we have moved into the trash via the GNOME GUI. If you don't have anything in your GNOME desktop trash, you can put something there if you like, or if you would rather just follow along here without typing in the $ rm command, that is fine as well.

First, we will $ cd into the ~/.local/share/Trash/files directory and do an $ ll. Notice that because 'Screenshot from 2021-02-18 10-05-16.png' has spaces, it is surrounded in single quotes (see Appendix B for more information). Now we will "empty" the trash with $ rm.

$ rm -i 'Screenshot from 2021-02-18 10-05-16.png'

```
                                            me@MyLinuxBox: ~/.local/share/Trash/files
me@MyLinuxBox:~/.local/share/Trash/files$ ll
total 24
drwx------ 2 me me 4096 Apr 23 07:55 ./
drwx------ 4 me me 4096 Nov 24 21:23 ../
-rw-rw-r-- 1 me me 14940 Feb 18 10:05 'Screenshot from 2021-02-18 10-05-16.png'
me@MyLinuxBox:~/.local/share/Trash/files$ rm -i 'Screenshot from 2021-02-18 10-05-16.png'
rm: remove regular file 'Screenshot from 2021-02-18 10-05-16.png'?
```

The -i [option] forces an i̲nteractive y/n prompt:

rm: remove regular file 'Screenshot from 2021-02-18 10-05-16.png'?

When we enter y, the file is gone. There is no -n [option] for $ rm (since $ rm by definition "clobbers" what is in the <operand>), so it is important that we train ourselves to include the -i [option] with $ rm as though $ rm will not function without it. Later in this guide, we will download and install a utility package called trash-cli which will give us the capability to easily move things into the ~/.local/share/Trash/files directory from the command line. With trash-cli installed, you may want to adopt a policy where your only use of $ rm is to empty the trash (if that).

Your new persistent prompt

Now that we have a backup of our ~/.bashrc file, we can resume with our modification of the Bash command line prompt. Let's head back to ~ and reopen .bashrc in $ vim. Scroll down again to the line in .bashrc where our PS1 shell variable is defined (see p. 103).

```
if [ "$color_prompt" = yes ]; then
    PS1='${debian_chroot:+($debian_chroot)}\[\033[01;32m\]\u@\h\033[00m\]:\[\033[01;34m\]\w\[\033[00m\]\$
else
    PS1='${debian_chroot:+($debian_chroot)}\u@\h:\w\$ '
fi
```

To make our modification, first we need to copy the line highlighted above. We will do this by selecting the line with the mouse/trackpad and pressing ctrl + shift + c to copy to the clipboard (see p. 36).

Next, we need to add a # in front of the line to turn it into a **comment** (see p. 79 for a refresher on basic editing in $ vim). By adding the # and "commenting out" the line, we are telling Bash to ignore what is there. This gives us an extra bit of backup convenience in case we want to quickly revert to the original PS1 definition.

```
if [ "$color_prompt" = yes ]; then
    # PS1='${debian_chroot:+($debian_chroot)}\[\033[01;32m\]\u@\h\033[00m\]:\[\033[01;34m\]\w\[\033[00m\]\$ '
else
    PS1='${debian_chroot:+($debian_chroot)}\u@\h:\w\$ '
fi
```

Now we are going to insert a blank line below our comment by moving the cursor to the end of the line and pressing enter (in normal mode in $ vim, $ jumps to the end of the line), and on the new blank line right below the comment, we are going to paste the "stock" PS1 variable definition from the clipboard. When the cursor is in position below the comment, go ahead and paste using ctrl + shift + v.

Are you ready to start doing some work on PS1 and saving the changes to .bashrc? At this point, we are going to make a suggestion for how you *might* want to modify your PS1 variable. You can use this approach as the basis for your modifications, or if you have something else in mind, of course you are welcome to do whatever you want!

On the next page you will see three segments where we have made modifications to PS1. The smaller segment (outlined in orange) shows where the first color code has been changed from 32m (green) to 33m (brown). This affects the rendering of the \u special character (<username>). The two longer segments (outlined in yellow) are color codes (+ escape sequences) that we have inserted—36m (cyan) for the string literal @, and 35m (purple) for the special character \h (<hostname>).

Below is the modified part of the PS1 variable string with color codes, special characters, and string literals highlighted for ease of viewing (so as not to get distracted by the escape sequences).

Be aware that in defining PS1, the entire string would need to be enclosed in single quotes to capture the string literal   space at the end. Also, there is the beginning part of the string (not shown above) that still needs to be included. The full definition for the new (modified) PS1 as it would appear in .bashrc (without the $ vim text coloring) is shown below.

When you come to a point where you are satisfied with your PS1 mod, let's move forward with saving .bashrc and restarting the shell so that we can view the results. In $ vim, to save work and quit the program, first hit the esc key, then :, and then type wq at the : prompt followed by enter (see p. 79). This will take you back to the Bash command line prompt. Now, let's $ exit (or ctrl + d) and then open a new terminal window.

And here we meet the new prompt!

It's just a couple of colors that have changed, but somehow it feels like an altogether different shell. Echoing back to the last chapter, it is not an accident that PS1 is defined as a shell variable. If we were to $ su as another user (e.g., as <newusername> again), PS1 as it is currently defined in this shell would <u>not</u> transfer into the child shell. This behavior follows from the notion that PS1 customization in the parent shell is not necessarily wanted in the child shell; hence, it is best to keep the scope of PS1 limited to the shell in which it is defined.

As an experiment, you could try doing an $ su as <newusername> again to see how your new prompt compares with the stock Bash prompt. In situations with more than one user account, the utility of a customized prompt really shines through as it becomes much easier to visually identify "who you are" when switching between accounts on the command line.

Summary:

The shell is in a temporary state by design, and in order to make any lasting changes, we need to modify the configuration files that Bash loads at startup. For example, by editing ~/.bashrc, we can make shell customizations persist from one session to the next. Configuration files are where shell settings live, so if we do alter a configuration file like ~/.bashrc, we should make a backup first. One of the easiest ways to make backups of files and directories on the command line is to use the $ cp command (for copy). The $ cp command along with $ mv and $ rm are members of the file management family of commands in Linux. When we perform file management operations on the command line, we run the risk of overwriting our own files and directories, so we must remember to include either the -n or -i [option] for safety when we call these commands.

Commands:

$ cp $ ls
$ mv $ cd
$ rm $ vim

Concepts:

- Bash configuration files
- ~/.bashrc.bak backup
- Linux file management commands
  - -n [option]
  - -i [option]
  - -r [option] (for directories)
  - -a [option] (for directories)

- ctrl + shift + c (copy in terminal)
- ctrl + shift + v (paste in terminal)
- Wildcard * globbing
- Renaming files and directories in Linux
- Emptying the GNOME desktop trash
- # comments in Bash scripts
- PS1 as a shell variable

Challenge:

The Unix convention of hiding dot files from view was originally introduced as a way of protecting important files and directories from accidental deletion. We can give ourselves some extra deletion insurance by backing up all of the dot files present in the home directory. Try making a new directory called .backups inside the home directory (see p. 57). Then form a single command that will copy the dot files you see in the home directory into your new .backups directory. For this task we only want to copy dot files (not dot directories), so don't use the -r or -a [option] here. Depending on how you construct your command, when you run it, you might receive a message from the shell stating that it was unable to copy the dot directories. This message is normal, but if you would rather not see this message, you can redirect stderr to /dev/null using the 2> redirection operator (see p. 67). As always with Linux file management commands, please practice caution by using either the -n or -i [option].

From script to command

We are now setting course in approach of our final goal, which is to be able to create our own custom commands on the Linux command line.

We have already discussed much of the framework that supports customizations in Bash, and now we need to add just a few more bits and pieces to have a complete toolkit for building our own callable commands. Then when everything is in place, we will connect the pieces together and see our commands come to life.

What makes up a command in Linux?

Commands in the Linux shell can be grouped into three categories (see p. 33): **built-in commands**, **external commands**, and **scripted commands**[72] (we are bunching callable shell scripts and shell functions together as "scripted commands"). Among the different types, all of them are essentially programs that execute when called by name on the command line. Some commands are stored as executable files (external commands and callable shell scripts), while others are either baked into the Bash program itself (built-in commands) or loaded at startup from configuration files (shell functions).

In calling commands by name, we are effectively giving instructions to the computer—just like we would in any programming language. Depending on context, we might instruct the computer to display information (`$ man`, `$ help`, `$ whoami`, `$ id`, `$ pwd`, `$ ls`, `$ stat`, `$ echo`, `$ cat`, `$ less`, `$ env`, `$ set`, etc.), carve out a place for information (`$ touch`, `$ mkdir`, etc.), filter information (`$ wc`, `$ grep`, `$ sed`, `$ sort`, `$ head`, `$ tail`, `$ uniq`, etc.), append information (`$ cat`, etc.), define information (`$ export`, etc.), move/manage information (`$ cp`, `$ mv`, `$ rm`, etc.), and so on.

The common denominator among all of these commands is that their names encode the actions they perform. By the same token, to *create* a command in the Linux shell involves assigning a name[73] to an action produced by a series of instructions. Because commands themselves *are* instructions that we give the computer, we can *create* a custom command in Bash by stringing existing shell commands together and assigning their combined operation a name. Then we can *call* our custom command (by name) and have it carry out its action in the same way we would call any other command in the shell. A custom command like this is known as a **scripted command** because we put the instructions (i.e., the constituent shell commands) into a human-readable "script" and then have Bash "run through" the

---

[72] For our purposes here, when we refer to "scripted commands", we are only talking about Bash as the scripting language, but in Linux, there are other scripting languages in common use such as Python, Perl, and Ruby.
[73] The longtime trend has been for Unix command names to be as short and compact as possible. Originally, to conserve memory, Unix had an eight-character limit on the maximum length allowed for command names. Although this limit has been relaxed in modern Unix-like systems, most command names still follow the tradition.

script at our beck and call. A scripted command can appear in the form of a **shell script** (stored in an executable file) or a **shell function** (defined in a configuration file, which gets loaded at shell startup).

We have already seen a hint of custom command creation in making our own alias (see p. 80), but an alias in Bash has only a limited capacity to process arguments. As we make progress building our own command line solutions, we will see where aliases would or would not be the right choice—depending on the use case.

Commands as executable files in the Linux shell

To start fitting the pieces together to form our own commands, first we will be taking a closer look at commands that operate as **executable files**.

Take, for example, any external command that we might call in the shell. When we enter an external command (like $ ls, for example), the name[74] we type in is indeed the name of an executable file somewhere in the Linux file system. By typing the external command and pressing enter, we are telling the shell to launch the executable file that goes by that name—wherever that file may be (as in, <pathname>/ls). But this begs the question: Where *is* the file? And for that matter, how does the shell know the path to the file?

$ whereis

To answer our first question above, we have the handy $ whereis utility, which will reveal the executable file location for any external command we put in the argument (assuming the external command is installed). Let's see if we can find the location of the executable file that launches when we call the $ ls command. With $ whereis, we will use the -b [option] (for binary) to show us the <pathname>/ls information only (and no extra details like the location of $ man pages for $ ls).

$ whereis -b ls

Ah ha. The executable program file for the $ ls command is located in the /usr/bin directory. How about we pay a visit to /usr/bin and see what's there?

---

[74] The $ ls that we call in Ubuntu Bash is actually an alias for $ ls –color=auto (see the footnote on p. 122). Nevertheless, the aliased $ ls -color=auto command launches the /usr/bin/ls executable file.

We could $ cd into /usr/bin and then do an $ 11, but this time let's try a slightly different method. As an experiment, type in the **group command** shown below and press enter. This demonstrates how we can use the ; operator to string multiple commands together as a single operation.

$$\$ \; cd \; /usr/bin \; ; \; 11$$

```
-rwxr-xr-x  1 root  root       2206 Dec 13  2019  zless*
-rwxr-xr-x  1 root  root       1842 Dec 13  2019  zmore*
-rwxr-xr-x  1 root  root       4553 Dec 13  2019  znew*
me@MyLinuxBox:/usr/bin$ █
```

After pressing enter, you will be transported into /usr/bin with a (very long) list of items going before the command line prompt.

Try scrolling up or using shift + pg up in the terminal window to find ls in the list.

```
-rwxr-xr-x  1 root  root      51192 Jun  2  2017  lp_solve*
-rwxr-xr-x  1 root  root      39520 Apr 24  2020  lpstat*
-rwxr-xr-x  1 root  root     142144 Sep  5  2019  ls*
-rwxr-xr-x  1 root  root      14656 Feb 14  2020  lsattr*
-rwxr-xr-x  1 root  root     133352 Jul 21  2020  lsblk*
```

And there it is—the executable program file we call every time we list the contents of a directory (of course, this is the same file that launches when we enter $ 11 or any other alias for $ ls—see the footnote on p. 122 about $ ls as an alias for itself). Note the permissions for ls show an x in all three executable slots (see p. 53), as do most permissions for other files in this directory.

While we're here in /usr/bin (short for "binaries"[75]), let's browse through the list and see if we can find anything else that looks familiar. If you scroll up towards the beginning, you will see the bash executable binary file*. This is the program we are using right now as our shell!

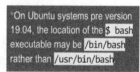

*On Ubuntu systems pre version 19.04, the location of the $ bash executable may be /bin/bash rather than /usr/bin/bash

In /usr/bin, you will recognize the executable files for many commands that we've worked with. You will also notice that certain commands like $ cd, $ set, and $ export are not represented in the list. This is because these commands are built-ins, which means they solely exist as part of the Bash program itself. Despite built-ins not being executable files, it is still possible to call $ bash like any other external command in the shell. In fact, launching the /usr/bin/bash executable from within a

---

[75] A "binary" is a program that has been compiled into machine language (i.e., binary 1s and 0s) to run directly on the CPU. For a command to be an "external" command (external to the shell) generally means the command is a compiled binary. When we call an external command and launch its executable binary file, the kernel assigns a new process to run the external command separately from the shell process where the command was called.

shell session is the very definition of entering a **child shell** (see p. 90)! This can happen either explicitly by calling $ bash on the command line (see p. 93), or "silently" (i.e., automatically) in a series of steps that occur when we, for example, call an e<u>x</u>ecutable shell script. We will be investigating how this calling process works for shell scripts as e<u>x</u>ecutable files soon.

Locating executable files as commands

Returning to our second question earlier, we'd like to know how the shell finds executable files when we call them by name. The general answer is that we must tell the shell where to look every time we launch an executable file. One way is by specifically entering $ <pathname>/<filename>, which leads the shell down <pathname> into the right destination directory where it can find and launch <filename>. The other way of informing the shell where to look for executable files involves keeping <pathname> stored in the PATH environment variable and then letting the shell automatically find <pathname>/<filename> when we make a call for $ <filename> as a command (this is the mechanism we have relied on to run external commands in the shell). After we get some experience with the first method (entering $ <pathname>/<filename>), we will move on to see how the PATH variable helps the shell find and launch executable files called by name.

Since we're still in the /usr/bin directory, let's check what happens when we try to call an external command by spelling out *where* the shell needs to look for the executable file. Usually when we call an external command, we just type in the name and let the shell take care of finding the executable, but this time, we will directly specify the path for the shell to go down—as in, $ <pathname>/<filename>.

Inside the /usr/bin directory, type in the command as shown below and press enter. Notice the relative path to the cwd is formed by ./ (see p. 50).

$ ./ls

Aside from the color[76] of the text in the output, $ ./ls executes in the /usr/bin directory just as $ ls would. By entering $ ./ls, we are effectively telling the shell, "Hey, look here in ./ for an executable file called ls and then launch it." Now, as a further experiment, let's try taking a step back with $ cd .. into the /usr directory and performing $ ./ls one more time. We will use the ; operator as we did before to combine both commands into a single operation.

$ cd .. ; ./ls

---

[76] If you go to ~/.bashrc and look at line #78 (try :set number in $ vim to view line numbers), you will see that the $ ls command as we know it is actually itself an alias: alias ls='ls –color=auto'. This means if we call $ ./ls in /usr/bin, unless we include the same color [option] as defined for the $ ls alias (i.e., $ ./ls -color=auto), the list of items in the $ ./ls command's output will be displayed in plain white text.

And we get an error: `bash: ./ls: No such file or directory`.

As the message says, there is no "`ls`" file in the /usr directory! What this points out is—if we are trying to launch an executable file and we specify a path (i.e., `$ <pathname>/<filename>`), nothing will happen unless the path correctly leads to the file we want to launch. From a general-use perspective, it would be burdensome if every time we wanted to run a command, we had to pre-fix a path to get the command to do anything. But having this `<pathname>` requirement turns out to be an advantage in certain situations. A typical use case would be when we want to reserve an executable file for operation only in a particular directory, perhaps because the file is an installer. Clearly, however, it would be preferable not to have to type in a path to an executable file every time we call a command!

Turning files into commands with the PATH variable

As the shell has no way of launching an executable file without being told where to find it, $PATH comes to the shell's assistance and supplies the missing information needed to retrieve an executable file when we call it by name. And what information is missing when we call an executable file by name only? In the shell's eyes, the information missing is the path to the executable file. It is $PATH that comes to the rescue and supplies the shell with the information required (e.g., /usr/bin in the case of $ ls). This fills in a critical piece of the Bash environment that allows us to call commands without having to think about where they are located.

We need to have a look at $PATH to get a sense of how this works. When you are ready, $ cd back into ~ and try the following.

$ echo $PATH

```
 ⊡                                          me@MyLinuxBox: ~
me@MyLinuxBox:~$ echo $PATH
/usr/local/sbin:/usr/local/bin:/usr/sbin:/usr/bin:/sbin:/bin:/usr/games:/usr/local/games:/snap/bin
me@MyLinuxBox:~$ █
```

You will see that $PATH is made up of several paths. Here we have nine to be exact. You will also see that each path is separated by a colon (:)—in a **colon-separated list**. That's really all the PATH variable is—a list of paths. But paths to what? These paths all lead to destination directories where an executable file *could* be located. When we call an external command by name only (i.e., when we don't prepend a path to the executable file), the shell checks in each of these $PATH destination directories until it finds an executable file with a name matching the command we typed in. Then, with a verified path to the executable file, the shell follows that path and launches the file—letting the program in the file execute—which produces the resultant output of the command. That's it!

Thus far we have been talking about this process of calling executable files in terms of **external commands**, but it is in fact the same process that gets applied when we call an executable **shell script**[77] by name (which is a type of **scripted command**[78]). Just like external commands, callable shell scripts are executable files in the Linux file system. The main difference between an external command (like `$ ls`) and a shell script is that an external command is by definition a **compiled binary** (see the footnote on p. 121), whereas a callable shell script is an executable file containing a sequence of human-readable shell commands (in principle the same as stringing `$ cd <pathname> ; ll` together as a single operation). To be able to call a shell script by name as a command, we simply need to put the script into an executable file and then help the shell find the file when we call for it—in the same way we tell the shell where to look for an executable file when we call an external command by name. This is all made possible with the help of $PATH, which supplies the shell with the list of places to look for executable files.

Let's pause for a moment and take stock of what we have collected so far about shell scripts as commands. We know that callable shell scripts are executable files, and we know that to call them as commands (by name), we have to place the executable files somewhere within the sights of the $PATH list of destinations. Now the question becomes

> *In what $PATH destination directory should we put our executable shell scripts so that the shell can locate the files when we call them by name?*

Considering that these are <u>our own</u> custom shell scripts we are talking about here, the best practice is to place them in a directory inside the home directory (~). But if you look at $PATH, there is (currently) no path such as `/home/<username>/<directoryname>` listed. This will have to change. We are going to have to make a directory within ~ just for our own shell scripts, and we are going to have to <u>add</u> (i.e., append or prepend) this directory to the PATH variable. That is, we will grab the absolute path to the directory and add it to the PATH variable's list of paths. So, rather than nine paths stored in the PATH variable, there will be ten when we're done.

There is a tradition in Unix/Linux of giving the name "bin" (for "<u>bin</u>aries") to directories that hold executable files (i.e., programs). If you look at the names of the destination directories listed in $PATH, "bin" certainly is a popular choice ("sbin" stands for "<u>s</u>ystem <u>bin</u>aries"). Does this mean we should follow suit and name our own directory for executable shell scripts "bin" as well—as in, `/home/<username>/bin`?

---

[77] In the world of Bash, you will often hear the term "Bash script" in substitution for "shell script".
[78] The two types of **scripted commands** that we are building in this guide are **callable shell scripts** (which we are talking about here) and **shell functions** (which we will talk about soon).

As always, you are welcome to do as you wish, but yes, in this guide we are recommending naming the directory for home-spun shell scripts "bin"[79]. We do this partly out of tradition, but there is also another compelling reason for "bin". It just so happens that Ubuntu comes set up with a special configuration that makes it a snap to add our own "bin" directory to the PATH variable.

To see what we're talking about, in the home directory, if you do an $ ll, you will notice there is a shell configuration file called .profile. Let's open ~/.profile in $ vim and take a look at what's there (to display line numbers in $ vim, enter :set number—see p. 79).

```
19 # set PATH so it includes user's private bin if it exists
20 if [ -d "$HOME/bin" ] ; then
21     PATH="$HOME/bin:$PATH"
22 fi
```

This is interesting. The comment in line #19 tells us that this bit of Bash code will add the "user's private bin" directory to the PATH variable *if* the directory exists. That is, *if* /home/<username>/bin exists, then PATH="$HOME/bin:$PATH". This is helpful! This means just by *having* a ~/bin directory, the path to the directory will automatically get added to the PATH variable when we log in (see the comment in the beginning of ~/.profile about the file being "executed...for login shells").

Let's break down exactly what happens in line #21 in ~/.profile *if* we have a ~/bin directory. You will see that line #21 is a variable definition (see p. 84) for PATH. In fact it is a *redefinition*[80]. The initial $PATH variable on the right is prepended with $HOME/bin: to create the newly defined PATH variable on the left. In the definition of the new PATH variable, $HOME and $PATH undergo **variable expansion** (see p. 86) and are glued with /bin: between them as a **string literal** (see p. 105).

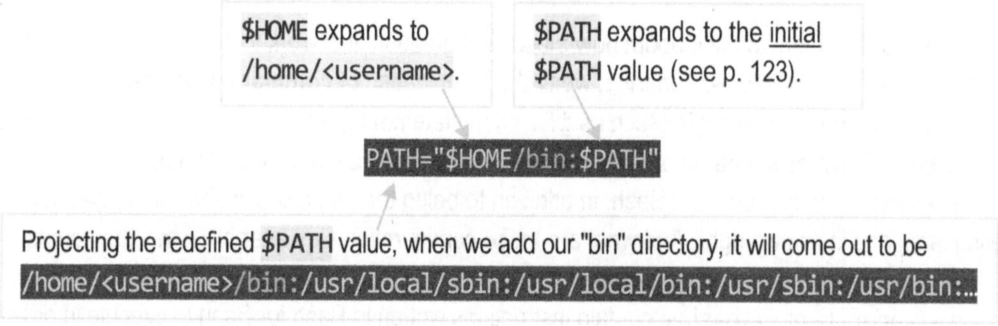

$HOME expands to /home/<username>.

$PATH expands to the initial $PATH value (see p. 123).

PATH="$HOME/bin:$PATH"

Projecting the redefined $PATH value, when we add our "bin" directory, it will come out to be
/home/<username>/bin:/usr/local/sbin:/usr/local/bin:/usr/sbin:/usr/bin:...

Figure 10 PATH variable definition diagram

---

[79] Even though "bin" sounds like it's intended for executable binaries, the name is just a holdover from the early days of Unix when programs had to be in binary form to run. Nowadays it is common for users to put scripts written in Bash or other interpreted languages into a private "bin" directory inside the home directory. Of course, we can still put compiled binaries in our private "bin" directory too!

[80] Note that since PATH is already an environment variable, we can *redefine* PATH as shown in line #21 and PATH will remain an environment variable without need of calling the $ export command.

With the code in ~/.profile just sitting there, waiting for its chance to detect a ~/bin directory and add /home/<username>/bin to the PATH variable, we should take advantage of this and let it help us set up a place to put our shell scripts. All we need to do is make a ~/bin directory and see to it that the shell loads (i.e., runs) ~/.profile.

So, let's do that. Inside ~, enter the following.

$ mkdir bin

Now, we could log out and log back in (see the comment in line #1), and in that process, the shell would load ~/.profile and run the code in lines #20-22, resulting in /home/<username>/bin getting added to the PATH variable. This is indeed what we want to happen whenever we log into Ubuntu—to make our /home/<username>/bin directory's spot in the PATH variable persist.

But in a situation like this where we would like a change to take effect immediately, we can employ another method of launching the configuration file, and it will not require logging out or even closing and re-opening the terminal window (which we have done previously to get the shell to freshly load ~/.bashrc after making changes).

Sourcing from configuration (and other) files

It's worth taking a moment to think about how these configuration files work to *configure* the shell. If we look inside ~/.profile or ~/.bashrc, we find a combination of **commands**, **variable definitions**, and **control flow logic** (such as if...then statements)—all written in Bash. Here we are using the word "Bash" as the name of the **programming language** that the shell understands. We haven't stressed this very much, but Bash, in addition to being the name of our shell, is a powerful scripting language in its own right. And what are these configuration files after all? They are scripts!

Files like ~/.profile or ~/.bashrc contain instructions written in Bash for Bash to execute in order to configure the current shell. Bash automatically loads and runs each configuration file in a pre-set sequence at startup, but if at any point we decide we would like to *re-launch* a file to make a change in the shell's configuration (e.g., to redefine the PATH variable), we can do so by telling the shell to **source** the code from the file that we want to re-launch. Then, any changes will take effect immediately. Re-launching configuration files by sourcing their code is much more convenient than the rigmarole of leaving and returning to the shell every time we want to put a persistent change into effect.

$ source

Meet the $ source[81] command—an extremely useful built-in for executing Bash code contained in configuration files (as well as other "source" files). To re-launch ~/.profile so that our ~/bin directory gets added to the PATH variable, in ~, enter the command shown below.

$ source .profile

Now if we print $PATH again, we should see the absolute path to our ~/bin directory in the list.

$ echo $PATH

```
me@MyLinuxBox:~$ echo $PATH
/home/me/bin:/usr/local/sbin:/usr/local/bin:/usr/sbin:/usr/bin:/sbin:/bin:/usr/games:/usr/local/games:/snap/bin
me@MyLinuxBox:~$
```

There we are! Our ~/bin directory is now officially on the list of places where the shell will look when we call executable files by name (most importantly, our own executable files).

There are a couple of things to note about how we use $ source to trigger the execution of a script in the shell. For one thing, you might have noticed that neither ~/.profile, nor ~/.bashrc, nor any of the other shell configuration files have executable permissions (see p. 54). Yet, we are able to "execute" these files' scripts with $ source. This is because executable permissions don't necessarily determine *whether* we can execute a script contained in a file, but rather—*how* we can execute the script.

There is a subtle but important distinction between what happens when we $ source a script from a file (such as ~/.profile) as opposed to when we "call" an executable file containing a shell script. When we $ source a script, this means we are executing the script in the current shell. This is why we can use $ source to *reconfigure the shell*—the code execution happens within the current shell and not a child shell. On the other hand, when we call an executable file containing a shell script, rather than executing the script, the current shell automatically spawns a child shell (see p. 93) in which a separate instance of $ bash executes the script. This means we cannot call an executable

---

[81] The $ source command has a direct "synonym" in $., known as the "dot" command. If substituted for $ source ~/.profile shown above, the dot command version would be $. ~/.profile.

shell script to reconfigure the current shell. We can, however, do other things with callable shell scripts, as we shall soon find out!

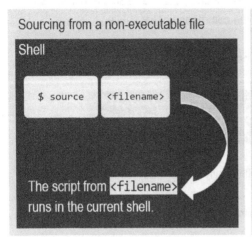

Figure 14 Script launch comparison diagram

What's in an executable shell script?

We are very close to having the supporting structure we need to call our own shell scripts as commands on the command line. We now just have to work out the details of preparing executable files to hold our scripts so that they will launch properly.

First things first, we need to make a file to hold our very first shell script. There are several ways we could do this, but for simplicity's sake, let's call our old friend $ touch to make a blank file for us. We will start by $ cd-ing into the ~/bin directory. Once in ~/bin, enter the command shown below. The choice of name for our first shell script is "bak". You may be able to deduce where this is heading, but one thing behind this name choice is that if you try to call $ bak, you'll find there is no existing command with that name (nor anything in the list of packages recommended for installation[82]).

$ touch bak

Following with an $ ll, we can check the permissions that have been assigned to our new bak file.

```
me@MyLinuxBox:~/bin$ touch bak
me@MyLinuxBox:~/bin$ ll
total 8
drwxrwxr-x  2 me me 4096 Jun 27 12:36 ./
drwxr-xr-x 21 me me 4096 Jun 27 12:31 ../
-rw-rw-r--  1 me me    0 Jun 27 12:36 bak
me@MyLinuxBox:~/bin$
```

---

[82] This is because "bak" is not in the list of downloadable packages stored in the $ apt package manager cache.

As indicated in the `-rw-rw-r--` permissions for ~/bin/bak (see p. 54), when we make a new file like this, it is initially without e<u>x</u>ecutable permissions. But we will need to turn on the file's e<u>x</u>ecutable permissions in order to launch $ bak as a command[83]. Let's see what we can do about that.

$ chmod

The $ chmod command (for "<u>ch</u>ange <u>mode</u>") is our one-stop do-it-all utility for changing file permissions in the Linux shell. If we own a file, then we have the rights with $ chmod to change the permissions however we like. Here we will use $ chmod with the +x [option] to make our new file e<u>x</u>ecutable. Try the command below and then do an $ ll to check on the result.

$ chmod +x bak

```
                                                    me@MyLinuxBox: ~/bin
me@MyLinuxBox:~/bin$ chmod +x bak
me@MyLinuxBox:~/bin$ ll
total 8
drwxrwxr-x  2 me me 4096 Jun 27 12:36 ./
drwxr-xr-x 21 me me 4096 Jun 27 12:31 ../
-rwxrwxr-x  1 me me    0 Jun 27 12:36 bak*
me@MyLinuxBox:~/bin$
```

Note that our bak file is now green with an asterisk—just like the e<u>x</u>ecutable files we saw in the /usr/bin directory earlier in this chapter (see p. 121). Also, just as we would have hoped, bak now shows an x in all of the e<u>x</u>ecutable permissions slots (see p. 54). For our purposes on a single-user system, the only x that matters is the one in the owner permissions slot (4th slot from the left). However, in a multi-user system, the `-rwxrwxr-x` permissions would mean that <u>anybody</u> logged in who is able to access our /home/<username>/bin directory could launch $ ./bak. This may be nothing to worry about, but in case we wanted to set the ~/bin/bak <u>r</u>ead and e<u>x</u>ecute permissions only for users in our primary <u>g</u>roup and exclude all <u>o</u>ther users (aside from root—see p. 40), then we could enter the command $ chmod u=rwx,g=rx,o= bak inside the ~/bin directory. The resulting permissions for ~/bin/bak would then be -rwxr-x---. Check $ man chmod for a full treatment of the command's capabilities in managing file and directory permissions.

Now we are ready to begin writing the instructions (i.e., the code) that will go into our $ bak shell script. First, let's open ~/bin/bak in $ vim. As this is currently an empty file, you will see $ vim displays tildes where there would otherwise be lines of text. This is just a $ vim convention to indicate that nothing is in those lines (you can disregard the tildes).

---

[83] Also, <u>r</u>ead permissions (which we have here) are needed to launch an executable shell script (see p. 55).

Starting at the very top of the script, after pressing the `i` key to change into insert mode in `$ vim` (see p. 79), type in these two lines* as separated by a blank line (the blank line is for readability only):

```
#!/usr/bin/bash

echo 'Calling $ bak <filename> will create a backup of <filename> in the cwd.'
```

Once you are done typing, your script should appear in `$ vim` as shown below.

*On Ubuntu systems pre version 19.04, the location of the `$ bash` executable may be `/bin/bash` rather than `/usr/bin/bash`

Getting there! Now let's write (i.e., save) our `~/bin/bak` file to disk and quit `$ vim` to return to the Bash command line.

So, what did we just do? We created our first executable shell script! You might be wondering what the purpose of the `#!/usr/bin/bash` line is. The `#!` character combination[84] is called a **shebang**. When we run `$ bak` as a command, the line with the `#!` (the "shebang line") gives instructions to the kernel to launch `/usr/bin/bash` in order to provision a child shell where `~/bin/bak` will run. Read on below for a technical description of how the launch sequence works (if you would rather just skip to running `$ bak`, turn to the next page!).

To launch an executable program (whether shell script or external command), Bash spawns a **child process** to allow the program to run in its own environment. The way Bash sets up a child process for an executable program is as follows. First, to spawn a child process, Bash makes a copy of itself in RAM. This operation where Bash copies itself in RAM is known as a **fork** in Unix/Linux. Then Bash asks the kernel to decide how to execute the program (the shell script or external command we want to launch) *in place of* the newly created fork. That is, the kernel now *replaces* the forked copy of Bash in RAM with a child process. If the program to be executed is an external command, then the kernel replaces the fork with the external command's compiled binary code as the child process. The external command's binary code then runs directly on the CPU, with output sent to stdout. When complete, the external command's process terminates. If the program is a shell script like our `~/bin/bak` file, then the kernel looks at the script's **shebang line** for the path to the **interpreter**[85] (`/usr/bin/bash` in our case) required to run the code in the script. For our script, the kernel *replaces* the forked copy of Bash in RAM with a new, separate instance of `/usr/bin/bash` as the child process running (i.e., "interpreting") the script. This makes for a **non-interactive**[86] **child shell** in which the script runs and outputs to stdout. When the script completes, the child shell process terminates and the user (who never left the calling shell's environment) sees the script's output appear in stdout.

---

[84] Note that `#!/usr/bin/bash` appears as a comment to Bash (see p. 116). Therefore, Bash ignores the shebang line.

[85] We say that Bash works as an "interpreter" when running the shell script code because the CPU doesn't understand instructions written in Bash (nor does the kernel—the kernel only recognizes the shebang line).

[86] A non-interactive shell has no command line, as opposed to an interactive shell, which by definition has a command line.

We're ready to try calling our ~/bin/bak shell script on the command line. Let's do a $ cd to place ourselves in the home directory just to demonstrate that we don't need to be inside ~/bin to make this call. When you are all set, enter the following.

$ bak

Bravo! You now have your own callable shell script to work with. Of course, the script isn't doing anything yet but printing a message to stdout. Still, this shows that calling $ bak runs as expected.

There are several ways that we can check on the status of $ bak as a callable command.

$ type

The $ type utility is similar to $ whereis (which we tried earlier in this chapter—see p. 120), but in addition to info about the location of executable files, $ type can return other information as well—like if a command is built-in or not. Let's see what $ type has to say about our $ bak script.

$ type bak

Like $ whereis, $ type returns the path to the executable file connected with $ bak. If you try $ type -t bak, you will see $ type recognizes ~/bin/bak as a "file" (i.e., not a built-in command).

$ file

And then there is the $ file utility for displaying detailed filetype information. When we supply ~/bin/bak in the argument, we get the full picture.

$ file ~/bin/bak

Summary:
Of the three families of commands in Linux (built-in, external, and scripted), the scripted command category includes commands programmed with already existing shell commands as the instructions. To make a custom scripted command like this, we string shell commands together to execute their combined action as a single operation. By assigning the operation a name, we can "call" our scripted command as we would any other command on the Linux command line. Callable shell scripts, which are one type of scripted command, are stored as files in the Linux file system. For a shell script file to be "callable", we need to turn on the executable permissions for the file. This is done with the $ chmod command. Additionally, in the beginning of a callable shell script, there needs to be a #! (shebang) followed by a path to the command interpreter chosen to run the instructions in the script. With these things all set to go, once we place the shell script's executable file in a destination directory listed in $PATH, we can call the file by name on the command line and the instructions in the script will execute as a command.

Commands:

```
$ whereis          $ chmod
$ source           $ type
$ vim              $ file
```

Concepts:

- Scripted commands
  - Callable shell scripts
  - Shell functions
- Executable files
- Grouping commands with the ; operator
- Launching $ ./<filename>
- PATH environment variable
- : separated list
- ~/.profile for adding to PATH variable
  - ~/bin directory

- Bash as a scripting language
- Sourcing from configuration scripts
  - Code runs in the current shell
- Calling an executable shell script
  - Code runs in a child shell
- File permissions w/ $ chmod
- #! (shebang)
  - Bash as a command interpreter
  - Non-interactive shell
- Checking command location and status

Challenge:
After some time on the command line, we start to notice routine usage patterns that really ought to be cut down to just one step. One of these patterns occurs with $ cd: Every time we do a $ cd to visit a directory, we end up immediately entering $ ll (or another variant of $ ls) to view the directory's contents. If we're always entering these two commands in succession ($ cd and then $ ll), couldn't they just be combined into one action? Yes, they can. Make an alias called $ cdll that will $ cd into the home directory and automatically do an $ ll (or a variant) in one operation. Use the ; operator to combine the two commands sequentially. As an exercise, try making a callable shell script (with a different name) that performs the same action. Spoiler: It won't quite work. Try it, though, and see what happens. Why do you think it behaves the way it does? Hint: child shell.

From function to command

Our next step in pursuit of our own custom commands will be to explore **shell functions**, which are another type of **scripted command** used in the Linux shell.

On many levels, shell functions (a.k.a. "functions") are similar to shell scripts. The most immediate similarity is that both are programmed in Bash (the scripting language), which means both are coded with commands we use on the Bash command line. Just like shell scripts rely on Bash (the shell program) to interpret and execute code, functions also work by feeding their code to Bash line by line as though the lines are being typed in. This is why we say both shell scripts and functions are "scripted"—because Bash reads their code instructions from top to bottom, navigating the logical flow of the program and performing each action sequentially until the operation is complete. With a *callable* shell script, we can tell Bash to carry out an operation by calling the operation's name as a command, and this is no different with shell functions since they also run when called by name. So, are these two types of scripted commands basically the same?

Despite their similarities, callable shell scripts and functions operate in virtually separate compartments in Linux. The main difference between the two is in the way Bash handles executing their code. As we found out in the last chapter (see p. 128), when we launch an executable (i.e., callable) shell script, the script does not execute in the shell where it is called. Instead, an executable shell script runs in a non-interactive child shell (see p. 130). Then, when the script operation completes, the child shell terminates. Contrast that with what happens when we call a function[87]. A function runs not in a child shell but inside the current shell (the shell in which it is called). Then when the function completes its operation, the function's code remains in the current shell's memory as the session carries on. This difference in the execution environment affects command behavior, and we will look out for this as we compare how these two types of commands run in different contexts.

Another major difference between callable shell scripts and functions is in how they are loaded and stored. Whenever we call an executable shell script on the command line, we are launching a file. In this way, the name of the shell script's executable file determines the name of the command that we call. A function, on the other hand, does not need to be kept in an executable file. Rather, a function's code usually resides in a configuration file like `~/.bashrc`, and when the code in the file is loaded at shell startup (and/or taken in via `$ source`), the function gets *defined* for that shell session and stored in the shell's memory—where it remains indefinitely. In this sense, a function is not wholly different from a variable. For example, we assign a name to the function when we define it, and then whenever we call the function's name during that shell session, it returns a result. The difference naturally is that invoking

---

[87] In this guide, we are only working with functions that execute in the current shell (functions with the { } syntax around the code instructions), but Bash does also support functions that run in a subshell (defined with ( ) rather than { } around the code instructions).

$<variable> (e.g., after $ echo) returns the variable's stored value, whereas calling a function as a command causes the shell to execute the function's code—producing the command's output.

	Callable Shell Script	Shell Function
Storage	Stored in an executable file.	Stored in a configuration file[88].
Name (as a command)	The name of the executable file is the name we call as a command.	The name assigned in the definition is the name we call as a command.
Launching (as a command)	Each time we call the command, its executable file launches and the kernel sets up a separate execution environment to run the code.	First, the code is loaded into the shell's memory. Then when we call the command, the shell executes the function's code held in memory.
Execution Environment	Runs in a non-interactive child shell and outputs to stdout.	Runs in the current shell and outputs to stdout.

As we get to know how shell scripts and shell functions behave in operation, we will develop our sense of when to use one or the other for a given job.

Defining a shell function

We'll start playing with shell functions by defining one directly on the command line, and then we'll graduate to making a function persist in a configuration file.

The general syntax[89] for defining a shell function is outlined here.

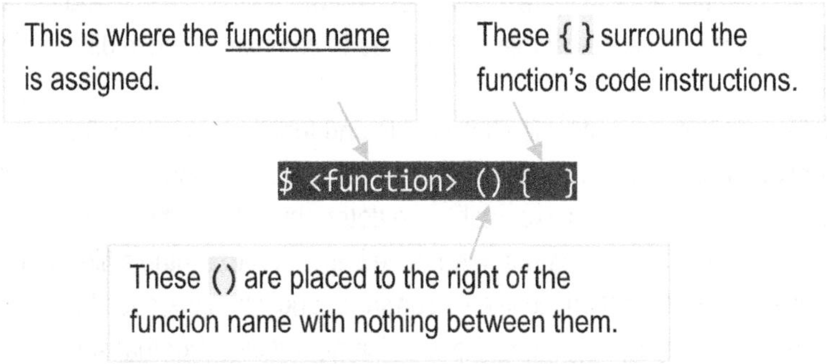

This is where the <u>function name</u> is assigned.

These { } surround the function's code instructions.

```
$ <function> () { }
```

These () are placed to the right of the function name with nothing between them.

Figure 11 Shell function syntax diagram

---

[88] Sometimes you may find a function defined inside an executable shell script for use within that script only. If we want a function to be generally available as a command, however, then we need to define it somewhere in a configuration file that gets loaded at shell startup.

[89] There is also the $ function <function> { } syntax, which uses the function keyword in Bash (other examples of keywords in Bash are if and then). In this guide, we are focusing on the $ <function> () { } syntax shown above. There is no difference in effect between these two syntaxes for defining shell functions in Bash.

For our very first shell function, we'll type in the definition as shown below.

```
$ howdy () { echo 'Hey there!'; echo 'I am a function!'; }
```

A couple of things to note about the syntax: see how the outer { and } both have a space on the inside? These spaces are necessary when we define a function on one line as we have done here. Also, in a one-line function definition, we always need to place a single ; (or &[90]) *after* the last command instruction. Below is a diagram highlighting where spaces are a required part of the syntax and where one has been added for improved readability.

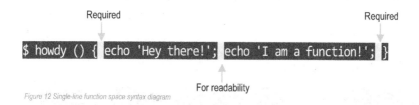

Figure 12 Single-line function space syntax diagram

Once you press enter, calling $ howdy on the command line will cause the shell to execute the function's code.

```
$ howdy
```

```
me@MyLinuxBox: ~
me@MyLinuxBox:~$ howdy () { echo 'Hey there!'; echo 'I am a function!'; }
me@MyLinuxBox:~$ howdy
Hey there!
I am a function!
me@MyLinuxBox:~$
```

Good!

We can use $ type to check on our new function.

```
$ type howdy
```

```
me@MyLinuxBox: ~
me@MyLinuxBox:~$ type howdy
howdy is a function
howdy ()
{
    echo 'Hey there!';
    echo 'I am a function!'
}
me@MyLinuxBox:~$
```

---

[90] If we replaced the final ; with &, then the function would execute as a background job (in a subshell) when we call it.

In the $ type command's output, we see our function definition displayed with different formatting. Rather than   spaces separating the { } from the code instructions, we have **newline separation** showing each curly bracket on its own line. Because this newline formatting is often easier for humans to read, it is generally preferred as the format for defining a function in a configuration file. Shall we add our function definition to ~/.bashrc using this newline format?

$ unset

Before we add our function definition to ~/.bashrc, first we'll call the $ unset built-in to remove our currently defined function from the shell's memory. This way we can start with a clean slate when we do a $ source ~/.bashrc to load our reformatted function definition into memory.

$ unset howdy

```
me@MyLinuxBox: ~

me@MyLinuxBox:~$ unset howdy
me@MyLinuxBox:~$ howdy
howdy: command not found
me@MyLinuxBox:~$ █
```

Now when you enter $ howdy, you should receive a howdy: command not found error.

Alright. In the home directory, open .bashrc in $ vim (enter :set number in $ vim to view line numbers—see p. 79). Scroll down to the end of the file (around line #120) and enter the function definition as shown.

```
119
120 howdy ()
121 {
122         echo 'Hey there!'
123         echo 'I am a function!'
124 }
125
```

You will find when you press enter after {, $ vim automatically indents the cursor before you start typing the function's code instructions. This indent is added for readability only and the number of   spaces is arbitrary. Also, notice that you do not need to add a semi-colon after lines of code when they are newline-separated (as they are here). When you reach the end of the second line of code instructions (the end of the second $ echo command), press enter, type }, and $ vim should automatically stop indenting. Then write your changes to disk and quit $ vim.

Now, back on the command line, we need to $ source the code in ~/.bashrc for our newly added function to take effect.

$.

Here we will get our first taste of the $. command, known colloquially as the "dot command". The dot command and $ source are **synonyms**. That is, there is <u>no difference</u> in behavior between $. and $ source. Because $. is easier to type than $ source, you may find yourself using $. from now on, but either way works. In the home directory, enter the following.

$$\texttt{\$ . .bashrc}$$

```
me@MyLinuxBox:~$ . .bashrc
me@MyLinuxBox:~$ howdy
Hey there!
I am a function!
me@MyLinuxBox:~$
```

Now if you call $ howdy again, you should see the same output as before.

Positional parameters

We're ready to pick up some tools Bash has in store for capturing what we put into the argument of a scripted command. We're approaching these things first in the context of shell functions, but the same framework[91] applies to executable shell scripts as well.

Let's talk for a moment about command arguments. Consider a command like $ cd. We know when we call $ cd, whatever is in the argument will completely determine the command's resultant action or output. We might put a <pathname> in the argument of $ cd, or nothing, or even something invalid (which would return an error), but whatever we do will stimulate a response from the command.

Generally, this is what makes commands useful—their ability to produce an action or output based on a given input. So, what would happen if we sent an argument to our shell function? Let's find out. Try this below.

$$\texttt{\$ howdy Ken}$$

```
me@MyLinuxBox:~$ howdy Ken
Hey there!
I am a function!
me@MyLinuxBox:~$
```

---

[91] With the exception of the FUNCNAME variable (see p. 138), the same framework applies to callable shell scripts.

Our function doesn't seem to know or care that we placed text in its argument! Nor does it seem to be aware that it is answering to the wrong proper name (the function's name is howdy—not Ken)! What we are realizing here is that unless we tell a scripted command how to react to an argument, the command will just blindly go on as though the argument isn't there or doesn't matter. But the argument <u>does</u> matter (if we want our command to be responsive to input)!

To improve our function's awareness of who it is and what we put into it, we're going to go back to `~/.bashrc` and make a couple of small changes. Open `~/.bashrc` in `$ vim` again, scroll down to our function definition, and make these additions as shown.

```
120 howdy ()                         shell variable
121 {
122         echo ⓤHey there! My name is $FUNCNAME. Not $1.ⓤ
123         echo 'I am a function!'
124 }                                positional parameter
125
```

Here we have added $FUNCNAME and $1, plus we have surrounded the whole first string in **double quotes**. Let's discuss the effect that each of these changes has on the command's output.

→ $FUNCNAME expands to the name of the function we are calling (the shell stores the function's name in the FUNCNAME variable[92] when the function's code is executed).

→ $1 is a **positional parameter**. We can think of a positional parameter as a <u>special variable</u> whose name refers to the <u>position</u> of a block of text in a command's argument. This $1 captures the <u>first block of text</u> that we put in the argument of the command (hence the 1). If we supply two blocks of text in the argument of a command (separated by a   space), then $1 captures the first block and $2 captures the second block, and so on. Positional parameters nominally range from $0 to $9 ($0 expanding to the name of the calling command[93]). If we need to capture more than nine positional parameters in an argument, then we can invoke the ${#} form (e.g., ${10}, ${11}, and onward).

→ The double quotes have been added so that $FUNCNAME and $1 can be expanded to their values rather than treated as literal text. Whenever we have a string[94] in **single quotes**, <u>all</u> text[95] in the string is treated literally—as in, no characters carry any special meaning. Hence, we use double quotes here.

---

[92] The FUNCNAME shell variable is actually an <u>array variable</u> which can keep track of multiple function names in the event that we call a function within a function (the level of function nesting allowed in the shell is defined in the FUNCNEST variable). In the case above, we are only calling one function, so $FUNCNAME returns just that name.

[93] The shell's method of resolving the value for $0 does not reliably capture the name of a scripted command. This is why we use $FUNCNAME instead of $0 to retrieve the name of the function above.

[94] Except in a variable definition like for PS1—where single quotes surround the string because the variable gets <u>re-defined</u> with the string in "" double quotes (effectively) every time the shell prints the command line prompt.

[95] The exception would be single quotes (' ') themselves, which cannot be literal *within* a single-quoted string.

Once you've finished updating the function definition in $ vim, proceed with a write and quit. Also, don't forget to enter $ . .bashrc to source the code changes. When ready, let's try this command again and see what comes back.

$ howdy Ken

```
me@MyLinuxBox:~$ howdy Ken
Hey there! My name is howdy. Not Ken.
I am a function!
me@MyLinuxBox:~$
```

Not bad! Here we can see that Ken is the text returned as the $1 positional parameter value. But what if we put more than one block of text into the argument? Let's try that and see what happens.

$ howdy Ken Thompson

```
me@MyLinuxBox:~$ howdy Ken Thompson
Hey there! My name is howdy. Not Ken.
I am a function!
me@MyLinuxBox:~$
```

This works, but we still need a way to receive the full input if more than one item (i.e., more than one block of text) is in the argument. We could add more positional parameters to the string in the form of "Hey there! My name is $FUNCNAME. Not $1 $2.". But there is a better way which will let us take in the whole argument without having to guess the number of text blocks to capture. Let's go back to ~/.bashrc in $ vim and make another small change.

```
120 howdy ()
121 {
122         echo "Hey there! My name is $FUNCNAME. Not $*."
123         echo 'I am a function!'
124 }                                        special variable
125
```

This time we have switched out the $1 for $*. This $* special variable is the shell parameter in Bash that captures all text present in the argument when we call a command. The * symbol is reminiscent of the * wildcard operator, implying that $* comprises the value of *any* positional parameter (excluding the value of $0). When ready, go ahead with the write, quit, and $ . .bashrc routine again, and then try the following one more time.

$ howdy Ken Thompson

```
                                              me@MyLinuxBox: ~
me@MyLinuxBox:~$ howdy Ken Thompson
Hey there! My name is howdy. Not Ken Thompson.
I am a function!
me@MyLinuxBox:~$
```

Improvement! Our function is becoming more elastic in its response to input.

But then there is the possibility for things to get confused. Case in point, try calling our function as we did originally with nothing in the argument.

$ howdy

```
                                              me@MyLinuxBox: ~
me@MyLinuxBox:~$ howdy
Hey there! My name is howdy. Not .
I am a function!
me@MyLinuxBox:~$
```

Oh dear. It looks like our function has gotten all mixed up about who it is and who it is not. To remedy this, we need to take a deeper dip into the Bash scripting language.

Working with if...then...else statements in Bash

When we need to control a scripted command's behavior based on different factors in the command's **execution environment**[96], we can fit a command with if...then...else statements to create rules for when the command will or will not do certain things. This type of **control flow logic** allows code to run *if* a **condition** in the execution environment is true. If a condition is not satisfied, then control is given to the else[97] part of the statement for other instructions to be executed.

We can have if check for anything in the execution environment and use that as a basis for scripted command behavior (e.g., $ if ["$PWD" = "/"]; then echo 'root directory'; else echo 'not root directory'; fi). But the use case for if...then...else statements that we are most interested in here is the control they give over command behavior in response to the command's argument. We'll approach this first by looking closely at the structure and syntax of an if...then...else statement in Bash. Then we'll experiment with building one of these statements into our function to fine-tune its response to given input.

---

[96] A command's <u>execution environment</u> includes the command's positional parameters plus all currently defined shell *and* environment variables. Special variables such as $* (argument string), $? (command/test exit status), and others are included as well.

[97] An if...then statement does not require an else clause (i.e., including an else clause is always optional).

With the **keyword**[98] if in Bash, there is a segment directly afterward that performs a **test** to check whether or not something in the execution environment is true. The result of this test[99] ("true" or "false") informs Bash whether to proceed and execute the then clause (in the case of a "true" result) or jump and execute the else clause (in the case of a "false" result). Because the test result (true or false) depends on how the facts of the execution environment line up (or not) with the assertion in the test, the test is termed a **conditional expression** in Bash. See the diagram below.

```
$ if [ "$PWD" = "/" ]; then echo 'root directory'; else echo 'not root directory'; fi
    └──────────────┘ └───────────────────────────┘ └───────────────────────────────┘
         test              then clause                      else clause
```

Figure 13 if … then … else statement diagram

The syntax[100] we use for the test is with [   ] surrounding the **logical comparison** (the assertion being tested). The single   space separating each square bracket from the enclosed text is necessary, as are the   spaces surrounding the = **comparison operator**. The   spaces around = delineate this as <u>not</u> a variable definition (see p. 84). Since this is all on a single line, a ; is used to separate each keyword segment (if…; then…; else…; fi). Note that Bash always requires the fi keyword at the end of an if…then or if…then…else statement.

Let's now go back to ~/.bashrc and try our hand at adding an if…then…else statement to our function. The goal here is to give the function a better means of responding to input received in the command's argument. Try typing in the several additions shown below. Indenting is for readability only.

```
120 howdy ()
121 {
122     if [ -n "$*" ]; then
123             echo "Hey there! My name is $FUNCNAME. Not $*."
124             echo 'I am a function!'
125     else
126             echo 'Hey there!'
127             echo 'I am a function!'
128     fi
129 }
130
```

Instead of using a comparison operator like in the earlier example, here the test is checking $* with the -n [option] to see if the length of the argument string is <u>non</u>-zero.

---

[98] Keywords (or "reserved words") in Bash are pieces of the language generally used to frame instructions within a control flow scheme. Keywords are different from commands in that a keyword alone cannot perform any action. Aside from if, other examples of Bash keywords we have seen include then, else, and fi.
[99] The result of the test is an <u>exit status</u> in Bash, with exit code 0 representing "true" (or "success") and any other exit code (1 through 255) representing "false" (or "failure"). Every command or test in the shell returns an exit status. The shell parameter $? always holds the exit status of the most recently executed command or test.
[100] Surprisingly, $ [is a built-in (as in, a built-in <u>command</u>)! The $ [command is a near synonym for the $ test built-in. Try $ type [and you will see built-in in the output.

Effectively, our conditional expression is asking, *"Is there anything in the argument of the command?"* If yes, then the first two $ echo instructions are executed. If no, then Bash looks to the else clause and executes the other two $ echo instructions.

When you're done typing everything in, be sure to <u>w</u>rite, <u>q</u>uit, and do $ . .bashrc. Then, whenever you're ready, let's try this again on the command line.

$ howdy

```
me@MyLinuxBox:~$ howdy
Hey there!
I am a function!
me@MyLinuxBox:~$ 
```

We got our old behavior back! Now if you tried typing in $ howdy Ken Thompson (or any other name in the argument), you should get an output as before. But wait a minute. *Any* other name? What if we typed in the function's name <u>in the argument</u>? Let's check what happens with this.

$ howdy howdy

```
me@MyLinuxBox:~$ howdy howdy
Hey there! My name is howdy. Not howdy.
I am a function!
me@MyLinuxBox:~$ 
```

Our poor function is lost again. But not to worry. We can fix this by refining the logic used for testing the command's argument. Let's open .bashrc one more time and add two additional tests to enhance the conditional expression's logic. Now the if decision will cover three possible tests.

```
120 howdy ()
121 {
122    if [ -n "$*" ] && [ "$*" != "howdy" ] && [ "$*" != "Howdy" ]; then
123        echo "Hey there! My name is $FUNCNAME. Not $*."
124        echo 'I am a function!'
125    else
126        echo 'Hey there!'
127        echo 'I am a function!'
128    fi
129 }
130
```

Here you see we're using **&&**, the **logical AND operator**, to absorb two more tests into our conditional expression. The **&&** operator in Bash has a unique property where it will only allow continuation into the next test (or command) if the previous test (or command) finishes with a 0 **exit status**.

In Linux, a command (or test) returning an exit status of 0 means the command (or test) completed successfully (interpreted as "true" in the case of a test). Otherwise, a command or test will finish with a non-zero exit status (between 1 and 255), indicating failure to execute (interpreted as "false" in the case of a test). See the footnote on p. 141 for more information.

Looking back at the conditional expression, we've also brought in the != comparison operator for our two additional tests. The != means "not equal to". Altogether, the conditional expression is now asking,

"Is there anything in the argument of the command AND is it not equal to 'howdy' AND not equal to 'Howdy'?"

If yes, then the first two $ echo instructions are executed. If no, Bash skips to the else clause and executes the other two $ echo instructions. Note that the exit status of the conditional expression itself is 0 if "yes" and non-zero if "no". It is this returned exit status (from the full conditional expression) that Bash uses to determine whether to proceed to then or skip to else.

After you've typed everything in, written the file to disk, quit $ vim, and done a $ . .bashrc, let's try this one more time.

$ howdy howdy

Thank goodness. And, for thoroughness:

$ howdy Howdy

Now, we can imagine many other inputs that would throw our function off or warrant different responses, like $ howdy howdy!, $ howdy Howdy., and so on. This points out the challenge of making a robust command interface capable of handling a broad range of inputs for modifying command behavior. In real-world use, these inputs would often be the command's [options]. Fortunately, there are specialized tools such as $ getopts for parsing [options] without requiring an exhaustive set of [ ] tests. In time, you will pick up these tools for easily adding [options] to your own commands.

Summary:

In the realm of Bash, we have two types of scripted commands programmed in the Bash scripting language: callable shell scripts and shell functions. These two types of scripted commands are similar in that both require Bash (the shell) to execute their instructions. The main difference between the two is in the way Bash arranges for their code to be executed. Shell functions, unlike callable shell scripts, have to be loaded into the shell's memory before they can be called as commands. Once a shell function is defined in the shell's memory, then we can call the function by name and Bash will execute its instructions in the current shell. Within a shell function's (or callable shell script's) execution environment, we can sample the command's argument stored in positional parameters, which get consolidated as a single string in the $* special variable. The $* special variable's string can then be tested in an if...then...else statement against conditions needed for code execution, thus letting us shape command behavior around what is (or is not) included in the command's argument.

Commands:

$ unset $ type
$. $ echo

Concepts:

- Shell functions
  - -vs- callable shell scripts
  - Function definition syntax
  - ; single line formatting
  - Newline formatting
- $. and $ source as synonyms
- Positional parameters
- FUNCNAME shell variable
- $* special variable
- Double quotes vs single quotes

- Execution environment
- Keywords in Bash
- if...then...else statements
  - Control flow logic
  - [ ] tests
  - Conditional expressions
  - Logical comparisons
  - = and != comparison operators
  - && logical AND operator
- Exit status

Challenge:

When we speak about if...then...else statements, for brevity we often neglect to mention an additional component available to us in Bash: the elif (else if) keyword. The full if...then...else structure in Bash is really if...then...elif...then...else...fi. One big advantage of using elif...then is that on top of a single else clause (which is always optional), we can include as many elif...then statements as needed to cover a range of conditions. As a challenge, insert an elif...then statement before the else clause in the $ howdy function. Base the test in your elif...then statement on a misspelling of "howdy" (e.g., "howdie", "hwdy", etc.). As an added challenge, give your elif...then statement a conditional expression capable of testing for more than one misspelling of "howdy". If you try this, you'll want to use || (the **logical OR operator**) to join the tests together (formatted like we did with the && operator between the tests following if—see p. 142).

Practical commands of our own

Continuing in the direction of forming our own commands, we are now going to take what we have gathered about callable shell scripts and shell functions and see what kinds of practical commands we can build ourselves. As we put together our own custom commands, we will also be making some important last-minute additions to our standard Linux toolbox.

Using links in the Linux shell

For our first project here, we will be going back to our `$ bak` callable shell script (see p. 128) and giving it purpose as a utility for making backups of files and directories.

To prepare the ~/bin/bak file for edits, we are going to create a **link** between ~/bin/bak and a new "identical twin" file which we will place in another location (away from ~/bin). In doing this, when we make edits to either file (~/bin/bak or its identical twin), the edits will simultaneously appear in <u>both</u> files as if they are <u>the same file</u> in two different places. The advantage of this is that as we work on our script, we can keep our test files and script together in a "workshop" location (away from ~/bin) while leaving a single, up to date ~/bin/bak file in the ~/bin directory (we don't want to litter the ~/bin directory with random files that we keep in our "workshop" directory for testing our script).

$ ln

The command we will use to create an identical twin for ~/bin/bak is `$ ln`, short for "l<u>in</u>k". One of the most powerful tools in all of Linux, `$ ln` by itself with no [option(s)] takes a <target> file given in the argument and makes a **hard link** to a new file (which we also name in the argument). The general syntax for `$ ln` follows this template: `$ ln [option(s)] <target> <link>`.

Let's try using `$ ln` on our ~/bin/bak script as the <target> so that we can have a new hard <link> to it in the ~/Projects/MyScripts directory.

$ ln ~/bin/bak ~/Projects/MyScripts/bak

Now if we look in ~/Projects/MyScripts, we see a new bak file.

```
me@MyLinuxBox: ~/Projects/MyScripts
me@MyLinuxBox:~/Projects/MyScripts$ ll
total 24
drwxrwxr-x 2 me me 4096 Sep  1 19:00 ./
drwxrwxr-x 7 me me 4096 Jul 20 19:33 ../
-rwxrwxr-x 2 me me  117 Jul  5 15:09 bak*
-rw-rw-r-- 1 me me   35 Jun 26 20:43 my_second_file
-rw-rw-r-- 1 me me  135 Jan 24  2021 my_third_file
-rw-rw-r-- 1 me me   60 Jan 29  2021 my_very_first_file
me@MyLinuxBox:~/Projects/MyScripts$
```

Any edits we make to the ~/Projects/MyScripts/bak file will immediately show up in the ~/bin/bak file (and vice-versa). This is because both files now share the same underlying resource[101] in the Linux file system database. That is to say, these files are <u>not</u> linked *together*, but rather they both *point* to the same data[102] on the physical storage medium.

Because of this, we could even delete the ~/bin/bak file, and ~/Projects/MyScripts/bak would remain untouched (because we wouldn't be deleting the ~/bin/bak *data*—we would just be deleting the file as a reference to that data). If we deleted both ~/bin/bak and ~/Projects/MyScripts/bak, then their mutual resource[101] would be removed from the file system's database and the files' data would be overwritten (sooner or later).

In addition to hard links, the $ ln command with the -s [option] lets us create a **soft link**, otherwise known as a **symlink** (short for <u>sym</u>bolic <u>link</u>). One big difference between a hard link and a soft link is that a soft link can point to a <u>file</u> or <u>directory</u> as its <target>, whereas a hard link cannot be created for a directory (a hard link can only exist as a regular file).

Soft links are essentially shortcuts to the files or directories they point to, and they are very common. To get some soft link practice, let's create a soft link in ~ that points to the ~/Projects/MyScripts directory.

$ ln -s ~/Projects/MyScripts ~/MyScripts

Now if we list the contents of ~, we will see a MyScripts entry pointing to ~/Projects/MyScripts.

```
drwxr-xr-x  2 me    me     4096 Nov 18  2020 Music/
lrwxrwxrwx  1 me    me       27 Sep  4 07:27 MyScripts -> /home/me/Projects/MyScripts/
drwxr-xr-x  2 me    me    20480 Sep  1 19:02 Pictures/
```

Note the filetype for ~/MyScripts is l (see p. 54), indicating that this is a soft <u>l</u>ink.

Building and testing a callable shell script

And here is where we begin putting all the pieces together. Let's outline what we want our $ bak command to do. Originally, when we started our script (see p. 130), we imagined that

Calling $ bak <filename> will create a backup of <filename> in the cwd.

---

[101] The resource these files share is called an <u>inode</u> (for <u>index node</u>), which is a record in the database maintained by Linux for keeping track of files and directories in the Linux file system. An inode stores information about a file, such as where the file's data is located on the physical storage medium.

[102] To be precise, the files both point to the same inode, which keeps track of the location of the files' mutually shared data on the physical storage medium. Try $ ll -i ~/bin/bak ~/Projects/MyScripts/bak to view the two files' shared <u>i</u>node number.

This is a good starting goal. But we can do even more by including an if...then...elif...then...else statement to give our script the logic it needs to be able to back up <u>directories</u> in addition to <u>regular files</u>. Our revised goal would read, "Calling $ bak <filename> or $ bak <directoryname> will create a backup of <filename> or <directoryname> in the cwd."

That's better. So then, what pieces of Bash would allow us to accomplish this?

- For backup, we know we can use the $ cp command.

- For capturing the <filename> or <directoryname> that we want to back up, we have the $* special variable for sampling the argument of $ bak.

- Since we want $ bak to operate on either a regular file or a directory, we would construct an if...then...elif...then...else statement as follows (in pseudocode).

  - if backing up a regular file, then make a new file <filename>.bak.
  - elif backing up a directory, then make a new directory <directoryname>.bak.
  - else don't do anything because the backup file or directory already exists.

Before you look at the full script* below, see if you can come up with your own solution that approximates the initial goal for $ bak as described on p. 146. As a starting point, you could make $ bak into a simple script that uses $ cp to back up <filename> when we call $ bak <filename>.

*On Ubuntu systems pre version 19.04, the location of the $ bash executable may be /bin/bash rather than /usr/bin/bash

```
#!/usr/bin/bash
cp -n "$*" "$*.bak"
```

Building on this simple core operation, we can wrap it in an if...then...elif...then...else statement to control the code execution based on whether we have a <filename> or a <directoryname> in the argument of $ bak. The script shown below follows from these requirements. Open $ vim bak in ~/Projects/MyScripts and type in the new script as shown.

```
me@MyLinuxBox: ~/Projects/MyScripts
#!/usr/bin/bash

if [ -f "$*" ] && [ ! -f "$*.bak" ] && [ ! -d "$*.bak" ]; then
    cp -n "$*" "$*.bak"

elif [ -d "$*" ] && [ ! -d "$*.bak" ] && [ ! -f "$*.bak" ]; then
    cp -nr "$*" "$*.bak"

else
    echo "$*.bak already exists. Please delete or rename $*.bak and try again."
    exit 1
fi
```

Notice the tests for the presence of a file [-f "$*"] or a directory [-d "$*"] in the execution environment. These tests with the -f and -d [options] look in the cwd (automatically retrieved from $PWD) for a <filename> or <directoryname> matching $* (double quotes "$*" are used in each test to safely expand the $* variable—see p. 85 and p. 138).

The main reason we need to test to see whether $* matches the name of a file or directory is because we cannot simply $ cp -n <source> <target> for a non-empty directory. Instead, we need to invoke either the -r (recursive) or -a (archive) [option] (see p. 111) for $ cp to copy all of a directory's contents. We have chosen -r here because we want the timestamp for the backup to reflect when the backup was made (-a preserves the timestamp of when <source> was created).

Also, in our two conditional expressions, you will see in some of the tests that we are using the ! **logical NOT operator**. For example, [! -f "$*.bak"] means, *"Is there no file named <filename>.bak in the cwd?"* This is to make sure that we are not overwriting an existing <filename>.bak file (which is doubly ensured by the -n [option] with $ cp—see p. 111). In the event of a non-zero exit status from these tests (see p. 143), Bash skips to the else clause, which prints a message to stdout informing us to delete or rename <filename>.bak or <directoryname>.bak. Because executing the else clause amounts to an error, we have the $ exit command broadcast a 1 exit status at the end of the clause (this is to make the $ bak command play well with other commands that might depend on receiving the $ bak command's exit status).

Let's take our new $ bak command out for a spin and run it through some tests. In the ~/Projects/MyScripts directory, enter the following command.

$ bak my_second_file

Following with an $ ll, we see a new my_second_file.bak file in the list.

```
                                              me@MyLinuxBox: ~/Projects/MyScripts
me@MyLinuxBox:~/Projects/MyScripts$ bak my_second_file
me@MyLinuxBox:~/Projects/MyScripts$ ll
total 28
drwxrwxr-x 2 me me 4096 Sep  5 15:26 ./
drwxrwxr-x 7 me me 4096 Sep  5 11:52 ../
-rwxrwxr-x 2 me me  493 Sep  5 05:49 bak*
-rw-rw-r-- 1 me me   35 Jun 26 20:43 my_second_file
-rw-rw-r-- 1 me me   35 Sep  5 15:26 my_second_file.bak
-rw-rw-r-- 1 me me  135 Jan 24  2021 my_third_file
-rw-rw-r-- 1 me me   60 Jan 29  2021 my_very_first_file
me@MyLinuxBox:~/Projects/MyScripts$ bak my_second_file
my_second_file.bak already exists. Please delete or rename my_second_file.bak and try again.
me@MyLinuxBox:~/Projects/MyScripts$
```

Then if we attempt to run $ bak my_second_file again, our script returns an error message.

Now we'll remove the `my_second_file.bak` file we just made. This will be good practice in case we ever need to replace a backup file with a newer version.

$ rm -i my_second_file.bak

```
                                                        me@MyLinuxBox: ~/Projects/MyScripts
me@MyLinuxBox:~/Projects/MyScripts$ ll
total 28
drwxrwxr-x 2 me me 4096 Sep  5 15:26 ./
drwxrwxr-x 7 me me 4096 Sep  5 11:52 ../
-rwxrwxr-x 2 me me  493 Sep  5 05:49 bak*
-rw-rw-r-- 1 me me   35 Jun 26 20:43 my_second_file
-rw-rw-r-- 1 me me   35 Sep  5 15:26 my_second_file.bak
-rw-rw-r-- 1 me me  135 Jan 24  2021 my_third_file
-rw-rw-r-- 1 me me   60 Jan 29  2021 my_very_first_file
me@MyLinuxBox:~/Projects/MyScripts$ rm -i my_second_file.bak
rm: remove regular file 'my_second_file.bak'? y
me@MyLinuxBox:~/Projects/MyScripts$
```

Using the `-i [option]` with `$ rm` requires us to enter y at the interactive prompt to continue.

Next we'll create a new directory to test the `$ bak` command's directory backup capabilities.

$ mkdir files

And we'll copy our three original files to use as test subjects in the new `./files` directory.

$ cp -n my* files

```
                                                        me@MyLinuxBox: ~/Projects/MyScripts
me@MyLinuxBox:~/Projects/MyScripts$ mkdir files
me@MyLinuxBox:~/Projects/MyScripts$ cp -n my* files
me@MyLinuxBox:~/Projects/MyScripts$ ll
total 28
drwxrwxr-x 3 me me 4096 Sep  5 15:29 ./
drwxrwxr-x 7 me me 4096 Sep  5 11:52 ../
-rwxrwxr-x 2 me me  493 Sep  5 05:49 bak*
drwxrwxr-x 2 me me 4096 Sep  5 15:29 files/
-rw-rw-r-- 1 me me   35 Jun 26 20:43 my_second_file
-rw-rw-r-- 1 me me  135 Jan 24  2021 my_third_file
-rw-rw-r-- 1 me me   60 Jan 29  2021 my_very_first_file
me@MyLinuxBox:~/Projects/MyScripts$ ll files
total 20
drwxrwxr-x 2 me me 4096 Sep  5 15:29 ./
drwxrwxr-x 3 me me 4096 Sep  5 15:29 ../
-rw-rw-r-- 1 me me   35 Sep  5 15:29 my_second_file
-rw-rw-r-- 1 me me  135 Sep  5 15:29 my_third_file
-rw-rw-r-- 1 me me   60 Sep  5 15:29 my_very_first_file
me@MyLinuxBox:~/Projects/MyScripts$
```

An `$ ll` shows the new `files` directory inside `~/Projects/MyScripts`, and an `$ ll files` confirms that our three copied test subjects arrived in their destination.

With the `./files` directory ready to go, we'll try backing it up with the `$ bak` command.

$ bak files

Doing an `$ ll` afterward shows a new `files.bak` directory inside `~/Projects/MyScripts`.

```
                                                    me@MyLinuxBox: ~/Projects/MyScripts
me@MyLinuxBox:~/Projects/MyScripts$ bak files
me@MyLinuxBox:~/Projects/MyScripts$ ll
total 32
drwxrwxr-x 4 me me 4096 Sep  5 15:30 ./
drwxrwxr-x 7 me me 4096 Sep  5 11:52 ../
-rwxrwxr-x 2 me me  493 Sep  5 05:49 bak*
drwxrwxr-x 2 me me 4096 Sep  5 15:29 files/
drwxrwxr-x 2 me me 4096 Sep  5 15:30 files.bak/
-rw-rw-r-- 1 me me   35 Jun 26 20:43 my_second_file
-rw-rw-r-- 1 me me  135 Jan 24  2021 my_third_file
-rw-rw-r-- 1 me me   60 Jan 29  2021 my_very_first_file
me@MyLinuxBox:~/Projects/MyScripts$ bak files
files.bak already exists. Please delete or rename files.bak and try again.
me@MyLinuxBox:~/Projects/MyScripts$ 
```

And if we try to use `$ bak` on `./files` a second time, we get the same warning that a backup already exists.

Again for practice, we'll delete both the `./files` and `./files.bak` directories that we just made.

$ rm -ir files*

```
                                                    me@MyLinuxBox: ~/Projects/MyScripts
me@MyLinuxBox:~/Projects/MyScripts$ rm -ir files*
rm: descend into directory 'files'? y
rm: remove regular file 'files/my_very_first_file'? y
rm: remove regular file 'files/my_third_file'? y
rm: remove regular file 'files/my_second_file'? y
rm: remove directory 'files'? y
rm: descend into directory 'files.bak'? y
rm: remove regular file 'files.bak/my_very_first_file'? y
rm: remove regular file 'files.bak/my_third_file'? y
rm: remove regular file 'files.bak/my_second_file'? y
rm: remove directory 'files.bak'? y
me@MyLinuxBox:~/Projects/MyScripts$ 
```

The `-r` [option] with `$ rm` (for recursive) is necessary for removing non-empty directories. By including the `-i` [option] along with `$ rm -r`, we get an interactive prompt for y confirmation on every file we want to delete. This is useful as a safety measure, but if a directory has a large number of files, the `-i` [option] with `$ rm` might be more trouble than it's worth. In that case, if you don't want to confirm the deletion of each and every file, you can press ctrl + c and the `$ rm -ir` process will terminate. Then just run `$ rm -r files*` without the `-i` [option], and the task will complete.

It appears that our $ bak command is working. Now, we could stop here and be satisfied with what we have, but there are two more checks that we could add to the script's logic to take our command up a notch in robustness.

Like we saw in the last chapter, it's a good idea to try to cover as many input scenarios as we can (see p. 140). Currently, the command's behavior is undefined if we call $ bak with nothing in the argument or if the argument we send is invalid (e.g., if what we enter does not exist in the cwd). We can fix this by adding two more elif…then statements to our script (see below).

```
#!/usr/bin/bash

if [ -f "$*" ] && [ ! -f "$*.bak" ] && [ ! -d "$*.bak" ]; then
    cp -n "$*" "$*.bak"

elif [ -d "$*" ] && [ ! -d "$*.bak" ] && [ ! -f "$*.bak" ]; then
    cp -nr "$*" "$*.bak"

elif [ -z "$*" ]; then
    echo "Usage: $ bak <filename> or $ bak <directoryname>"
    exit 1

elif [ -n "$*" ] && [ ! -f "$*" ] && [ ! -d "$*" ]; then
    echo "$*: No such file or directory."
    exit 1

else
    echo "$*.bak already exists. Please delete or rename $*.bak and try again."
    exit 1
fi
```

Here we have added a [-z "$*"] test to check if $* is of zero length, and another conditional expression to check if a non-zero-length input string does not match anything in the cwd. Once you have added these lines, let's run two additional tests for $ bak.

$ bak

$ bak t

```
me@MyLinuxBox:~/Projects/MyScripts$ bak
Usage: $ bak <filename> or $ bak <directoryname>
me@MyLinuxBox:~/Projects/MyScripts$ bak t
t: No such file or directory.
me@MyLinuxBox:~/Projects/MyScripts$ 
```

And we receive the corresponding error message for each input. It's helpful to include this kind of error messaging in the event that someone who is unfamiliar with the command ever tries to use it!

Summary:
One of the most useful features in Linux is its support for file system links, and the $ ln command gives us access to this capability on the command line. With $ ln, we can make hard-linked "identical twin" regular files that remain in sync in different locations across the file system, and we can use the -s [option] to create soft links that point as shortcuts to target files or directories in separate parts of the file system as well. By making a hard link to a callable shell script and placing the linked file in its own directory, we can test and make changes to the script without keeping test files in the ~/bin directory. To begin building a callable shell script, we can start with a simple operation and develop it by wrapping the operation in an if...then...elif...then...else statement. Then we can add conditional expressions with tests for the presence of files or directories in the cwd, and we can trigger error messages based on input received in the argument.

Commands:

$ ln	$ mkdir
$ rm	$ cp

Concepts:

- Links in the Linux file system
  - Hard links
  - Soft links
- Testing for files or directories in cwd
  - [-f "$*"] file test
  - [-d "$*"] directory test
- ! logical NOT operator
- $ exit [#] for broadcasting exit status
- $ cp -nr for copying directories
- $ rm -ir for removing directories
- [-n "$*"] non-zero length test
- [-z "$*"] zero length test

Challenge:
Now it's your turn to make a scripted command! If you worked on the challenge from two chapters ago (see p. 132), you will have experimented with creating an alias called $ cdll that, when called, performs a $ cd to change the cwd to the home directory and an $ ll to list the contents, all in one operation. You might have noticed that if you try calling this alias with a path to a directory in the argument (e.g., $ cdll <pathname>/<directoryname>), the alias lists the contents of the destination directory and changes the cwd to ~ (always, regardless of what directory we include in the argument). This is because aliases are limited in their capacity to handle input arguments. Now your task is to fix this by turning the $ cdll alias into a <u>shell function</u>. Before you do this, you will need to call $ unalias cdll to free up the $ cdll name to be redefined as a function. You will also need to # comment out the alias definition in the ~/.bash_aliases file (or wherever you stored the alias) so that your new $ cdll function will persist. When that is all taken care of, make a new $ cdll shell function that will change the cwd to a destination directory (included in the argument) and then list the directory's contents, all in one operation. As an extra challenge, try making a callable shell script (with a different name) using the same code. You will find that it doesn't quite work as expected. Why is this? Hint: callable shell scripts run in a child shell execution environment.

A package arrives

As we send you off on your Linux journey ahead, we will be filling in these last bits for you to take along as you move into more advanced Linux territory.

Finding things in the Linux file system

If there were ever a place where a search tool would come in extremely handy, it would be in the Linux file system. Earlier when we introduced $ grep, we looked at how to search for a <pattern> in a file's contents (see p. 69). Combining this capability with a method of searching across files and directories will open a new degree of independence for us on the command line.

$ find

The way we will combine these search capabilities together is with the $ find utility: an incredibly versatile tool that allows us to search for items in the file system by name, type, size, permissions, and a host of other parameters. In its baseline configuration, $ find prints a list of items to stdout that match the search criteria. This is useful, but the true power of $ find is in its ability to locate items in the file system and *act upon* them with commands (or command equivalents) that we put in the $ find command's argument. See the diagram below for the general $ find command structure.

The <pathname> sets the enclosing directory where the search happens.

Here we set the [action] to perform on the search results.

```
$ find [option(s)] <pathname> [expression] [action]
```

This is where we define the search criteria (e.g., -type -f to limit the results to files).

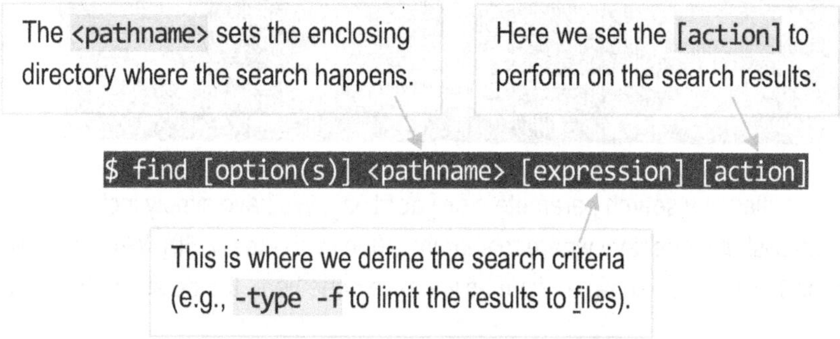

Figure 14 $ find command structure diagram

The default behavior for $ find is to perform a **recursive search** through all sub-directories within the <pathname> directory. By default, the $ find command will not follow any soft links (that is, by default, $ find will not search *through* soft-linked directories or act on soft-linked target files but simply regard the links themselves as items in the search). Unless we explicitly state the [action] that we want $ find to perform, the default [action] is -print (i.e., print every matching search result to stdout).

Before we begin experimenting with $ find, let's go back to the ~/Projects/MyScripts directory and make a backup of the ~/Projects/MyScripts/bak file with our $ bak command. This will be helpful in producing a certain search result later (in addition to being a generally good thing to do).

$ bak bak

```
                                            me@MyLinuxBox: ~/Projects/MyScripts
me@MyLinuxBox:~/Projects/MyScripts$ bak bak
me@MyLinuxBox:~/Projects/MyScripts$ ll
total 28
drwxrwxr-x 2 me me 4096 Sep 16 06:13 ./
drwxrwxr-x 6 me me 4096 Sep 16 06:06 ../
-rwxrwxr-x 2 me me  493 Sep  5 05:49 bak*
-rwxrwxr-x 1 me me  493 Sep 16 06:13 bak.bak*
-rw-rw-r-- 1 me me   35 Jun 26 20:43 my_second_file
-rw-rw-r-- 1 me me  135 Jan 24  2021 my_third_file
-rw-rw-r-- 1 me me   60 Jan 29  2021 my_very_first_file
me@MyLinuxBox:~/Projects/MyScripts$
```

Alright. Now we will start with $ find in its most basic form: $ find <pathname>. In the ~/Projects/MyScripts directory, type in the command as shown below.

$ find .

```
                                            me@MyLinuxBox: ~/Projects/MyScripts
me@MyLinuxBox:~/Projects/MyScripts$ find .
.
./my_very_first_file
./my_third_file
./bak
./bak.bak
./my_second_file
me@MyLinuxBox:~/Projects/MyScripts$
```

Here we haven't specified any search parameters or [action]. We have simply included a <pathname> to establish the directory where to search: . (the cwd—see p. 50). When we call the command using the $ find <pathname> form as we have done here, the default behavior is for $ find to

1) search for all filetypes (regular files, directories, soft links, and special system files[103]) within <pathname>,
2) recurse through any directories (except soft-linked directories—this being the default behavior), and
3) print all results to stdout.

---

[103] These "special system files" are character device files, block device files, sockets, and named pipes. We are not covering these filetypes in this guide, but eventually you will want to familiarize yourself with these.

Notice the .̲ directory shortcut (see p. 45) is included in the search results whereas the .. directory shortcut is not in the results. This omission of .. is to prevent $ find from blindly recursing through the parent directory and acting on files or directories outside of the hierarchical tree structure stemming from <pathname>. If we invoke the -L [option], $ find *will* follow <u>soft links</u> from within <pathname> to files and directories in other places (and act upon them—even the parent directory of <pathname> if it is linked!). With the -L [option], $ find treats these <u>soft-linked</u> files and directories as being *within* the <pathname> tree structure ($ find is built to detect any infinite loops in the soft-link-extended tree structure and terminate with an error if it gets stuck). Still, $ find will not recurse into the parent directory via .. because .. is <u>not</u> a soft link and the user has no control over the presence of .. in <pathname> (i.e., .. is not a result of the user's configuration, so $ find ignores ..).

We'll continue getting acquainted with $ find by moving one step back into the ~/Projects directory and calling $ find <pathname> again.

$ cd ..

$ find .

Here $ find searched through <pathname> (i.e., ~/Projects), located the ./MyScripts directory, and printed the directory path to stdout. Then $ find recursed through ./MyScripts—finding and printing all of the ./MyScripts contents.

If we continue in this trend and jump another step backward, we will be in ~. When you run $ find . in the home directory, the number of search results can become quite large. Prepare to have your terminal window inundated with every file, directory, and soft link in the home directory (there won't be any special system files[103] in ~).

$ cd ..

$ find .

You will see a long list flash before you with the command line prompt directly below it. How many items was that? Let's find out. We'll run the same command again, but this time we'll pipe into $ wc (see p. 64). By using the -l [option] with $ wc, we'll tell the command not to do an actual word count but instead to count the number of lines that $ find returns in its search results.

$ find . | wc -l

```
me@MyLinuxBox:~$ find . | wc -l
39181
me@MyLinuxBox:~$
```

The number you get might be quite different from above—depending on how many software packages you have installed. At a minimum, a typical Ubuntu home directory would have around 250 items.

To find out exactly how many *files* there are in the home directory, we can call $ find again using the -type -f flag in the [expression] position (see p. 153) to narrow the search results down to just regular files (i.e., no directories or soft links). Let's try this.

$ find . -type -f | wc -l

```
me@MyLinuxBox:~$ find . -type f | wc -l
36752
me@MyLinuxBox:~$
```

Continuing in this way, we can use -type d to give us specifically the number of directories in ~.

$ find . -type -d | wc -l

```
me@MyLinuxBox:~$ find . -type d | wc -l
2147
me@MyLinuxBox:~$
```

And why not the number of soft links as well with -type l.

$ find . -type l | wc -l

```
me@MyLinuxBox:~$ find . -type l | wc -l
282
me@MyLinuxBox:~$
```

Doing a little arithmetic, $\boxed{282}$ + $\boxed{2147}$ + $\boxed{36752}$ = $\boxed{39181}$. Nice. Be aware that if you have installed any web browsers or other large software applications that happen to be running when you perform these searches through all of ~, the number of files can vary dynamically from one second to the next—which can make it seem like the total is off. A group command would be a good remedy for this (see p. 121).

Now we'll modify the $ find search with the -name flag to look for items whose <u>n</u>ames match a text <pattern> (i.e., search term) that we specify as an argument. The <pattern> we are searching for here is the familiar .bashrc filename.

$ find . -name .bashrc

```
me@MyLinuxBox:~$ find . -name .bashrc
./.bashrc
me@MyLinuxBox:~$
```

That was predictable! When we search for a <pattern> with no wildcard operator (e.g., no *), $ find won't return any results unless there is an exact verbatim match. Sometimes this may be what we want, but it is often more useful for a search to return a set of closely matching results. Let's try performing a **wildcard search** with the * operator to find all items in <pathname> whose names start with .bash.

$ find . -name .bash*

```
me@MyLinuxBox:~$ find . -name .bash*
find: paths must precede expression: `.bash_history'
find: possible unquoted pattern after predicate `-name'?
me@MyLinuxBox:~$
```

What? Didn't we enter it correctly? This $ find error is a famous showstopper in Linux—having perplexed many-a-Linux-user. The problem here has to do with the way <u>the shell</u> expands the .bash* glob (see p. 113) to every matching item in the cwd *before* $ find even receives input. In this case, since the shell sees more than one match in ~ for .bash*, $ find ends up with <u>several</u> filenames listed after -name and doesn't know what to do with them.

The way to fix this is by simply enclosing .bash* in **double quotes**[104]: ".bash*". Among the many things that double quotes do in Linux, one of their main uses is to *hide* (i.e., suppress) certain

---

[104] Single quotes would work here as well because $ find simply wants a string literal .bash* in its argument.

metacharacters from the shell's view—one of these being the * operator. Hiding * effectively means the shell cannot perform a * glob for matching names in the cwd. In our case here, double quotes will allow `$ find` to receive the literal string `.bash*` after `-name` (and not a list of every name in ~ starting with the `.bash <pattern>`).

But the `.bash*` string that `$ find` receives in its input can't be interpreted literally as the `<pattern>` to search for, right? How does the `.bash*` wildcard get evaluated if not by the shell? The `$ find` command itself has this capability! Unlike most commands, `$ find` has its own wildcard expansion faculties and does <u>not</u> rely on the shell to perform * globbing. This makes sense considering that `$ find` needs to be able to conduct * wildcard searches recursively in sub-directories within `<pathname>` (traditionally, globbing performed by the shell is only in the context of the cwd[105]).

Let's try our wildcard search again, but this time with double quotes around the search `<pattern>`.

`$ find . -name ".bash*"`

```
me@MyLinuxBox: ~
me@MyLinuxBox:~$ find . -name ".bash*"
./.bash_history
./.bash_aliases
./.bash_logout
./.bashrc
./.bashrc.bak
me@MyLinuxBox:~$
```

Now we're getting somewhere! In the results we see the `./.bashrc.bak` file that we made four chapters ago. Let's try searching through the home directory for any other items whose names end with `.bak`.

`$ find . -name "*.bak"`

```
me@MyLinuxBox: ~
me@MyLinuxBox:~$ find . -name "*.bak"
./Projects/MyScripts/bak.bak
./.bashrc.bak
me@MyLinuxBox:~$
```

Ah, yes. We just made this `./Projects/MyScripts/bak.bak` file earlier. Notice that `$ find` has recursed into `./Projects/MyScripts`, but it hasn't recursed through the `./MyScripts` soft link that we set up in the last chapter (see p. 146). This is because the default behavior for `$ find` is <u>not</u> to

---

[105] Since Bash version 4.0, the shell is capable of doing recursive glob searching through sub-directories within the cwd. This is achieved with the ** ("globstar") operator, which is enabled through `$ shopt -s globstar`.

follow soft links; however, we can change this by invoking the `-L` [option]. Just for educational purposes, let's see what happens when we include `-L` as an [option].

$$\$ \text{ find -L . -name "*.bak"}$$

```
me@MyLinuxBox:~$ find -L . -name "*.bak"
./MyScripts/bak.bak
./Projects/MyScripts/bak.bak
./.bashrc.bak
me@MyLinuxBox:~$
```

You can see why this is not the default behavior for `$ find`! In the results we have two instances of the same file. Enabling the `-L` [option] with `$ find` is really only useful if soft links extend beyond the internal <pathname> directory structure.

Moving along, now we will specify an [action] (other than the default `-print`) for `$ find` to perform on search results. The first [action] we'll try is `$ ls` (`$ ls -dils`, in effect). We won't be calling `$ ls` directly, but instead we will do a search with `$ find` and include the `-ls` flag in the [action] position (see p. 153). With the `-ls` flag, `$ find` automatically calls `$ ls -dils` in the background to return a formatted list of the search results. Try it as shown below.

$$\$ \text{ find . -name "bak*" -ls}$$

```
me@MyLinuxBox:~$ find . -name "bak*" -ls
 5253102     4 -rwxrwxr-x   2 me        me             493 Sep  5 05:49 ./Projects/MyScripts/bak
 5773518     4 -rwxrwxr-x   1 me        me             493 Sep 16 06:13 ./Projects/MyScripts/bak.bak
 5253102     4 -rwxrwxr-x   2 me        me             493 Sep  5 05:49 ./bin/bak
me@MyLinuxBox:~$
```

Here in this list we see the three items in <pathname> whose names start with bak. The `-i` [option] in the `$ ls -dils` command (called in the background by `$ find`) stands for "inode". An **inode** is a record in the file system database that Linux maintains for keeping track of where[106] each item's data is located on the physical storage medium. You can see the **inode number** for each file in the left-most column. Notice that ./Projects/MyScripts/bak and ./bin/bak have the same inode number, whereas ./Projects/MyScripts/bak.bak has a different inode number. This is because we used `$ ln` to create ./Projects/MyScripts/bak as a hard link to the same data that underlies ./bin/bak. The ./Projects/MyScripts/bak.bak file, however, was not linked but *copied* (with `$ cp`), so it received its own inode (see the footnotes on p. 146 for more information).

---

[106] Inodes also store other metadata about files—such as filetype, permissions, and access/modify/change times.

Also, in the third column from the left, we can see that all of these files have the same permissions. Let's try doing a search with `$ find` using the `-perm` flag and specifying these files' p̲ermissions as the search criteria. We will also use the `-type f` flag to limit the results to f̲iles.

```
$ find . -type f -perm u=rwx,g=rwx,o=rx
```

```
me@MyLinuxBox: ~
me@MyLinuxBox:~$ find . -type f -perm u=rwx,g=rwx,o=rx
./Projects/MyScripts/bak
./Projects/MyScripts/bak.bak
./bin/bak
me@MyLinuxBox:~$
```

All of these files have r̲ead, w̲rite, and e̲x̲ecutable permissions set for the u̲ser (i.e. owner) and the primary g̲roup (see p. 40). The "o̲ther" category is set with r̲ead and e̲x̲ecutable permissions (see p. 54).

These permissions are fine for a single-user system, but what if we wanted to restrict e̲x̲ecutable permissions to just the u̲ser and primary g̲roup in a multi-user system? We could perform `$ chmod` on each file, but why do that when we can accomplish this more efficiently with the `$ find` command? To make this work we will apply the `$ find` command's powerful `-exec` flag, which lets us act on search result files using any external command that we specify as an argument after `-exec`. To demonstrate, we will append the `$ find` command above with `-exec chmod` to set the files' permissions to `-rwxr-x---` (see p. 129 for reference). For `$ chmod` to take effect, we include `{}` to represent each search result in the `<operand>` of the `$ chmod` command. We also place a `;` to indicate to `$ find` the end of the `$ chmod` segment (while using `\` to escape `;`—see p. 56).

```
$ find . -type f -perm u=rwx,g=rwx,o=rx -exec chmod u=rwx,g=rx,o= {} \;
```

```
me@MyLinuxBox: ~
me@MyLinuxBox:~$ find . -type f -perm u=rwx,g=rwx,o=rx -exec chmod u=rwx,g=rx,o= {} \;
me@MyLinuxBox:~$ find . -name "bak*" -ls
 5253102    4 -rwxr-x---    2 me        me        493 Sep  5 05:49 ./Projects/MyScripts/bak
 5773518    4 -rwxr-x---    1 me        me        493 Sep 16 06:13 ./Projects/MyScripts/bak.bak
 5253102    4 -rwxr-x---    2 me        me        493 Sep  5 05:49 ./bin/bak
me@MyLinuxBox:~$
```

Following with `$ find . -name "bak*" -ls` as before, we see that the permissions for each search result now show `-rwxr-x---`.

The `-exec` flag with `$ find` gives us new potency on the command line, but we must be careful with it because, if mishandled, we can cause widespread damage[107]. Fortunately, combinations between

---

[107] In addition to `-exec`, extra caution needs to be practiced with the `$ find` command's `-delete` flag.

160

$ `find` and other commands are harmless if we are just *searching* for information, and one of the most powerful such partnerships in all of Linux is $ `find` combined with $ `grep`.

We will try this[108] with $ `grep` searching through file contents using the `-l [option]`, which makes $ `grep` return the name of any file containing a `<pattern>` match.

$$\$ \text{ find . -type f -exec grep -l "howdy" \{\} \textbackslash;}$$

```
                                                              me@MyLinuxBox: ~
me@MyLinuxBox:~$ find . -type f -exec grep -l "howdy" {} \;
./.bash_history
./.bashrc
me@MyLinuxBox:~$
```

Those are the files where the "howdy" `<pattern>` would be, if anywhere. We encourage you to continue searching for things in the file system and testing different search criteria. There are dozens more features for both $ `find` and $ `grep` waiting for you to explore in the $ `man` pages.

Basic Linux process management

A key part in anyone's Linux journey is learning how to work with processes, and here we are going to be introducing some of the basic tools used for process management in the shell.

What are processes in Linux?

In the most general sense, a process is a program running on the computer. Since there are many programs to run and only so many CPUs available, the Linux kernel must ration the amount of time each program spends on the CPU to make sure there is enough CPU time to go around for all programs that need it. The way the Linux kernel keeps track of these programs waiting in queue for the CPU is by assigning each program a **Process ID** (PID) and then selectively switching between the processes in a round-robin fashion—giving highest priority to the processes that are most urgent and/or resource hungry.

In this sense, a process in Linux is a program in action, and the activity is labeled with a Process ID (PID) which follows the program as it is executed or waiting to be executed. When a program's task is complete, the kernel terminates the process and retires its PID (until the PID is later recycled).

---

[108] We could achieve the same results with $ `grep -sl "howdy" * .*` (which effectively puts every `<filename>` and `<directoryname>` from the cwd into the argument of the command). We could even do a recursive search with $ `grep` by adding the `-r [option]`. Basing a search like this on $ `find` may become a better choice, however, if we need to use certain file attributes as search parameters. To each their own!

To get some practice with Linux process management, let's call a command that will give us a long-running process. This way we will have ample time to inspect the process before it terminates. In the home directory, enter the command as shown below.

A note on the following command: so that we don't accumulate a mountain of search results in the terminal window, we are using the &> redirection operator to send both stdout and stderr into a new file named find_output (written in the cwd). Also, by including the & operator at the trailing end, we are telling Bash to run this command as a **background job**. This will allow us to continue using the shell while the command executes in the background.

$ find / -type f -exec grep "bak" {} \; &> find_output &

```
                                                            me@MyLinuxBox: ~
me@MyLinuxBox:~$ find / -type f -exec grep "bak" {} \; &> find_output &
[1] 2652
me@MyLinuxBox:~$
```

In the output, the shell displays a [1], signifying that our command's background job number is 1. Next to the job number is 2652, which is the $ find command's **PID** assigned by the kernel.

$ jobs

Jobs, not to be confused with processes, are a construct in Linux for keeping track of commands running in the background (e.g., when we call a command with an & at the end). Sometimes a command can initiate more than one process—such as ours above where we are running both $ find and $ grep together ($ find and $ grep constitute one process each—so, two processes). The "job" in this case would be the logical grouping of the two processes together ($ find and $ grep). If we had a single-process command running in the background, it would also be tracked as a job (because any command running in the background is treated as a job). We can use the $ jobs utility to confirm that our command above is running as a background job.

$ jobs

```
                                                            me@MyLinuxBox: ~
me@MyLinuxBox:~$ jobs
[1]+  Running                 find / -type f -exec grep "bak" {} \; &> find_output &
me@MyLinuxBox:~$
```

Great. Now let's take a look at a list of the most CPU-hungry processes currently active on the machine.

$ top

Calling the $ top command displays a dynamically updating list of processes ordered by CPU consumption (this is the default $ top configuration). The processes listed are those currently at the "top" of the kernel's process-scheduling priority.

$ top

```
 ⊓                                                    me@MyLinuxBox: ~
top - 06:24:59 up 3 min,  1 user,  load average: 1.39, 1.13, 0.50
Tasks: 250 total,   1 running, 249 sleeping,   0 stopped,   0 zombie
%Cpu(s): 10.0 us, 16.2 sy,  0.4 ni, 66.8 id,  0.5 wa,  0.0 hi,  6.0 si,  0.0 st
MiB Mem :  15944.6 total,  10875.6 free,    732.0 used,   4337.1 buff/cache
MiB Swap:   2048.0 total,   2048.0 free,      0.0 used.  14764.4 avail Mem
add filter #1 (ignoring case) as: [!]FLD?VAL USER=me
   PID USER      PR  NI    VIRT    RES    SHR S  %CPU  %MEM     TIME+ COMMAND
  2652 me        20   0   11184   3532   3008 S  13.6   0.0   0:12.70 find
  1598 me        20   0  742920  49636  23236 S   8.3   0.3   0:05.94 Xorg
  1749 me        20   0 4328580 230412  82456 S   5.6   1.4   0:10.21 gnome-shell
  2602 me        20   0  814560  50780  38276 S   5.3   0.3   0:02.67 gnome-terminal-
 11391 me        20   0  439796  48868  15044 S   1.7   0.3   0:00.93 tracker-store
```

Here we see our find process and its PID of 2652 at the very top of the list (likely different on your machine), reportedly consuming 13.6 percent of the CPU time available. There is a lot of information here, so we will focus on the points most relevant to monitoring our $ find command process.

To filter the output of $ top to display just processes associated with your <username>, you can type a lowercase u and then enter your <username> (when prompted for Which user), or you can type a lowercase o and then enter USER=<username> at the [!]FLD?VAL prompt (as shown above).

Take a look at the Tasks field in the second line (directly below where it says top). There are 250 total tasks (i.e., processes) that the kernel has under its watch, with 1 running and 249 sleeping. Is the running process our $ find command?

If you look at the S column (for State), you will see our find process shows an S (for Sleeping). But how can a process be sleeping and yet consume a substantial percentage of the CPU? This points out the need for a little patience with $ top. If you stare at the find row for a while as the list updates, you might occasionally see an R flash momentarily (for Running) in the S column. This means as $ top updates, there is a greater probability that it will catch our $ find process waiting (i.e., sleeping) than it will catch the process running on the CPU. This sleeping occurs because the $ find process is requesting disk access and has to wait for the kernel to complete an I/O operation before proceeding to the next step. Depending on machine specs and other factors, the sleep-run-sleep-run switching for $ find can happen several hundred times (or more) per second—on the order of milliseconds (or less) for the duration of each process state (sleeping or running). You can verify this on your machine by entering $ `sudo strace -p <PID>` while the $ `find` command is running (we will talk about this soon—if you do try this now you'll need to quit $ `top` first by pressing q).

So, where is our grep command process? Wasn't $ `find` supposed to call $ `grep` to search through every file for the `bak <pattern>` and return each positive match? How long it takes $ `grep` to start is dependent on a number of factors, but sooner or later $ `find` will initiate the $ `grep` process. When $ `grep` does kick in, you may see the find and grep rows vying back and forth for the top spot, but eventually, when $ `grep` starts sifting through large system files, find will take a backseat and grep will assume the top position.

```
 ⌐⌐                                                      me@MyLinuxBox: ~

top - 06:31:30 up 9 min,  1 user,  load average: 1.45, 1.27, 0.79
Tasks: 240 total,   2 running, 238 sleeping,   0 stopped,   0 zombie
%Cpu(s): 16.1 us,  9.0 sy,  0.0 ni, 74.9 id,  0.0 wa,  0.0 hi,  0.0 si,  0.0 st
MiB Mem :  15944.6 total,   9067.5 free,    726.0 used,   6151.1 buff/cache
MiB Swap:   2048.0 total,   2048.0 free,      0.0 used.  14764.6 avail Mem

    PID USER      PR  NI    VIRT    RES    SHR S  %CPU  %MEM     TIME+ COMMAND
 209281 me        20   0    8908   2456   2216 R 100.0   0.0   0:51.50 grep
   2652 me        20   0   11784   4148   3008 S   0.0   0.0   1:11.89 find
   3733 me        20   0  162264   6308   5672 S   0.0   0.0   0:00.04 gvfsd-metadata
   3752 me        20   0  420420  31488  22036 S   0.0   0.2   0:00.22 update-notifier
  14871 me        20   0  314100   8400   7460 S   0.0   0.1   0:00.04 gvfsd-network
  15853 me        20   0  314988   8308   7352 S   0.0   0.1   0:00.01 gvfsd-dnssd
  26351 me        20   0   12016   4088   3300 R   0.0   0.0   0:01.10 top
 209283 me        20   0  439788  48956  15316 S   0.0   0.3   0:00.23 tracker-store
 209358 me        20   0  735092  45896  35060 S   0.0   0.3   0:00.50 gnome-screensho
```

Such can be seen happening above. In this process state, $ `find` is truly sleeping waiting for $ `grep` because it takes $ `grep` a long time to get through the mountains of gibberish in some system files (even running at `100.00 %CPU`!). The $ `grep` process, unlike $ `find`, does not have to wait for disk I/O, so $ `grep` is able to consume a higher percentage of the CPU when it runs (in this case, anyway). If you stare at the grep row for any length of time, you will notice that its PID changes every now and then. This is because every time $ `grep` finishes searching through a file, that particular $ `grep` process terminates, and then $ `find` calls $ `grep` again to search through another file. When $ `grep` is called again, the kernel assigns a new PID and we see the PID number for $ `grep` go up incrementally. Depending on system configuration, eventually the kernel will hit its PID ceiling and will have to start recycling lower-number PIDs—so we see the PID for $ `grep` jump back to a lower number (and start crawling up again).

The $ `top` utility has a deep feature set and is highly customizable. Pressing the h key for help gives an overview of the many key commands available. Taking some time to absorb the $ `man` pages for $ `top` is also recommended. Let's now quit $ `top` by pressing q and return to the command line.

$ ps

The $ ps command (for process status) gives us a static snapshot view of processes currently active on our machine. This can be useful when we want to get a quick look at what is happening without all the commotion of $ top. Calling $ ps with the -a [option] tells the command to filter down to "all" of the processes that we have initiated directly (excluding the Terminal app and its descendants, one of which is Bash). Many of the processes running are initiated automatically by the Terminal app after we launch it, or from the cascade of other processes originating from when Linux boots up.

$ ps -a

```
me@MyLinuxBox:~$ ps -a
    PID TTY          TIME CMD
   1598 tty2     00:00:15 Xorg
   1624 tty2     00:00:00 gnome-session-b
   2652 pts/0    00:01:11 find
 209281 pts/0    00:01:11 grep
 209395 pts/0    00:00:00 ps
me@MyLinuxBox:~$
```

This shows that the same grep process with PID 209281 is still churning away. If you want to view the entire list of all ~250 active processes, try entering $ ps -aux. At the very top of the list, you will see that PID 1 is init (or init splash), which is the first program that the kernel launches during the boot sequence.

Now we'll get a peek into exactly what our $ find process is doing.

$ strace

The $ strace command is a powerful tool that lets us see in low-level detail a "system trace" of what is actually going on behind the curtain as a process executes. We can call $ strace with any external command in the argument (as in, $ strace <command>), and $ strace will return a running report on the command's **system calls**. System calls are requests that external commands make to the kernel for services like accessing the file system, storing things in memory, and other tasks that require the kernel's direct negotiation with the machine. As an example, if you enter $ strace ls, you'll get an eye into how the $ ls command petitions the kernel to read the contents of the cwd. Try it!

We are going to call $ strace with the -p [option] to inspect the current state of our $ find command process. Because using $ strace this way essentially lets us put a "wiretap" on an active process, we have to assume elevated status with $ sudo to make this happen (see p. 98).

```
$ sudo strace -p <PID>
```

And here is how we know that our $ find command is waiting specifically for the current $ grep process to finish. The $ find command's wait4() system call (end parenthesis added for clarity) is telling the kernel not to proceed with execution of $ find until the $ find command's **child process** (PID 209281—i.e., the current $ grep process) returns an exit status of 0 (meaning that $ find needs its child $ grep process to complete successfully in order for $ find to continue—see p. 143).

This illustrates how processes in Linux[109] have parent/child relationships—in direct analogy to the parent shell/child shell relationship that we've talked about (a child shell is a child process spawned from its parent shell as the parent process—see p. 130).

$ pstree

To further investigate the parent/child process relationship, we can call $ pstree to display a tree structure diagram of all currently active processes. We'll pipe into $ grep to filter the results down to our currently active $ find command process.

```
$ pstree | grep find
```

```
                                                    me@MyLinuxBox: ~
me@MyLinuxBox:~$ pstree | grep find
       |            |-gnome-terminal--+-bash-+-find---grep
me@MyLinuxBox:~$ █
```

In this line we see that the parent of grep (PID 209281 from above) is find, that the parent of find is bash, and that the parent of bash is the gnome-terminal. You could call $ pstree by itself and trace the lineage through the entire family tree all the way back to init. Note here that bash as the parent of find is an example of the way Bash handles execution of external commands ($ find is an external command). If you opened another shell and did an $ strace -f -p <PID> (<PID> being the PID of the first shell here) to monitor Bash during the launch process for $ find, you would

---

[109] The Linux kernel itself is technically not a process—having no parent. The kernel does CPU bookkeeping for itself with what are called threads (processes are just "fat threads" to the kernel).

observe Bash making a `clone(2)` system call to create a copy of itself in RAM (i.e., a "fork") and an `execve(2)` system call to replace the copy of itself with the `/usr/bin/find` executable binary (which then would run as the `$ find` command—see p. 130 for reference).

$ kill

And when we're done with a process and ready for it to end, we can expedite this by calling the `$ kill` command with the `<PID>` in the argument. Let's try this now on our `$ find` command process. We'll do another `$ ps -a` first to make sure that the process is still active.

$ ps -a

$ kill <PID>

```
                                              me@MyLinuxBox: ~
me@MyLinuxBox:~$ ps -a
    PID TTY          TIME CMD
   1598 tty2     00:00:21 Xorg
   1624 tty2     00:00:00 gnome-session-b
   2652 pts/0    00:01:11 find
 209777 pts/0    00:00:00 grep
 209778 pts/0    00:00:00 ps
me@MyLinuxBox:~$ kill 2652
me@MyLinuxBox:~$
```

Now if you call `$ ps -a` again, you will see that the `find` line is no longer there. If a `grep` child process is still running, it will continue on as an **orphan process** until it terminates. Of course, you could also do a `$ kill <PID>` on the running `grep` process if you don't want to wait. Another alternative would be, rather than killing the processes one at a time, to use the `$ kill` command with the commands' job number (see p. 162) in the argument. In this case, this would be done by entering `$ kill %1` (the % symbol in front distinguishes the job number as not a PID). Then both processes would terminate at (nearly) the same time.

Software package management

One of the amenities of using a well-established Linux distribution like Ubuntu, Mint, Fedora, CentOS, or Red Hat Enterprise Linux is the package management support that comes built-in to the system. These and other major distros feature integrated "package manager" utilities for monitoring the version numbers of all software present on a machine. Package manager utilities (a.k.a. "package managers") are capable of tracking, installing, updating, and/or removing software, including GUI applications, command line programs, and system components (even the Linux kernel). In Ubuntu, package management is handled through the APT (Advanced Packaging Tool) framework, which keeps a local database of installed software and matches it against large public software repositories maintained by Debian (Ubuntu's parent distribution) and other organizations. Ubuntu's APT services are available on the command line through the `$ apt` family of commands.

What is a "package" in Linux?

From a command line point of view, each external command[110] (including the shell itself) has a corresponding software "package" that it originates from. These "packages" in Linux are basically equivalent to "installers" in other operating systems, except that Linux packages are generally kept out of sight from the user—under the careful eye of the package manager (APT in the case of Ubuntu). Aside from making things easier for the user, keeping packages out of the user's hands gives a greater guarantee that the package manager's database for installed and installable packages won't get corrupted.

We can think of packages as being like downloadable "pods" from which our command line tools spring when they are installed or updated. Each one of these packages (or pods if you like) has a version number, and the package manager monitors the repositories online, checking for any package updates (reflected in the version numbers). If an update is released for an installed package, depending on settings, the package manager will notify the user of the available update. Then, the user may choose to proceed with downloading the update and installing it.

If and when we want to install, for instance, a new external command[110] on the command line, we simply call the package manager to take care of finding, downloading, and cataloging the command's package—from which the executable(s) and any supporting files are automatically installed. Furthermore, if we need to remove a command (or other software) from our system, the package manager will take care of this as well. One of the most convenient things about the APT framework is in the way it automatically tracks and updates all **dependencies** that a command (or other software) may have. Letting APT manage dependencies relieves us of having to worry about which additional programs need to be installed/updated in order to use a piece of software.

$ apt update

Whenever we do any package management tasks on the command line in Ubuntu, it is good practice to start with the `$ apt update` command. Calling this command causes APT to scan all of our installed packages and report on any available updates. Make sure you are connected to the internet, and then try this (package management tasks like this require elevated privileges through `$ sudo`).

```
$ sudo apt update
```

---

[110] The same is true of published scripted commands. For example, the `trash-cli` package, which we will download and install soon, contains a suite of commands written in Python.

```
me@MyLinuxBox: ~

me@MyLinuxBox:~$ sudo apt update
[sudo] password for me:
Hit:1 http://us.archive.ubuntu.com/ubuntu focal InRelease
Get:2 http://us.archive.ubuntu.com/ubuntu focal-updates InRelease [114 kB]
Hit:3 http://dl.google.com/linux/chrome/deb stable InRelease
Hit:4 http://packages.microsoft.com/repos/code stable InRelease
Get:5 http://security.ubuntu.com/ubuntu focal-security InRelease [114 kB]
Get:6 http://us.archive.ubuntu.com/ubuntu focal-backports InRelease [101 kB]
Fetched 328 kB in 1s (278 kB/s)
Reading package lists... Done
Building dependency tree
Reading state information... Done
14 packages can be upgraded. Run 'apt list --upgradable' to see them.
me@MyLinuxBox:~$
```

In the output list we see several software repositories where $ apt update has checked for updates to our currently installed packages. The entries marked with Hit indicate where our installed packages are up-to-date, and the Get entries indicate bundles that contain updates for us to download. At the bottom we learn that 14 packages can be upgraded. Let's take the suggestion given and view a list of these packages to upgrade (of course, different on your machine).

$ apt list

If you enter the next command within fifteen minutes of the previous one, you probably won't have to repeat $ sudo.

$ apt list --upgradable

```
me@MyLinuxBox: ~

me@MyLinuxBox:~$ apt list --upgradable
Listing... Done
gir1.2-udisks-2.0/focal-updates 2.8.4-1ubuntu2 amd64 [upgradable from: 2.8.4-1ubuntu1]
gnome-control-center-data/focal-updates,focal-updates 1:3.36.5-0ubuntu3 all [upgradable from: 1
gnome-control-center-faces/focal-updates,focal-updates 1:3.36.5-0ubuntu3 all [upgradable from:
gnome-control-center/focal-updates 1:3.36.5-0ubuntu3 amd64 [upgradable from: 1:3.36.5-0ubuntu2]
libnss-systemd/focal-updates 245.4-4ubuntu3.13 amd64 [upgradable from: 245.4-4ubuntu3.11]
libpam-systemd/focal-updates 245.4-4ubuntu3.13 amd64 [upgradable from: 245.4-4ubuntu3.11]
libsystemd0/focal-updates 245.4-4ubuntu3.13 amd64 [upgradable from: 245.4-4ubuntu3.11]
libudev1/focal-updates 245.4-4ubuntu3.13 amd64 [upgradable from: 245.4-4ubuntu3.11]
libudisks2-0/focal-updates 2.8.4-1ubuntu2 amd64 [upgradable from: 2.8.4-1ubuntu1]
systemd-sysv/focal-updates 245.4-4ubuntu3.13 amd64 [upgradable from: 245.4-4ubuntu3.11]
systemd-timesyncd/focal-updates 245.4-4ubuntu3.13 amd64 [upgradable from: 245.4-4ubuntu3.11]
systemd/focal-updates 245.4-4ubuntu3.13 amd64 [upgradable from: 245.4-4ubuntu3.11]
udev/focal-updates 245.4-4ubuntu3.13 amd64 [upgradable from: 245.4-4ubuntu3.11]
udisks2/focal-updates 2.8.4-1ubuntu2 amd64 [upgradable from: 2.8.4-1ubuntu1]
me@MyLinuxBox:~$
```

It looks like all of these packages are for programs and files used by the system. We place a lot of trust in APT on what to upgrade. Since we know the repositories listed above are all reputable sources, we can assume these upgrades are safe. Let's go ahead with it then.

$ apt upgrade

$ sudo apt upgrade

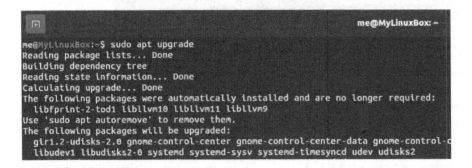

Good. Now we're going to try downloading a package from which we will install some new scripted commands. Several chapters ago, we spoke about installing a command line utility package called trash-cli (see p. 115).

To install trash-cli, first we will do a search to see if we can locate the correct package.

$ apt search

Again, you might not have to enter $ sudo if you enter this command within fifteen minutes of the previous command. We'll use trash as the <pattern> to search for here.

$ apt search trash

Scrolling through the search results reveals the entry shown below.

```
trash-cli/focal,focal,now 0.17.1.14-2ubuntu1 all
  command line trashcan utility
```

This is the package that we want. Now we can install this one by name.

$ apt install

$ sudo apt install trash-cli

```
me@MyLinuxBox: ~
me@MyLinuxBox:~$ sudo apt install trash-cli
[sudo] password for me:
Reading package lists... Done
Building dependency tree
Reading state information... Done
The following packages were automatically installed and are no longer required:
  libfprint-2-tod1 libllvm10 libllvm11 libllvm9
```

Great. Notice that $ apt has automatically taken care of installing some dependencies that the commands in our new trash-cli package require in order to function.

Once installed, looking at $ man trash, it says we can use $ trash-put to move files into ~/.local/share/Trash/files (the GNOME desktop trash directory—see p. 115). Let's try this on the ~/find_output file left behind from when we were testing the $ find command process.

$ trash-put find_output

```
me@MyLinuxBox: ~
me@MyLinuxBox:~$ trash-put find_output
me@MyLinuxBox:~$ ▮
```

Now let's check that the file made it into the ~/.local/share/Trash/files directory.

$ trash-list

```
me@MyLinuxBox: ~
me@MyLinuxBox:~$ trash-list
2021-04-23 07:55:54 /home/me/Pictures/Screenshot from 2021-02-18 10-05-16.png
2021-09-04 08:39:50 /home/me/Pictures/Screenshot from 2021-09-04 07-52-19.png
2020-11-24 21:23:26 /home/me/Pictures/Screenshot from 2020-11-23 15-03-25.png
2021-09-18 08:01:22 /home/me/find_output
2021-09-17 04:53:01 /home/me/Pictures/Screenshot from 2021-09-17 04-45-54.png
2021-09-17 05:21:46 /home/me/Pictures/Screenshot from 2021-09-17 05-08-52.png
```

There it is. Whenever you like, you can use the command below to empty the trash.

$ trash-empty

That's it! We hope you find use for $ trash-put as a safe alternative to $ rm.

Summary:

The $ find command has the important duty of locating things in the Linux file system given a set of search criteria. But more than just locating things, $ find lets us act on the search results with other commands that we specify in the $ find command's argument. One powerful combination is to have $ find locate files narrowed by a set of attributes and $ grep search through file contents for a text <pattern>. We can also use this pairing of commands ($ find and $ grep) to investigate how their respective processes operate together as a background job. A key piece of information in analyzing any Linux process is the Process ID (PID)—the number assigned by the kernel to keep track of a process in its various states. There are powerful command line tools in Linux for observing and managing processes via their PIDs, and a lot can be learned about the innerworkings of an external command by tracing the activity of the command's process. Speaking of external commands, there are many more available beyond the ones that come pre-bundled with Ubuntu. If at any point we decide that we want to install new external commands (or published scripted commands), we can do so using the $ apt utility, which is part of Ubuntu's APT framework for browsing and managing software packages.

Commands:

$ find	$ kill
$ grep	$ sudo
$ jobs	$ apt update
$ top	$ apt list
$ ps	$ apt upgrade
$ strace	$ apt search
$ pstree	$ apt install

Concepts:

- Searching in the file system
  - Recursive search
  - Wildcard search with *
  - Double quotes "" to hide *
- Inodes
  - Inode number
- Processes in Linux
  - Process ID (PID)

- Background jobs
- System calls
- Parent/child processes
- Orphan processes
- Software package management
  - APT package manager
  - Dependencies
  - Installing new commands

Challenge:

On p. 166, we mentioned using $ strace to monitor the system calls that Bash makes during the launch process of an external command. To monitor these calls, first, open another shell tab in the Terminal app window by clicking on the ▣ icon. In this second shell tab, you'll need to get the PID of the shell in the first tab. Then, enter $ sudo strace -e clone,execve -f -p <PID> in the second shell. After that, if you go back to the first shell and enter an external command, you will see the clone(2) and execve(2) system calls from Bash appear in the output in the second shell.

Final Project

For your final project in this guide, you will be creating a new shell function as described below.

Function name: `$ hst`
Synopsis: `$ hst <pattern>`
Description: Calling `$ hst <pattern>` returns a list of all instances of `<pattern>` from the command history. The typical use would be to search the command history for times that `<pattern>` has been called as a command (e.g., `$ hst <command>`).

A bit of advice:
There are several ways you could accomplish this task, but basing your function on the `$ history` command would probably be the most convenient.

$ history

The `$ history` command returns a numbered list of the last `$HISTSIZE` (typically 2000) commands that have been called on the command line. Try it!

```
$ history
```

In the output, you will see a numerically ordered list of past commands. The special thing about this list is that if you want to *repeat* any of these commands, you can simply enter `!` directly followed by the command number (as in, `$ ![#]`), and that command will execute exactly as it was previously entered. To experiment, pick a command from the list that you'd like to run again and then try executing it using the `$ ![#]` method.

Now, for your `$ hst` function, if you incorporate the `$ history` command in the function's code, when you call the function with a past command as the `<pattern>` in the argument, the output should look something like shown below (`$ hst vim` is given as an example of `$ hst <command>`).

```
me@MyLinuxBox:~$ hst vim
 1104  vim .bashrc
 1565  vim ..
 1576  vim MyScripts/
 1578  vim .
 1735  less .viminfo
 2005  vim .bashrc
 2010  vim bak
 2012  vim .bashrc
 2024  vim .bashrc
 2034  hst vim
me@MyLinuxBox:~$
```

Best of luck!

Appendix A – More on permissions in Linux

Octal notation for permissions

We know the familiar nine-character scheme for representing permissions in the shell. These nine permissions "slots" are viewable in the output of $ ls -la (to focus on permissions, we have omitted the filetype slot that would normally appear in the first position on the left—see p. 54).

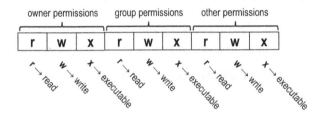

This view is informative, but it is not the only way permissions are represented in Linux. There is another method used in the shell for indicating permissions, and this other method is based on **octal** numbers. For a number to be "octal", the range of numerals in a single digit is not 2 (as in binary), or 10 (as in decimal), but 8 (as in, octal). This means octal numerals range from 0-7 (in comparison—binary numerals range from 0-1, and decimal from 0-9).

Below is a chart showing how Linux file system permissions are represented in **octal notation**.

Octal notation	Symbolic
0	---
1	--x
2	-w-
3	-wx
4	r--
5	r-x
6	rw-
7	rwx

Each value 0-7 encodes a different combination of the three permissions (rwx) given to a permissions class (owner, group, or "other") for an item in the file system.

For instance, if a directory's permissions are rwxrwxrwx (see the example above), the same permissions would be represented in octal notation as 777.

rwxrwxrwx
7 7 7

Umask

When we create a new file or directory in the Linux file system, there is a mechanism called **umask** ("user file-creation mode mask") for controlling what permissions get assigned to the new item. For example, when we make a new file with $ touch or a new directory with $ mkdir, the umask setting determines the permissions given to the new file or directory. This same umask setting applies to *all* new files and directories, regardless of what commands we use to create them ($ touch and $ mkdir are just common examples).

In the absence of a umask, the "user file creation mode" in Linux sets the *default* permissions (in octal) to 777 for new directories and 666 for new files. This means, with no umask, all newly created directories would have rwxrwxrwx permissions, and all newly created files, rw-rw-rw-. Note that for security reasons, Linux strictly forbids creation of e**x**ecutable files by default (meaning, if a file owner wants an e**x**ecutable file, they can only make a file e**x**ecutable *after* it has been created).

This restriction on the creation of executable files is a welcome security measure, but what if we want to further limit the permissions assigned to new files or directories? Surely we don't want to give rw- permissions to the "other" category for every new file we create, nor do we want every new directory to have full rwxrwxrwx permissions!

True to its namesake, the umask works as a "mask" to block these default "user file creation mode" permissions. The way this works is by setting the umask to a 3-digit octal number that effectively masks (i.e. blocks) permissions that new files or directories would otherwise be assigned.

Let's say we were to create a new directory in Linux without using a umask. By default, the "user file creation mode" permissions (in octal) for a directory are 777. With a umask of 000 (i.e., <u>no</u> umask), the resulting permissions would remain 777 for the new directory (i.e., no change from the default rwxrwxrwx).

But with a umask of 002, the resulting permissions assigned to a new directory would be 775 (rwxrwxr-x). And, if we created a new file, our 002 umask would cause the file permissions to be 664 (i.e., rw-rw-r--).

Now, it is tempting to believe that we are subtracting the octal number 002 from 777 or 666 to arrive at 775 or 664 when applying the umask. It does look like this, but technically, when applying a umask, we are not subtracting octal numbers. To see how the umask mechanism really works, we will convert these octal numbers into binary form and observe what happens when we "superimpose" one number on top of the other.

Octal notation	Binary	Symbolic
0	000	---
1	001	--x
2	010	-w-
3	011	-wx
4	100	r--
5	101	r-x
6	110	rw-
7	111	rwx

Here we have added a column with the equivalent binary form of each octal number (counting in binary, 000 is 0, 001 is 1, 010 is 2...and 111 is 7). Notice that each instance of the binary numeral 1 directly corresponds with a slot in the symbolic pattern where permission is given, and the binary numeral 0 corresponds with slots where permission is <u>withheld</u>.

Let's see what happens when we take a umask of octal 002, convert it into binary, and then place it "on top of" the binary form of octal permissions 777.

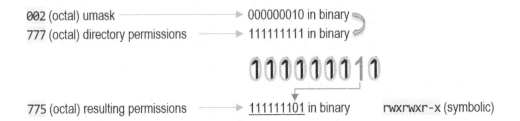

002 (octal) umask ⎯⎯⎯⎯⎯⎯⎯⎯⎯⎯⟶ 000000010 in binary

777 (octal) directory permissions ⎯⎯⟶ 111111111 in binary

010001010

775 (octal) resulting permissions ⎯⎯⟶ 111111101 in binary   rwxrwxr-x (symbolic)

When we "superimpose" this binary umask on top of the set of permissions, wherever there is an overlapping 1, the permissions bit changes to 0, and wherever there is a 0 on top of a 1, the permissions bit remains as a 1. This is what is meant by "masking" the default permissions—a bit with 1 in the umask "turns off" (i.e., "masks" or "hides") the corresponding bit in the default permissions. If a default permissions bit is already 0 (such as some of the bits we find in the "user file creation mode" rw-rw-rw- permissions for new files—110110110 in binary), then overlapping a umask bit of 1 will have no effect[111]—because the permissions bit with 0 is already "off". An overlapping umask bit of 0 on top of a 0 permissions bit also has no effect.

Even though we are technically not subtracting one octal number from another when we apply a umask (e.g., octal 6 (110) with a umask of octal 3 (011) results in octal 4 (100), yet 6 - 3 ≠ 4), the correct answer to many common umask calculations can be reached by "subtracting" the octal umask number from the octal permissions number (e.g., octal 777 permissions with umask 022 results in octal 755 permissions for directories). Because these results are correct often enough, many users find octal a convenient mode of working with the umask in Linux. We just have to be aware of when "subtracting" doesn't work (particularly when we mask[111] a 0 bit with a 1 bit).

$ umask

To view and/or customize umask settings, we have a command with the name of $ umask for this purpose. Entering the command by itself with no argument returns the current umask setting.

$ umask

---

[111] This is where binary "masking" differs from subtraction. In binary subtraction, a bitwise operation of 0 - 1 equals 1 with the 0 bit "borrowing" a 1 from the neighboring higher order bit to the left.

This 0002 in the output is the default umask setting for regular users in Ubuntu. To change the umask, we simply call the command with our preferred umask number in octal (e.g., $ umask 022—note that Linux automatically adds a leading 0 to make the resultant umask value 0022—we will discuss the reason for this soon). If we want to make our customized umask persist, we can place the command in ~/.bashrc and let the shell run the command at startup. Also, if you prefer not to use octal to set a custom umask, $ umask accepts symbolic permissions in the argument as well. Consult the $ man pages for more information.

You may be wondering to yourself where this extra 0 in front of 002 came from when we ran $ umask. Before we go into depth about why there is an extra 0 in the umask, there are two things you should know.

1. The umask setting is actually <u>four</u> octal digits rather than three.
2. Of the four octal digits in the umask, the first digit is always 0—as in, we can't change it.

If we can't change the leading 0, we could just ignore it because it has no effect (being 0). But why is it there?

The reason the umask setting has a 0 in the first digit is because, in truth, octal permissions are not just three digits in Linux. There is in fact *another* octal digit which adds extra control over file and directory permissions in addition to the three octal digits we have talked about. This additional octal digit, which is placed *before* the three digits, is reserved for what are known as "special permissions" in the Linux file system. Altogether, this makes for <u>four</u> digits in the octal permissions code carried by each file and directory. Because the umask is applied to every new file and directory, the umask is padded with a 0 in front to properly align with the four-digit code. Note that with its permanent 0 in the first octal digit, the umask has no effect on the "special permissions" assigned to a file or directory.

```
                                          me@MyLinuxBox: ~/Projects/MyScripts
me@MyLinuxBox:~/Projects/MyScripts$ stat my_first_file
  File: my_first_file
  Size: 0              Blocks: 0          IO Block: 4096    regular empty file
Device: 805h/2053d      Inode: 5768609    Links: 1
Access: (0664/ rw-rw-r--)  Uid: ( 1000/    me)   Gid: ( 1000/     me)
Access: 2020-12-26 16:59:19.152189027 -0500
Modify: 2020-12-26 16:59:19.152189027 -0500
Change: 2020-12-26 16:59:19.152189027 -0500
  Birth: -
me@MyLinuxBox:~/Projects/MyScripts$ 
```

Above we see the 0664 octal permissions code for a file. The 0 in the first digit indicates there are no special permissions assigned to this file. The file's permissions in symbolic form are rw-rw-r-- (visible to the right of the octal permissions code).

Special Permissions

Regarding special permissions in Linux, there are three of them for files and directories, and they are referred to as **SUID** (for Set User ID), **SGID** (for Set Group ID), and the **Sticky Bit.** In octal notation, special permissions are always represented in the first digit of the four-digit permissions code. Special permissions also have symbolic representation, as we shall see. Let's talk about what these special permissions do and how to detect their presence in files and directories.

SUID

We have seen how the processes we launch in the shell are associated with our `<username>` (see p. 163). We also know that our `<username>` is a more human-friendly representation of our **UID** (User ID—see p. 40). It is ultimately our UID that gets stamped onto the processes we launch in the shell, and what these processes can or cannot do in the file system is determined by our user status (as indicated by our UID, which is non-zero if we are not root). So, if, for example, we tried to use the `$ find` command to do a search in a directory to which we don't have access, we would get a `permission denied` error in return because the `$ find` process, being allowed only to do what is possible with our UID, doesn't have the privileges needed to access the directory. Sometimes this is tolerable, because, for example, the `$ find` command may just continue with its search elsewhere. But in other cases, being denied access to certain files or directories can break a command. This is where SUID ("Set User ID") special permissions come in.

SUID, also known as **setuid**, is a special permissions setting for compiled binaries[112] in the Linux file system. For a file to carry SUID permissions[113], the file must be

a) Executable
b) A compiled program (e.g., an external command, a binary GUI application, etc.)

When a regular user launches an executable file with SUID special permissions, even if the user is not the owner of the file, the process will run with privileges as if the *file owner* has launched the file. In this situation, we say that the **effective User ID** attached to the command process is the file owner's UID, and the **real User ID**[114] is the UID of the user who launched the file.

---

[112] For security reasons, the only types of files Linux allows to carry SUID or SGID permissions are executable binaries. This means we cannot have SUID or SGID permissions on executable shell scripts or other programs written in interpreted languages (Python, Perl, etc.). Directories, however, *can* be set with SGID permissions.
[113] If a file's SUID or SGID permissions are present and the file's executable permissions are removed (for example with `$ chmod -x <filename>`), an uppercase S will appear in the executable slot in the file owner's permissions (e.g., `rwSr--r--`) or the group permissions (e.g., `rw-r-Sr--`), respectively. This S indicates that the SUID or SGID permissions are inactive.
[114] To avoid conflicts, processes with root SUID permissions often change the real User ID to 0 (i.e., root's UID).

SUID permissions are most often applied where an external command's executable file is owned by root and the action performed by the command is something requiring root status to complete. If a regular user tries to run a command like this, without root SUID permissions set for the executable file, Linux will prohibit execution of the command because the regular user's UID (worn as a badge by the process) lacks the privileges needed to perform the command's action. Some regular users may get around this by calling `$ sudo <command>`[115], but this would require that the user is a member of the sudo group[116]. If the user is not a member of the sudo group, for the user to be able to run a process requiring root status, special permissions are needed so the process can set the effective User ID to the UID of the executable file owner (which is 0 for root).

A classic example of SUID permissions in action is when we use the `$ su` command to "<u>s</u>ubstitute" as another "<u>u</u>ser" on the command line (see p. 100). The default Ubuntu configuration[117] doesn't let us `$ su` as root. However, we can `$ su` as another regular user if we control the other user account. The feature that enables `$ su` to authenticate[118] the password we type in to access the other user account is the `/usr/bin/su` file's root SUID permissions.

```
                                                    me@MyLinuxBox: /usr/bin
me@MyLinuxBox:/usr/bin$ ll su ; stat su
-rwsr-xr-x 1 root root 67816 Jul 21  2020 su*
  File: su
  Size: 67816        Blocks: 136        IO Block: 4096    regular file
Device: 805h/2053d   Inode: 398561      Links: 1
Access: (4755/(rwsr-xr-x)  Uid: (   0/    root)   Gid: (   0/    root)
Access: 2021-09-29 13:54:16.905603584 -0400
Modify: 2020-07-21 03:49:28.000000000 -0400
Change: 2020-09-28 19:17:17.554309799 -0400
  Birth: -
me@MyLinuxBox:/usr/bin$
```

Here we see the `/usr/bin/su` file's permissions in both octal 4755 and symbolic rwsr-xr-x form. The 4 in the first digit of the octal code indicates that the `/usr/bin/su` file's SUID permissions are active. The same is indicated by the lowercase s in the file owner's executable permissions slot in symbolic form: rwsr-xr-x. Notice the Uid for the file owner is shown as 0/ root.

---

[115] The `$ sudo` command, which enables non-root users to run commands as root, itself relies on the root SUID permissions given to the `/usr/bin/sudo` file. To access `$ sudo`, a regular user must be a member of the sudo group. Aside from `$ sudo`, there are several other executables that have their root SUID permissions set. This makes these commands accessible to regular users without requiring the use of `$ sudo` (`$ su` being an example).

[116] Members of the sudo group are listed in the `/etc/sudoers` configuration file. Be careful with this file. You should never have to edit it because sudo group management is handled via the `$ sudo` command. If for some reason you ever try to edit the file (hopefully you won't), use the `$ visudo` special-purpose editor for this task. If you try to edit the file with a regular text editor like `$ vim`, you will damage the file (which can lead to catastrophic system failure).

[117] Users are unable to log in as root in Ubuntu systems because no password is set for the root account in the `/etc/shadow` file.

The file which the $ su command must access to obtain user account passwords is the /etc/shadow file (see below).

```
-rw-r-----   1 root shadow  1753 Mar 14  2021 shadow
-rw-r-----   1 root shadow  1623 Mar 14  2021 shadow-
```

Notice that only root and members of the shadow group may access this file. Hence, $ su must operate with root privileges in order to authenticate[118] typed-in passwords against those held in the /etc/shadow file.

In terms of setting SUID permissions for executable files, it is generally not something we should do ourselves because SUID permissions can pose security risks. It is best to leave the few files that have root SUID permissions as they are and not activate any other files' SUID permissions if we don't need to.

SGID

The SGID special permissions setting, short for "Set Group ID", is similar to SUID except the SGID permissions point to the **Group ID** (**GID**) associated with a binary executable, making the group's GID the **effective Group ID** attached to the process when it executes. This gives the process the group's privileges when a regular user launches the executable (whether the user is a member of the group or not).

Rather than the SUID octal value of 4, SGID permissions are represented by a 2 in the first digit of the four-digit octal code. A permissions code of 2755 in octal would translate to rwxr-sr-x in symbolic form (note the s is in the group permissions executable slot).

One use for SGID permissions that we don't see with SUID is the activation of SGID permissions on a directory. When SGID permissions are set on a directory, all new files and sub-directories created inside the directory will automatically take on the directory's group ownership as their group ownership as well. That is to say, the group that owns a parent directory with SGID permissions will automatically become the group owner for all new files and sub-directories created inside the directory. Despite this, a regular user who creates files and directories inside the SGID parent directory will still be those files' and directories' _user-owner_ (whether or not the user is a member of the parent directory's group). To set a directory with SGID permissions, the easiest way is to use $ chmod g+s <directoryname>. To remove SGID permissions from a directory, use $ chmod g-s <directoryname>.

---

[118] The $ su process itself isn't capable of authenticating passwords. Rather, when $ su obtains an encrypted password from /etc/shadow, $ su hands over the encrypted password along with the user's typed-in password to a subsystem in Linux called Pluggable Authentication Modules (PAM). Then PAM decrypts the stored password and authenticates the user's typed-in password against the stored one.

Sticky Bit

The sticky bit permissions setting gets its name from its former life in Unix when it was used on executable files to allow their code to "stick" around in swap space[119] rather than be deleted. This was important for optimizing computer performance in the 1970s. Nowadays, making code "stick" in swap space is unnecessary, and Linux ignores the sticky bit if it is set for files (in fact, the original application of the sticky bit has been obsolete since the mid-1980s and has never been implemented in Linux).

In its new life, the sticky bit works on <u>directories</u> as a special permissions setting which protects a directory's files[120] from deletion (now the only thing "sticky" about the sticky bit is its name). Normally in Linux, if a regular user has rwx permissions for a directory, then that user can delete (or rename) *any* file contained within the directory—even files that that user doesn't own! This is surprising, but it is due to the fact that the permissions to *access* or *edit* a file (e.g., having rw- permissions for a file as the file's owner) are separate from the mechanism in Linux that controls whether we can *delete, move, or rename* a file. Permissions to delete, move, or rename files are handled at the <u>directory</u> level (having rwx or -wx permissions on a directory). This means, normally, if we have permissions to access and write to a directory, then we have the permissions needed to delete files contained in that directory.

The sticky bit steps in to remedy this situation. When applied to a directory, the sticky bit restricts permissions such that no user can delete a file[120] in the directory unless the user is the *file owner*, the *directory owner*, or the *superuser*. The best-known example of a directory with its sticky bit enabled is the /tmp directory.

```
dr-xr-xr-x  13 root root        0 Nov  4 01:36 sys/
drwxrwxrwt  21 root root     4096 Nov  4 05:38 tmp/
drwxr-xr-x  14 root root     4096 Apr 23  2020 usr/
drwxr-xr-x  15 root root     4096 Jul 22  2020 var/
```

Notice the t in the executable permissions slot in the "other" category. This indicates that the /tmp directory's sticky bit is turned on. Having the sticky bit set for the /tmp directory makes sense since /tmp is a place where files belonging to various UIDs (including root) are stored. Most files in /tmp are created by processes (including root-owned processes), and there needs to be a way to protect these files from unauthorized deletion. The sticky bit answers this need. In octal, the sticky bit is represented by a 1 in the first digit of the four-digit octal permissions code. The permissions in octal for the /tmp directory shown above would be 1777. To activate the sticky bit for a directory, use $ chmod +t <directoryname>. To remove the sticky bit, use $ chmod -t <directoryname>.

---

[119] Swap space is a partition (or file) on a hard drive reserved by the system for copying binary images from RAM to free up memory for other applications. The binary copied to the swap space can later be loaded (i.e., "swapped") back into RAM if needed. Normally, if a binary in swap space is not accessed within a certain amount of time, then the system will overwrite that part of the swap space with other data copied from RAM. In pre-1985 Unix, if sticky bit permissions were set for an executable binary file, then the system was forbidden from overwriting that binary code if/when it was in swap space. This use of the sticky bit is no longer practiced due to improvements in hardware.
[120] In a directory with the sticky bit enabled, deletion protection also applies to sub-directories within that directory.

Appendix B – Quoting and escaping in Linux

How and when to use **single quotes** `' '`, **double quotes** `""`, and the **escape character** `\` in the shell can be a matter of confusion for Linux users. Here we will review these aspects of shell syntax and discuss the effect they have in different cases.

Let's start by thinking about the purpose of the shell. The main function of the shell program is to give users a means of running commands (i.e., programs). When we enter a command on the command line, the shell takes what we have entered in the argument, performs certain "preparatory" actions (depending on how we have structured the command), and then delivers the argument in its prepared form to the input of the command that we want to run. Then the command performs its own action(s) based on what it has received from the shell as input.

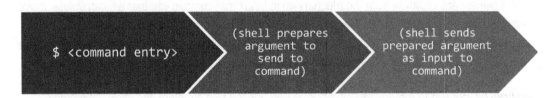

What the shell does to "prepare" the argument before sending it to a command depends on the pieces of shell syntax we include in our entry. For example, let's compare two commands that differ by only one small piece of shell syntax.

Command entered	After shell preparation	Command output
`$ echo $USERNAME`	`$ echo Brian Kernighan`	`Brian Kernighan`
`$ echo USERNAME`	`$ echo USERNAME`	`USERNAME`

The difference between these two commands is the inclusion of `$` before USERNAME. We can see that when we form $USERNAME in the argument of `$ echo`, the added `$` prompts the shell to *interpret* USERNAME as the name of a variable and to *expand* the $USERNAME field in our entry to the USERNAME variable's stored value (in this case, `Brian Kernighan`). We call this type of expansion **variable expansion**[121].

Without the `$` before USERNAME, the shell views USERNAME not as the name of a variable but as literal text, and the shell passes the argument as a string literal to the input of the `$ echo` command (hence, `$ echo` prints `USERNAME` in the output).

---

[121] Variable expansion is also sometimes called "parameter expansion".

The inclusion of the $ demonstrates how $ functions as a **special character** in the shell. Special characters are "special" because, when the shell "sees" them in the argument of a command, depending on context, they can control how the shell processes the argument. Listed below are some of the special characters that we have encountered, and some that you will learn about as you progress further. Notice that ", ', and \ are all special characters, as is the   space.

```
# ; & . ` " ' \ / ! ? * $ [ ] ( ) { } | < > = % ~
```

One important thing to note about how special characters operate is that they only have an effect in a command argument if the shell can "see" them. As an example, let's look at what happens when we add ' ' quotes around $USERNAME in the argument of the $ echo command.

Command entered
```
$ echo '$USERNAME'
```

After shell preparation   string literal
```
$ echo $USERNAME
```

Command output
```
$USERNAME
```

The effect of adding ' ' around $USERNAME is that the single quotes *hide* the $ from the shell's view as the shell prepares the argument to send to the input of the $ echo command. By "hide", we mean the single quotes hide the $ character's *"specialness"* from the shell. Another way of expressing this is to say that the single quotes "protect" the $ from the shell's view and therefore, from the shell's variable expansion. This demonstrates the function of ' ' as special characters in the argument of a command. Single quotes hide any other special characters they enclose, thus turning all enclosed characters into string literals from the shell's point of view. Note that in the shell's preparation of the argument, the ' ' are removed. We call this step **quote removal**.

Below we see what happens when we try to enter a command with a single ' in the argument.

Command entered
```
$ echo $USERNAME's account
```

Shell preparation (incomplete)
```
$ echo Brian Kernighan's acc
>
```

> Entering an un-paired ' in the argument of a command will cause the shell to produce a PS2 prompt > demanding that we enter another ' to go with the un-paired '.

If we tried to execute the command above and then typed a ' at the > prompt followed by enter, we would see Brian Kernighans account in the output. Note that the shell's quote removal would leave the n and s right next to each other.

Single quotes have the honorable title of **strong quotes** because they can hide *any* special character from the shell's view. Well, almost any. The only case in which single quotes fail to hide a special character from the shell is if a single, open-ended ' is placed between[122] two existing ' '. This is

---

[122] The shell always pairs single quotes by proximity, so no single quote is ever actually "between" others.

demonstrated if we try executing `$ echo '''`. Like the example on p. 183 with a single `'` in the argument, we get a `>` prompt when we enter `$ echo '''`. If the shell sees an unterminated `'`, the shell treats the `'` as undefined, and this is the case whenever we have an odd number of non-hidden `'` characters in the argument. If we press `enter` under these circumstances, the shell continues to show the `>` prompt until we pair the lone `'` with another `'` (or press `ctrl + c` to return to the `PS1` prompt).

But what if we *want* to have a single `'` appear in a command argument—for example as a string-literal apostrophe (see p. 183)? The key to this is to *hide* the single `'` from the shell's view so that the shell doesn't try to force pairing with another `'`. We can't accomplish this by adding more single quotes (because single quotes can hide everything *except* for an un-paired single quote). We do, however, have other ways of protecting a single `'` from the shell's scrutiny.

One way to hide a single `'` from the shell's view is to "escape" it with the shell's escape character: `\`.

Command entered	Shell preparation	Command output
`$ echo $USERNAME\'s account`	`$ echo Brian Kernighan's account`	↓
		`Brian Kernighan's account`

This is the function of the `\` special character when the shell sees it in the argument of a command. The `\` "escapes" (i.e. hides or protects) the special character immediately adjacent to the right. Note that in this case, the same quote removal step we saw with `''` also applies to `\`.

Another way of hiding a single `'` from the shell is by surrounding the `'` with double quotes: `""`.

Command entered	Shell preparation	Command output
`$ echo "$USERNAME's account"`	`$ echo Brian Kernighan's account`	↓
		`Brian Kernighan's account`

Here we see that double quotes `""` are able to protect the `'` from the shell's prying eyes, but not the `$USERNAME` field. Thus, the shell performs variable expansion on `$USERNAME`. This is an example of why double quotes go by the title of **weak quotes**. Unlike single quotes, there are certain special characters that double quotes alone cannot hide from the shell.

The "weak" designation may sound like an insult, but the fact that double quotes don't hide everything from the shell makes them tremendously useful. Double quotes allow us to safely construct argument strings that have literal text interspersed with variable expansions. This is very important, and something we cannot do with single quotes alone (see p. 183)! Also, note that the same quote removal step we saw with `''` and `\` applies to `""` as well.

Double quotes are so important in the shell (Bash in particular) that *not* using them to surround `$<variable>` expansions[123] is considered bad practice. At different points in this guide, for the sake of demonstration and/or simplicity in understanding, some `$<variable>` forms have been presented without wrapping them in double quotes. **However**, in the real world, the unequivocal best practice is to wrap <u>every</u> `$<variable>` expansion in the argument of a command with double quotes.

Say that we have a user with the `<username>` of `Brian Kernighan`. This user's home directory will therefore be `/home/Brian Kernighan`. Okay. Right away this should send off some alarm bells. One of the cardinal rules in Linux file naming conventions is to avoid using   spaces in file and directory names. The reality is, however, that real users in the real world do not always follow these conventions. To guard against potential errors (or deletions!) due to   spaces, we need to double quote every `$<variable>` expression (e.g., `"$USERNAME"`). Here we will demonstrate why.

<u>Command entered</u>
`$ cd /home/$USERNAME`

<u>Shell preparation</u> ↓ delimiter
`$ cd /home/Brian Kernighan`
field #1   field #2

<u>Command output</u>
`too many arguments`

Notice that without double quotes around `$USERNAME`, the shell has prepared the input for the `$ cd` command as <u>two</u> discrete arguments (i.e., two argument "fields"). This is due to the shell's interpretation of the unquoted (i.e., unhidden)   space character between `Brian` and `Kernighan`. Recall that the   space is a special character in the shell (see p. 183). The function of the   space as a special character is to indicate to the shell where **word splitting** should occur in a command's argument. When the shell "sees" a   space in the argument, the shell treats the   space as a **delimiter** between **fields**[124] (i.e., words). The result is that the shell splits the fields up and sends them to the input of the command as a list of arguments[125]. This is exhibited in the way the shell prepares a set of positional parameters for a scripted command (see p. 137).

For correctly interpreting a command with *multiple* fields (i.e., "words") in its argument, the shell's word splitting is needed. For example, if the shell can't "see" the   space between `<source>` and `<target>` in `$ cp "<source> <target>"`, then the two paths `<source> <target>` would be viewed as <u>one</u> path (e.g., `/home/me/pictures /home/me/photos` as though for some reason there were a `~/pictures /home` directory inside the home directory, which of course there shouldn't be). Hence, trying to call `$ cp` with double quotes around `<source> <target>` will return an error.

---

[123] In addition to variable expansions, it is also best practice to wrap command substitutions in double quotes (see p. 96 for reference).

[124] The term "field" here simply means a chunk of connected text.

[125] For external commands (i.e., compiled binaries), the shell prepares a string with each of the argument fields separated by a null character (`\0`), which the compiled binary uses to align and transfer the fields into its `argv` array (<u>arg</u>ument <u>v</u>ector).

However, if a *single* file or directory does have a　space in its name (such as with the example of /home/Brian Kernighan), then it is crucial that the shell doesn't "see" this　space when performing word splitting in the argument of a command. The /home/Brian Kernighan directory needs to be interpreted as <u>one</u> field and not split into two. The way to hide the　space from the shell when $USERNAME is expanded is by surrounding $USERNAME in double quotes: $ cd "/home/$USERNAME".

To further illustrate, let's imagine that in our hypothetical system, there are two files and one directory inside the /home directory.

/home/Brian	← file
/home/Brian Kernighan	← directory
/home/Kernighan	← file

If we entered $ cd /home/$USERNAME, we would get the same too many arguments error as before (see p. 185). However, if we were in the /home directory and we had the misfortune of typing into the shell $ cp /home/$USERNAME and pressing enter, then we would overwrite the contents of the /home/Kernighan file with the contents of the /home/Brian file.

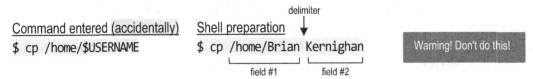

However unlikely this may seem, these kinds of things can happen when we least expect them if we are not careful. Fortunately, all of this can be avoided by hiding delimiting　spaces from the shell!

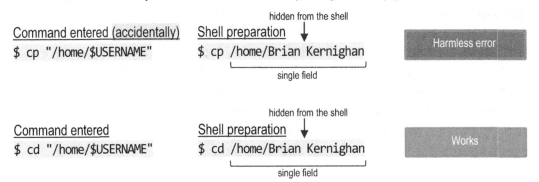

Hiding　spaces from the shell's view is one of the most important functions that double quotes perform as special characters. One potentially confusing thing about this is that the　spaces will still remain in the argument despite being "hidden" by double quotes. It's helpful to think of the　spaces as becoming "invisible" to the shell when enclosed in double quotes, thus losing their special meaning as "field delimiters" when the shell is preparing an argument to send to the input of a command. Rather than being split into a discrete field at every space, with double quotes, a single field is able to span across spaces after expansion (see p. 186). The result is that variable expansions and command substitutions (see p. 96) can happen without being subjected to the shell's word splitting.

Be aware that the space character is not the only special character that the shell views as a delimiter between fields in the argument of a command. The space character is one of <u>three</u> special characters defined in the IFS special variable (for <u>I</u>nternal <u>F</u>ield <u>S</u>eparator), all of which are interpreted as field separators/delimiters when "seen" by the shell. The name given to this category of special characters is "whitespace characters". Altogether, the three whitespace characters defined by default in the IFS variable are the space character, the unprintable <newline> character, and the unprintable <tab> character. Double quotes, single quotes, and the \ character all work to hide the three different whitespace characters from the shell's view.

\ Escape Character:

- In the argument of a command, hides/escapes the special character immediately to the right.
    - → the\ name\ in\ quotes is the same as 'the name in quotes' (see p. 56)
    - → $ find . -type f -exec grep -l "howdy" {} \; (see p. 161)
- In the context of a PS1 shell variable definition, used to escape unprintable special characters.
    - → \u becomes <username>, etc. (see p. 105)

' ' Single Quotes:

- In the argument of a command, hide all enclosed special characters (except for ') from the shell's view (preventing word splitting, variable expansion, command substitution, etc.).
    - → $ rm -i 'Screenshot from 2021-02-18 10-05-16.png' (see p. 115)
- In the context of a PS1 variable definition (i.e., <u>not</u> in the argument of a command), single quotes serve to capture the definition as a string literal. The special PS1 backslash-escaped characters aren't evaluated/expanded at the time of definition (unlike calling a command, where the argument is evaluated at the time of entry). The special PS1 backslash-escaped characters are evaluated when the command line prompt is <u>rendered</u> in the shell. For this reason, the prompt string needs to be *defined* first as a literal string (to establish a reference).
    - → PS1='\[\033[01;32m\]MyCustomShellPrompt\[\033[00m\]\$ ' (see p. 107)

" " Double Quotes:

- In the argument of a command, double quotes permit $<variable> expansions and $(<command>) substitutions to go forward while hiding special characters such as spaces and the wildcard (globbing) character * from the shell's view.
    - → $ echo "Hey there, my name is $FUNCNAME! Not $1." (see p. 138)
    - → $ find . -name ".bash*" (see p. 158)

Appendix C – Linux Command Line How-to (General)

Directory Operations

How to display the current working directory
- `$ pwd`

How to list the contents of the current working directory
- `$ ls`
  (list non-hidden files and directories)
- `$ ls -a`
  (list all files and directories)
- `$ ls -al`
  (list all files and directories, displayed in long format)
- `$ ls -alt`
  (list all files and directories, displayed in long format, sorted by time of modification)
- `$ ll`
  (alias for `$ ls -alF`)

How to change your location in the file system
- `$ cd <pathname>`
  (change to the destination directory specified in `<pathname>`)
- `$ cd -`
  (change to the previous directory)
- `$ cd /`
  (change to the root directory)
- `$ cd ~`
  (change to the home directory)
- `$ cd`
  (change to the home directory)

How to get info about a directory
- `$ stat <pathname>`
- `$ ls -lad <pathname>`

How to get the size of a directory
- `$ du -sh <pathname>`

How to make a new directory
- `$ mkdir <pathname>`

How to copy a directory
- `$ cp -rn <source> <target>`

How to rename a directory
- `$ mv -n <source> <target>`

How to move a directory
- `$ mv -n <source> <target>`

How to create a soft link to a directory
- `$ ln -s <target> <link>`

How to remove a soft link to a directory
- `$ unlink -s <link>`

How to delete an empty directory
- `$ rmdir <pathname>`
- `$ rm -d <pathname>`

How to delete a non-empty directory
- `$ rm -ri <pathname>`

File Operations

How to view the contents of a file
- `$ cat <filename>`
- `$ less <filename>`
- `$ nano <filename>`
- `$ vim <filename>`
- `$ emacs <filename>`

How to get info about a file
- `$ stat <filename>`
- `$ file <filename>`
- `$ ls -la <filename>`

How to get the size of a file
- `$ size <filename>`

How to make a new file

- `$ touch <filename>`

How to edit a file

- `$ nano <filename>`
- `$ vim <filename>`
- `$ emacs <filename>`

How to make a copy of a file

- `$ cp -n <source> <target>`

How to rename a file

- `$ mv -n <source> <target>`

How to move a file

- `$ mv -n <source> <target>`

How to search for a file by name

- `$ find <pathname> -type f -name <pattern>`

How to search for text within files

- `$ find <pathname> -type f -exec grep -Hn <pattern> {} \;`

How to create a hard link to a file

- `$ ln <target> <link>`

How to create a soft link to a file

- `$ ln -s <target> <link>`

How to remove a soft link to a file

- `$ unlink -s <link>`

How to delete a file

- `$ rm -i <filename>`

Environment Operations

How to display all environment variables

- `$ env | less`

How to display all environment and shell variables
- `$ set | less`

How to display $PATH
- `$ echo $PATH`

User Operations

How to check your `<username>`
- `$ whoami`

How to check what groups you belong to
- `$ id`

Command Operations

How to check the location of an external command or executable shell script
- `$ type <command>`
- `$ whereis <command>`

How to check the type of a command
- `$ type -t <command>`

How to run a command as root (superuser)
- `$ sudo <command>`

Package Management Operations

How to list all installed packages
- `$ apt list --installed`

How to check for available updates to packages
- `$ apt update`

How to upgrade all installed packages
- `$ apt upgrade`

How to search for a package in the APT database
- `$ apt search <pattern>`

How to install a new package
- `$ apt install <package>`

How to uninstall a package
- `$ apt uninstall <package>`

System Operations

How to get system info
- `$ uname -a`

How to list all currently active processes
- `$ ps -aux`

How to view a dynamic list of processes by CPU consumption
- `$ top`

How to end a process
- `$ kill <PID>`

How to check the file system
- `$ fsck`

How to check the amount of free space in the file system disk
- `$ du`
- `$ df -h`

Network Operations

How to view information about a system's network configuration
- `$ ip -a`

How to view network settings and statistics
- `$ netstat -ie`

How to verify a network connection
- `$ ping <URI>`

How to view the network route to a host
- `$ traceroute <URI>`

References

Allen, Ian D. 2013. "Shell Command Line Quoting Mechanisms." *CST 8207 Course Home Page*. April.
 https://teaching.idallen.com/cst8207/13w/notes/440_quotes.html.

n.d. *Ask Ubuntu*. https://askubuntu.com.

n.d. *Baeldung on Linux*. https://www.baeldung.com/linux.

Ball, Thorsten. 2014. *Where did fork go?* 13 Jun. https://thorstenball.com/blog/2014/06/13/where-did-
 fork-go.

n.d. *Base64 - Wikipedia*. https://en.wikipedia.org/wiki/Base64.

n.d. *Boolean World*. https://www.booleanworld.com.

Both, David. n.d. "A sysadmin's guide to Bash scripting." *https://www.opensource.com*.

Brousse, Nicolas. 2021. *Shell Tips! Sharpen Your Tech Skills*. https://www.shell-tips.com.

n.d. *Computer Hope*. https://www.computerhope.com.

Cooper, Mendel. 2014. *Advanced Bash-Scripting Guide*. https://tldp.org/LDP/abs/html/index.html.

n.d. *Enterprise Open Source and Linux | Ubuntu*. https://ubuntu.com.

Francia, Andrea. 2021. "GitHub - andreafrancia/trash-cli: Command line interface to the
 freedesktop.org trashcan." *GitHub*. https://github.com/andreafrancia/trash-cli.

Galov, Nick. 2021. *111+ Linux Statistics and Facts - Linux Rocks!* August.
 https://hostingtribunal.com/blog/linux-statistics/#gref.

Harder, Douglas Wilhelm. n.d. "Command-line Arguments: main(int argc, char *argv[])." *Introduction
 to Computer Structures and Real-time Systems*.
 https://ece.uwaterloo.ca/~dwharder/icsrts/C/05/.

n.d. *History of Unix - Wikipedia*. https://en.wikipedia.org/wiki/History_of_Unix.

Kamathe, Guarav. 2019. *Understanding system calls on Linux with strace*. 25 October.
 https://opensource.com/article/19/10/strace.

Kerrisk, Michael. 2010. *The Linux Programming Interface*. No Starch Press.

n.d. *Linux Config - Learn Linux Configuration*. https://linuxconfig.org.

n.d. *Linux Hint*. https://linuxhint.com.

n.d. *Linuxize*. https://linuxize.com.

McKay, Dave. 2020. *Everything You Ever Wanted to Know About inodes on Linux*. 21 January.
 https://www.howtogeek.com/465350/everything-you-ever-wanted-to-know-about-inodes-on-
 linux.

n.d. *nixCraft*. https://www.cyberciti.biz.

O'Reilly. 1998. *Learning the bash Shell, Second Editition*. O'Reilly Media, Inc.

n.d. *Package Management | Ubuntu*. https://ubuntu.com/server/docs/package-management.

Prakash, Abhishek. 2020. *Linux Runs on All of the Top 500 Supercomputers, Again!* 20 November.
 https://itsfoss.com/linux-runs-top-supercomputers.

Raymond, Eric Steven. 2003. *The Art of Unix Programming*.
 https://homepage.cs.uri.edu/~thenry/resources/unix_art/index.html.

Ritchie, Dennis M. and Thompson, Ken. July 1974. "The UNIX Time-Sharing System." *Communications of the ACM* 365-375.

Ritchie, Dennis M. 1979. *The Evolution of the Unix Time-sharing System.* https://www.bell-labs.com/usr/dmr/www/hist.html.

Sarwar, Sayed Mansoor and Koretsky, Robert M. 2019. *Linux, The Textbook, Second Edition.* Boca Raton, FL: Chapman and Hall/CRC.

Shotts, William. 2019. *The Linux Command Line.* No Starch Press.

Sneddon, Joey. 2018. *27 Interesting Facts About Linux.* August. https://www.omgubuntu.co.uk/2018/08/interesting-facts-about-linux.

n.d. *Stack Overflow.* https://stackoverflow.com.

n.d. *Super User.* https://superuser.com.

n.d. *Tecmint: Linux Howtos, Tutorials & Guides.* https://www.tecmint.com.

n.d. *The GNU Operating System and the Free Software Movement.* https://www.gnu.org.

n.d. *The UNIX System -- History and Timeline -- Unix History.* https://unix.org/what_is_unix/history_timeline.html.

Thompson, Ken, interview by Brian Kernighan. 2019. *VCF East 2019 -- Brian Kernighan interviews Ken Thompson* https://www.youtube.com/watch?v=EY6q5dv_B-o.

n.d. *Unix & Linux Stack Exchange.* https://unix.stackexchange.com.

n.d. *Unix architecture - Wikipedia.* https://en.wikipedia.org/wiki/Unix_architecture.

n.d. *Unix philosophy - Wikipedia.* https://en.wikipedia.org/wiki/Unix_philosophy.

n.d. *Unix-like - Wikipedia.* https://en.wikipedia.org/wiki/Unix-like.

Ward, Brian. 2021. *How Linux Works: What Every Superuser Should Know.* San Fransisco: No Starch Press.

Wooledge, Greg. 2021. *Bash Guide - Greg's Wiki.* https://mywiki.wooledge.org/BashGuide.

—. 2021. *The Bash Hackers Wiki.* https://wiki.bash-hackers.org/start.

Made in the USA
Middletown, DE
16 February 2025

71407389R00109